Lecture Notes in Computer Science 8332

Commenced Publication in 1973
Founding and Former Series Editors:
Gerhard Goos, Juris Hartmanis, and Jε

T0214206

For further volumes:
http://www.springer.com/series/7407

Shaoying Liu · Zhenhua Duan (Eds.)

Structured Object-Oriented Formal Language and Method

Third International Workshop, SOFL+MSVL 2013
Queenstown, New Zealand, October 29, 2013
Revised Selected Papers

 Springer

Editors
Shaoying Liu
Hosei University
Koganei-shi, Tokyo
Japan

Zhenhua Duan
Xidian University
Xi'an
People's Republic of China

ISSN 0302-9743   ISSN 1611-3349 (electronic)
ISBN 978-3-319-04914-4   ISBN 978-3-319-04915-1 (eBook)
DOI 10.1007/978-3-319-04915-1
Springer Cham Heidelberg New York Dordrecht London

Library of Congress Control Number: 2014932685

LNCS Sublibrary: SL1 – Theoretical Computer Science and General Issues

Printed on acid-free paper

Springer is part of Springer Science+Business Media (www.springer.com)

Preface

Both formal methods and conventional software engineering techniques face various challenges; they must be properly integrated to establish more effective technologies for future software engineering. The development of the Structured Object-Oriented Formal Language (SOFL) over the last two decades has shown some possibilities of achieving effective integrations to build practical formal techniques and tool support for requirements analysis, specification, design, inspection, review, and testing of software systems. SOFL integrates: Data Flow Diagram, Petri Nets, and VDM-SL to offer a graphical and formal notation for writing specifications; a three-step approach to requirements acquisition and system design; specification-based inspection and testing methods for detecting errors in both specifications and programs; and a set of tools to support modeling and verification. Meanwhile, the Modeling, Simulation and Verification Language (MSVL) is a parallel programming language developed over the last decade. Its supporting tool MSV has been developed to enable us to model, simulate, and verify a system formally. The two languages complement each other.

Following the success of the second SOFL workshop held in Kyoto in 2012, the 3rd International Workshop on SOFL+MSVL (SOFL+MSVL 2013) is jointly organized by the Shaoying Liu research group at Hosei University, Japan, and the Zhenhua Duan research group at Xidian University, China, with the aim of bringing industrial, academic, and government experts and practitioners of SOFL or MSVL to communicate and to exchange ideas. The workshop attracted 22 submissions on formal specification, specification-based testing, specification pattern, modeling checking, specification animation, simulation, application of SOFL, and supporting tools for SOFL or MSVL. Each submission is rigorously reviewed by two Program Committee members on the basis of technical quality, relevance, significance, and clarity, and 13 papers were accepted for publication in the workshop proceedings. The acceptance rate is approximately 59 %.

We would like to thank the ICFEM 2013 organizers for supporting the organization of the workshop, all of the Program Committee members for their great efforts and cooperation in reviewing and selecting papers, and our postgraduate students for their help. We would also like to thank all of the participants for attending presentation sessions and actively joining discussions at the workshop. Finally, our gratitude goes to Alfred Hofmann and his team for their continuous support in the publication of the workshop proceedings.

January 2014

Shaoying Liu
Zhenhua Duan

Organization

Program Co-Chairs

Shaoying Liu (Co-chair)   Hosei University, Japan
Zhenhua Duan (Co-chair)   Xidian University, China

Program Committee

Michael Butler	University of Southampton, UK
Steve Cha	Korea University, Korea
Jian Chen	Shaanxi Normal University, China
Yuting Chen	Shanghai Jiaotong University, China
Jin Song Dong	National University of Singapore
Mo Li	Hosei University, Japan
Xiaohong Li	Tianjin University, China
Abdul Rahman Mat	University Malaysia Serawak, Malaysia
Huaikou Miao	Shanghai University, China
Weikai Miao	East China Normal University, China
Fumiko Nagoya	Aoyama Gakuyin University, Japan
Shengchao Qin	University of Teesside, UK
Wuwei Shen	Western Michigan University, USA
Jing Sun	University of Auckland, New Zealand
Cong Tian	Xidian University, China
Xi Wang	Hosei University, Japan
Jinyun Xue	Jiangxi Normal University, China
Fauziah Zainuddin	Hosei University, Japan
Hong Zhu	Oxford Brookes University, UK

Contents

Testing and Verification

Combining Specification-Based Testing, Correctness Proof,
and Inspection for Program Verification in Practice 3
  Shaoying Liu and Shin Nakajima

Theory of Test Modeling Based on Regular Expressions 17
  Pan Liu and Huaikou Miao

Simulation and Model Checking

Integrating Separation Logic with PPTL 35
  Xu Lu, Zhenhua Duan, Cong Tian, and Hongjin Liu

Improved Net Reductions for LTL\X Model Checking 48
  Ya Shi, Zhenhua Duan, Cong Tian, and Hua Yang

Formalizing and Implementing Types in MSVL 62
  Xiaobing Wang, Zhenhua Duan, and Liang Zhao

Present-Future Form of Linear Time μ-Calculus 76
  Yao Liu, Zhenhua Duan, Cong Tian, and Bo Liu

SOFL Tools

Prototype Tool for Supporting a Formal Engineering Approach
to Service-Based Software Modeling 89
  Weikai Miao and Shaoying Liu

A Supporting Tool for Syntactic Analysis of SOFL Formal Specifications
and Automatic Generation of Functional Scenarios 104
  Shenghua Zhu and Shaoying Liu

SOFL Specification Animation with Tool Support 118
  Mo Li and Shaoying Liu

Formal Specification and Application

An Approach to Declaring Data Types for Formal Specifications 135
  Xi Wang and Shaoying Liu

Detection Method of the Second-Order SQL Injection in Web Applications 154
  Lu Yan, Xiaohong Li, Ruitao Feng, Zhiyong Feng, and Jing Hu

Applying SOFL to Constructing a Smart Traffic Light Specification.   166
  Wahyu Eko Sulistiono and Shaoying Liu

Checking Internal Consistency of SOFL Specification: A Hybrid Approach. . . .   175
  Yuting Chen

Author Index   193

Testing and Verification

Combining Specification-Based Testing, Correctness Proof, and Inspection for Program Verification in Practice

Shaoying Liu[1](✉) and Shin Nakajima[2]

[1] Hosei University, Tokyo, Japan
sliu@hosei.ac.jp
[2] NII, Tokyo, Japan
nkjm@nii.ac.jp

Abstract. Specification-based testing is limited in detecting program errors; correctness proof based on Hoare logic is difficult to perform in practice; and inspection is heavily dependent on human decisions. Each of these three is difficult to do a satisfactory job alone, but they complement each other when they come together in an appropriate manner. This paper puts forward a new method that makes good use of Hoare logic and inspection to improve the effectiveness of specification-based testing in detecting errors. The underlying principle of the method is first to use specification-based testing to discover traversed program paths and then to use Hoare logic to prove their correctness, but when proof is impossible to conduct, a special inspection is applied. During the proof or inspection process, all faults on the paths are expected to be detected. A case study is conducted to show its feasibility; an example taken from the case study is used to illustrate how the proposed method is applied; and a discussion on the important issues to be addressed in the future is presented.

1 Introduction

Given a formal specification S and an implementation P, how to verify whether P satisfies S (or P is correct with respect to S) in practice still remains a challenge. Formal verification (or proof) based on Hoare logic (also Flody-Hoare logic) [1] provides a possibility to establish the correctness for programs, but due to the difficulty in deriving appropriate invariants for iterations and the difficulties in managing *side effect*, complex data structures, and invocations of subroutines (methods, functions, or procedures) in programming languages, formal proof for realistic programs is impractical.

On the other hand, specification-based testing (SBT) is a practical technique for detecting program errors. A strong point of SBT superior to formal correctness verification is that it is much easier to be performed, even automatically if

This work is supported by NII Collaborative Program, SCAT research foundation, and Hosei University.

S. Liu and Z. Duan (Eds.): SOFL+MSVL 2013, LNCS 8332, pp. 3–16, 2014.
DOI: 10.1007/978-3-319-04915-1_1, © Springer International Publishing Switzerland 2014

formal specifications are adopted [2,3], but a weak point is that existing errors on a program path may still not be uncovered even if it has been traversed using a test case. Liu's previous work on combining Hoare Logic and SBT presented a novel technique for formally proving the correctness of all of the traversed program paths [4], which shows the potential of strengthening testing by applying Hoare logic. In spite of the great potential of improvement of this technique, there still exists a difficulty when testing encounters crash or non-termination in running the program. Another practical technique that is likely to perform better in some circumstances than testing is software inspection [5], but inspection usually heavily depends on human decisions and therefore lacks repeatability [6]. We believe, as many others do, that each of these three approaches is difficult to do a satisfactory job, but they complement each other when they come together in an appropriate manner.

In this paper, we propose an approach to verifying programs by combining the specific SBT we have developed before with the Hoare logic and a formal specification-based program inspection technique. This new approach is known as *testing-based formal verification* (TBFV). The essential idea is first to generate a test case from each functional scenario, derived from the formal specification using pre- and post-conditions, to run the program, and then repeatedly apply the axiom for assignment in Hoare logic to formally verify the correctness of the path that is traversed by using the test case. When such a proof is impossible to conduct due to complex data structures or other reasons, the inspection method will be applied. As described in Sect. 2, any pre-post style formal specification can be automatically transformed into an equivalent disjunction of functional scenarios and each scenario defines an independent function of the corresponding program in terms of the relation between input and output. A test case can be generated from each functional scenario and can be used to run the program to find a traversed path, which is a sequence of conditions or statements, but the correctness of the path with respect to the pre-condition and the functional scenario is unlikely to be established by means of testing. This deficiency can be eliminated by repeatedly applying the axiom for assignment in Hoare logic or by specification-based inspection when Hoare logic is hard to apply. The superiority of our approach to both SBT and formal verification is that it can verify the correctness of all traversed paths and can be performed automatically because the derivation of invariants from iterations is no longer needed.

Our focus in this paper is on the explanation of the new idea in combining specification-based testing with Hoare logic. Therefore, we deliberately choose small examples to explain the principle, which is expected to facilitate the reader in understanding the essential idea. The feasibility of applying the new technique to deal with a realistic program system has been demonstrated in our case study.

The rest of the paper is organized as follows. Section 2 gives a brief introduction to both the functional scenario-based testing (FSBT) and the formal specification-based inspection method. Section 3 describes the essential idea of our TBFV approach. In Sect. 4, we give an example to illustrate the TBFV approach systematically. Section 5 elaborates on how method invocation is dealt with in TBFV. Section 6 discusses the potential challenges to the proposed approach. Section 7 gives a brief overview of the related work. Finally, in Sect. 8, we conclude the paper and point out future research direction.

2 Introduction to FSBT and Inspection

This section briefly introduces the relevant parts of FSBT and the inspection technique we use to pave the way for discussing the proposed TBFV. Since Hoare logic is well known in the field, we omit the introduction but will briefly explain the axioms when they are used.

2.1 FSBT

FSBT is a specific specification-based testing approach that takes both the pre-condition and post-condition into account in test case generation [3]. Applying the principle of "divide and conquer", the approach treats a specification as a disjunction of *functional scenarios* (FS), and to generate test sets and analyze test results based on the functional scenarios. A functional scenario in a pre-post style specification is a logical expression that tells clearly what condition is used to constrain the output when the input satisfies some condition.

Specifically, let $S(S_{iv}, S_{ov})[S_{pre}, S_{post}]$ denote the specification of an operation S, where S_{iv} is the set of all input variables whose values are not changed by the operation, S_{ov} is the set of all output variables whose values are produced or updated by the operation, and S_{pre} and S_{post} are the pre- and post-conditions of S, respectively. The characteristic of this style specification is that the post-condition S_{post} is used to describe the relation between initial states and final states. We assume that in the post-condition, a decorated variable, such as $\tilde{x}$, is used to denote the initial value of external (or state) variable x before the operation and the variable itself, i.e., x, is used to represent the final value of x after the operation. Thus, $\tilde{x} \in S_{iv}$ and $x \in S_{ov}$. Of course, S_{iv} also contains all other input variables declared as input parameters and S_{ov} includes all other output variables declared as output parameters.

A practical strategy for generating test cases to exercise the behaviors expected of all functional scenarios derived from the specification is established based on the concept of functional scenario. To precisely describe this strategy, we first need to introduce functional scenario.

Definition 1. *Let* $S_{post} \equiv (C_1 \wedge D_1) \vee (C_2 \wedge D_2) \vee \cdots \vee (C_n \wedge D_n)$, *where each* C_i $(i \in \{1, ..., n\})$ *is a predicate called "guard condition" that contains no output variable in* S_{ov}; D_i *a "defining condition" that contains at least one output variable in* S_{ov} *but no guard condition. Then, a functional scenario* f_s *of S is a conjunction* $\tilde{S}_{pre} \wedge C_i \wedge D_i$, *and the expression* $(\tilde{S}_{pre} \wedge C_1 \wedge D_1) \vee (\tilde{S}_{pre} \wedge C_2 \wedge D_2) \vee \cdots \vee (\tilde{S}_{pre} \wedge C_n \wedge D_n)$ *is called a* functional scenario form *(FSF) of S.*

The decorated pre-condition $\tilde{}S_{pre} = S_{pre}\tilde{}(\sigma/\sigma)$ denotes the predicate resulting from substituting the initial state $\tilde{}\sigma$ for the final state σ in pre-condition S_{pre}. We treat a conjunction $\tilde{}S_{pre} \wedge C_i \wedge D_i$ as a scenario because it defines an independent behavior: when $\tilde{}S_{pre} \wedge C_i$ is satisfied by the initial state (or intuitively by the input variables), the final state (or the output variables) is defined by the defining condition D_i. The conjunction $\tilde{}S_{pre} \wedge C_i$ is known as the *test condition* of the scenario $\tilde{}S_{pre} \wedge C_i \wedge D_i$, which serves as the basis for test case generation from this scenario.

To support automatic test case generation from functional scenarios, the vital first step is to obtain an FSF from a given specification. A systematic transformation procedure, algorithm, and software tool support for deriving an FSF from a pre-post style specification have been developed in our previous work [7]. Generating test cases based on a specification using the functional scenario-based test case generation method is realized by generating them from its all functional scenarios. The production of test cases from a functional scenario is done by generating them from its test condition, which can be divided further into test case generations from every disjunctive clause of the test condition. In the previous work [3], a set of criteria for generating test cases are defined in detail. To effectively apply FSBT, the FSF of the specification must satisfy the *well-formed* condition defined below.

Definition 2. *Let the FSF of specification S be* $(\tilde{}S_{pre} \wedge C_1 \wedge D_1) \vee (\tilde{}S_{pre} \wedge C_2 \wedge D_2) \vee \cdots \vee (\tilde{}S_{pre} \wedge C_n \wedge D_n)$. *If S satisfies the condition* $(\forall_{i,j\in\{1,\ldots,n\}} \cdot (i \neq j \Rightarrow (C_i \wedge C_j \Leftrightarrow false))) \wedge (\tilde{}S_{pre} \Rightarrow (C_1 \vee C_2 \vee \cdots \vee C_n \Leftrightarrow true))$, *$S$ is said to be well-formed.*

The well-formedness of specification S ensures that each functional scenario defines an independent function and the guard conditions completely cover the restricted domain (a subdomain of the operation in which all of the values satisfy the pre-condition). Thus, for any input satisfying the pre-condition, S is guaranteed to define an output satisfying the defining condition of only one functional scenario.

Under the assumption that S is well-formed, we can focus on test case generation from a single functional scenario, say $\tilde{}S_{pre} \wedge C_i \wedge D_i$, at a time using our approach. The test case is then used to run the program, which will enable one program path to be executed. Let us take operation $ChildFareDiscount$, a process of the *IC card system for JR commute train service* used in our case study that is briefly explained in Sect. 4, as an example. The functionality of the process is specified using the SOFL specification language [8] below, which is similar to VDM-SL for operation specifications.

process $ChildFareDiscount(a : int, n\_f : int) a\_f : int$
pre $a > 0\, and\, n\_f > 1$
post $(a > 12 => a\_f = n\_f)$
    and
    $(a <= 12 => a\_f = n\_f - n\_f * 0.5)$
end_process

The specification states that the input a (standing for age) must be greater than 0 and n_f ($normal\_fare$) must be greater than 1. When a is greater than 12, the output a_f ($actual\_fare$) will be the same as n_f ; otherwise, a_f will be 50 % discount on n_f.

According to the algorithm reported in our previous work [7], three functional scenarios can be derived from this formal specification:

(1) $a > 0$ and $n\_f > 1$ and $a > 12$ and $a\_f = n\_f$
(2) $a > 0$ and $n\_f > 1$ and $a <= 12$ and $a\_f = n\_f - n\_f * 0.5$
(3) $a <= 0$ or $n\_f <= 1$ and anything

where $anything$ means that anything can happen when the pre-condition is violated.

Assume the formal specification is refined into the following program (a Java-like method):

```
    int ChildFareDiscount(int a, int n_f) {
(1) If (a > 0 && n_f > 1){
(2)   if (a > 12)
(3)       a_f := n_f;
(4)   else a_f := n_f * *2 - n_f - n_f * 0.5;
(5)   return a_f; }
(6) else System.out.println("the precondition is violated.");
    }
```

where the symbol := is used as the assignment operator in order to distinguish from the equality symbol = used in the specification. It is evident that we can derive the following paths: $[(1)(2)(3)(5)]$, $[(1)(2)'(4)(5)]$, and $[(1)'(6)]$. In the path $[(1)(2)'(4)(5)]$, $(2)'$ means the negation of the condition $a > 12$ (i.e., $a <= 12$), and the similar interpretation applies to $(1)'$ in path $[(1)'(6)]$. We also deliberately insert a defect in the assignment $a\_f = n\_f * *2 - n\_f - n\_f * 0.5$ (thecorrectoneshouldbe $a\_f = n\_f - n\_f * 0.5$), where $n\_f * *2$ means n_f to the power 2 (i.e., n_f^2).

The weakness of the testing approach is that it can only find the presence of errors but cannot find their absence. For example, we generate a test case, $\{(a, 5), (n\_f, 2)\}$, from the test condition $a > 0$ and $n\_f > 1$ and $a <= 12$ of functional scenario (2), as illustrated in Table 1. Executing the program with this test case, the path $[(1)(2)'(4)(5)]$ will be traversed. The result of the execution is $a\_f = 2 ** 2 - 2 - 2 * 0.5 = 1$. This result does not indicate the existence of error because when the test condition $a > 0$ and $n\_f > 1$ and $a <= 12$ is satisfied by the test case, the defining condition $a\_f = n\_f - n\_f * 0.5$ is also satisfied by the output $a\_f = 1$ (because $1 = 2 - 2 * 0.5 <=> true$), which proves that in $this$ $case$, the program correctly implements the functional scenario. But obviously the path contains an error.

One solution to this problem is to perform a formal verification based on Hoare logic to check whether the traversed path is correct with respect to the functional scenario. But if the program path involves expressions in assignments

Table 1. A test example

Test case:	$a = 5,\ n\_f = 2$
Test condition:	$a > 0\ and\ n\_f > 1\ and\ a <= 12$
Functional scenario:	$a > 0\ and\ n\_f > 1\ and\ a <= 12\ and$
	$a\_f = n\_f - n\_f * 0.5$

with side effect or complex data structures, such as *arraylist* of objects in Java, the axioms in Hoare logic may not be applied successfully. In this case, the formal specification-based inspection method can be applied to replace the formal proof.

2.2   Formal Specification-Based Inspection

The formal specification-based inspection method we developed previously exploits the ability to decompose a pre-post style specification into a set of functional scenarios (or simply scenarios) and to decompose a program into a set of program paths (or simply paths) [9]. In principle, each functional scenario should be implemented by a set of paths (can be single path). If the program correctly implements the specification, every path of the program must contribute to the implementation of some functional scenario in the specification. Therefore, the underlying principle of inspection using the method is to check whether every scenario in the specification is implemented correctly by some paths in the program and whether every path in the program contributes to the implementation of some scenario in the specification. The characteristic of the method is that the checklist, containing a set of questions for inspection, is derived from the functional scenarios in the specification and the judgement of the correctness of each path with respect to the corresponding functional scenario will be made by the human inspector.

3   Principle of TBFV

TBFV proposed in this paper provides a specific technique for verifying the correctness of traversed program paths identified using FSBT. The principle underlying the technique includes the following three points:

- Using FSBT to generate adequate test cases to identify all of the *representative paths* in the program under testing; each path is traversed by using at least one test case. A representative path is formed by treating an iteration as an *if-then-else* construct to ensure that the body of the iteration is executed at least once and the iteration terminates, and by treating all of the other constructs as same as their original form.
- Let $\tilde{S}_{pre} \wedge C_i \wedge D_i\ (i = 1, ..., n)$ denote a functional scenario and test case t be generated from the test condition $\tilde{S}_{pre} \wedge C_i$. Let $p = [sc_1, sc_2, ..., sc_m]$ be a program path in which each $sc_j\ (j = 1, ..., m)$ is called a *program segment*, which is a decision (i.e., a predicate), an assignment, a "return" statement,

or a printing statement. Assume path p is traversed by using test case t. To verify the correctness of p with respect to the functional scenario, we form a *path triple*

$$\{\tilde{S}_{pre}\}\, p\, \{C_i \wedge D_i\} \ .$$

The path triple is similar in structure to Hoare triple, but is specialized to a single path rather than the whole program. It means that if the pre-condition $\tilde{S}_{pre}$ of the program is true before path p is executed, the post-condition $C_i \wedge D_i$ of path p will be true on its termination.

– Repeatedly applying the axiom for assignment or the axiom we provide below for other relevant statements, we can derive a pre-condition, denoted by p_{pre}, to form the following expression:

$$\{\tilde{S}_{pre}(\tilde{x}/x)\}\, \{p_{pre}(\tilde{x}/x)\}\, p\, \{C_i \wedge D_i(\tilde{x}/x)\} \ .$$

where $\tilde{S}_{pre}(\tilde{x}/x)$, $p_{pre}(\tilde{x}/x)$ and $C_i \wedge D_i(\tilde{x}/x)$ are a predicate resulting from substituting every decorated input variable $\tilde{x}$ for the corresponding input variable x in the corresponding predicate, respectively. These substitutions are necessary to avoid confusion between the input variables and the internally updated variables (which may share the same name as the input variables).

Finally, if the implication $\tilde{S}_{pre}(\tilde{x}/x) => p_{pre}(\tilde{x}/x)$ can be proved, it means that no error exists on the path; otherwise, it indicates the existence of some error on the path.

The axioms for the other relevant statements or decisions are given below.

$$\overline{\{Q\}S\{Q\}} \qquad [1],$$

where S is one of the three kinds of program segments: *"return" statement*, and *printing statement*. The axiom describes that the pre-condition and post-condition for any of the three kinds of program segments are the same because none of them changes states.

$$\overline{\{S \wedge Q\}S\{Q\}} \qquad [2],$$

where S is a condition (predicate), which may be used in a *if-then-else* statement or a *while* statement. this axiom states that if the program segment is a condition, the derived pre-condition should be a conjunction of the condition and the post-condition. We call axioms [1] and [2] *axioms for non-change segment*.

It is worth mentioning that since the application of the axioms for assignment and for non-change segment involves only syntactical manipulation, deriving the pre-condition $p_{pre}(\tilde{x}/x)$ can be automatically carried out, but formally proving the implication $\tilde{S}_{pre}(\tilde{x}/x) => p_{pre}(\tilde{x}/x)$, which we simply write as $\tilde{S}_{pre} => p_{pre}$ below in this paper, may not be done automatically, even with the help of a theorem prover such as PVS, depending on the complexity of $\tilde{S}_{pre}$ and p_{pre}. If achieving a full automation is regarded as the highest priority, as taken in our approach, the formal proof of this implication can be "replaced" by a test. That is, we first generate sample values for variables in $\tilde{S}_{pre}$ and p_{pre}, and then evaluate both of them to see whether p_{pre} is false when $\tilde{S}_{pre}$ is true. If this is true, it tells that the path under examination contains an error. Since the testing technique is already available in the literature [3,10], we do not repeat the detail in this paper for the sake of space. Our experience suggests that in many realistic circumstances, testing can be both practical and beneficial. However, if the correctness assurance is regarded as the highest priority, a formal proof of the implication must be performed.

In fact, both the testing and formal proof approaches have drawbacks. If the traversed path contains no bugs, the implication $\tilde{S}_{pre} => p_{pre}$ will always hold for all the possible values of free variables in the implication. Using testing to determine this fact usually requires an exhaustive testing, which is generally impossible in practice unless the scope of the program is small enough. In this case, inspection of the implication can be adopted after a sufficiently large number of testing have been carried out. The *rigorous inspection method* based on an inspection task tree notation proposed in our previous work [11] can be utilized for this task. The reader can refer to that publication for details. As far as the formal proof is concerned, inspection can also be adopted to detect bugs contained on the traversed path. If the path contains bugs, the formal proof of the implication $\tilde{S}_{pre} => p_{pre}$ should not be done successfully. Bugs on the path must be first removed before another trial of formal proof, but how to find the bugs is still an open problem for formal proof: no general way of using formal proof to locate bugs is suggested in the literature. In this case, our *rigorous inspection method* can also be adopted for debugging of the path.

4   Example

We have conducted a case study to apply our TBFV approach to test and verify a simplified version of the *IC card system for JR commute train service* in Tokyo. Our experience shows that the approach is feasible and can be effective in general but also faces some challenges or limitations that need to be addressed in the future research, as elaborated in Sect. 6. The system we used is designed to offer the following functional services: (1) Controlling access to and exit from a railway station, (2) Buying tickets using the IC card, (3) Recharging the card by cash or through a bank account, and (4) Buying a railway pass for a certain period (e.g., for one month or three months). Due to the limit of space, we cannot present all of the details, but take one of the internal operations used in the system, which is *ChildFareDiscount* mentioned above, as an example to illustrate how TBFV is applied to rigorously test the corresponding program. The program contains three paths, it is necessary to formally verify all of the three paths. Since the process of the verification is the same for all the paths, we only use the path $[(1)(2)'(4)(5)]$ that is traversed by using the test case $\{(a,5), (n\_f,2)\}$ as an example for explanation.

Firstly, we form the path triple:

$\{\tilde{a} > 0 \; and \; \tilde{n}\_f > 1\}$
$[a > 0 \; \&\& \; n\_f > 1$
  $a <= 12,$
  $a\_f := n\_f * *2 - n\_f - n\_f * 0.5,$
  $return \; a\_f\,]$
$\{\tilde{a} <= 12 \; and \; a\_f = \tilde{n}\_f - \tilde{n}\_f * 0.5\}$

where $\tilde{a} > 0 \; and \; \tilde{n}\_f > 1$ is the result of substituting $\tilde{a}$ and $\tilde{n}\_f$ for input variables a and n_f, respectively, in the pre-condition of the program, and $\tilde{a} <= 12 \; and \; a\_f = \tilde{n}\_f - \tilde{n}\_f * 0.5$ is the result of completing the similar substitution in the post-condition.

Secondly, we repeatedly apply the axiom for assignment or the one for non-change segment to this path triple, starting from the post-condition. As a result, we form the following path, known as *asserted path*, with derived internal assertions between two program segments:

$\{\tilde{a} > 0 \; and \; \tilde{n}\_f > 1\}$
$\{\tilde{a} <= 12 \; and$
$\tilde{n}\_f * *2 - \tilde{n}\_f - \tilde{n}\_f * 0.5 = \tilde{n}\_f - \tilde{n}\_f * 0.5\}$
  $a > 0 \; \&\& \; n\_f > 1$
$\{a <= 12 \; and \; \tilde{a} <= 12 \; and$
$n\_f * *2 - n\_f - n\_f * 0.5 = \tilde{n}\_f - \tilde{n}\_f * 0.5\}$
  $a <= 12$
$\{\tilde{a} <= 12 \; and$
$n\_f * *2 - n\_f - n\_f * 0.5 = \tilde{n}\_f - \tilde{n}\_f * 0.5\}$
  $a\_f := n\_f * *2 - n\_f - n\_f * 0.5$
$\{\tilde{a} <= 12 \; and \; a\_f = \tilde{n}\_f - \tilde{n}\_f * 0.5\}$
  $return \; a\_f$
$\{\tilde{a} <= 12 \; and \; a\_f = \tilde{n}\_f - \tilde{n}\_f * 0.5\}$

where the assertion $\tilde{a} <= 12 \; and \; \tilde{n}\_f * *2 - \tilde{n}\_f - \tilde{n}\_f * 0.5 = \tilde{n}\_f - \tilde{n}\_f *$ 0.5, the second from the top of the sequence, is the result of substituting $\tilde{a}$ for a and $\tilde{n}\_f$ for n_f in the derived assertion $\{\tilde{a} <= 12 \; and \; \tilde{a} <= 12 \; and \; n\_f *$ $*2 - n\_f - n\_f * 0.5 = \tilde{n}\_f - \tilde{n}\_f * 0.5$. As explained previously, this is necessary in order to keep consistency of the input variables a and n_f in the original pre-condition (appearing as $\tilde{a}$ and $\tilde{n}\_f$) and the derived pre-condition.

Thirdly, we need to judge the validity of the implication $\tilde{a} > 0 \; and \; \tilde{n}\_f > 1 => \tilde{a} <= 12 \; and \; \tilde{n}\_f * *2 - \tilde{n}\_f - \tilde{n}\_f * 0.5 = \tilde{n}\_f - \tilde{n}\_f * 0.5$. Using the test case $\{(\tilde{a}, 5), (\tilde{n}\_f, 8)\}$, we can easily prove that the implication is false (the evaluation detail is omitted due to space limit).

From this example, we can see that sometimes testing can be even more efficient than formal proof in judging the validity of the implication when an error exists on the path, but if the path contains no error, testing will be almost impossible to give a firm conclusion in general. In that case, the specification-based inspection can be applied to check whether the path correctly implements the corresponding functional scenario. The inspection can also be valuable if the path cannot be formally proved for the reasons as mentioned previously.

5   Dealing with Iteration and Method Invocation

For the sake of space, we only briefly discuss how our method deals with iterations and method invocations that are frequently used in programs.

5.1   Iteration

Let us take a *while* loop, *while B do S*, as an example. When using a test case to run the program that entails running of this loop, a subpath generated by executing the loop will be traversed. Assume the subpath is as follows:

[B, S, B, S, B, S, not B],

since this is a single program path, the same method explained in the previous section can be applied to derive a pre-condition, and the same principle of using formal proof or testing can also be used to determine the correctness of the path. Because there is no new technique involved in dealing with iterations, we omit the further discussion.

5.2   Method Invocation

If a method invocation is used as a statement, it may change the current state of the program. Therefore, the traversed path within the invoked method will have to be taken into account in deriving the pre-condition of the program under testing.

Let us change the program *ChildFareDiscount* and organize the implementation into a class called *FareDiscount* below.

```
class FareDiscount {
int tem;  //instance variable

       int ChildFareDiscount1(int a, int n_f) {
(1)      Discount(n_f);
(2)      if (a > 0 && n_f > 1){
(3)       if (a > 12)
(4)         a_f := n_f;
(5)       else a_f := n_f * *2 − n_f − tem;
(6)      return a_f; }
(7)      else System.out.println("the precondition is violated.j);
         }

       void Discount(int x){
       int r;
(1.1) r := x * 0.5;
(1.2) tem := r; }
       }
```

When running the method *ChildFareDiscount1* in which the method *Discount(n_f)* is invoked, we obtain three paths: [(1)(2)(3)(4)(6)], [(1)(2)(3)'(5)

(6)], and [(1)(2)′(7)], where segment (1) is a subpath [(1.1)(1.2)](n_f/x), denoting the path resulting from substituting actual parameter n_f for formal parameter x in the subpath [(1.1)(1.2)]. Thus, [(1)(2)(3)′(5)(6)] for example, actually means the path after inserting the traversed path in $Discount$ into the traversed path in $ChildFareDiscount1$, which is simply represented by [(1.1)(1.2)(2)(3)′(5) (6)]. Selecting the same test case $\{(a, 5), (n\_f, 2)\}$ as before to run the program, we make the path [(1.1)(1.2)(2)(3)′(5)(6)] traversed. We then form the asserted path as follows:

$\{\tilde{\ }a > 0\ and\ \tilde{\ }n\_f > 1\}$
$\{\tilde{\ }a <= 12\ and$
$\tilde{\ }n\_f * *2 - \tilde{\ }n\_f - \tilde{\ }n\_f * 0.5 = \tilde{\ }n\_f - \tilde{\ }n\_f * 0.5\}$
$r := n\_f * 0.5$
$\{\tilde{\ }a <= 12$
$n\_f * *2 - n\_f - r = \tilde{\ }n\_f - \tilde{\ }n\_f * 0.5\}$
$tem := r$
$\{\tilde{\ }a <= 12\ and$
$n\_f * *2 - n\_f - tem = \tilde{\ }n\_f - \tilde{\ }n\_f * 0.5\}$
$a > 0\ \&\&\ n\_f > 1$
$\{\tilde{\ }a <= 12\ and$
$n\_f * *2 - n\_f - tem = \tilde{\ }n\_f - \tilde{\ }n\_f * 0.5\}$

$a <= 12$
$\{\tilde{\ }a <= 12\ and$
$n\_f * *2 - n\_f - tem = \tilde{\ }n\_f - \tilde{\ }n\_f * 0.5\}$
$a\_f := n\_f * *2 - n\_f - tem$
$\{\tilde{\ }a <= 12\ and\ a\_f = \tilde{\ }n\_f - \tilde{\ }n\_f * 0.5\}$
$return\ a\_f$
$\{\tilde{\ }a <= 12\ and\ a\_f = \tilde{\ }n\_f - \tilde{\ }n\_f * 0.5\}$

where the subpath $[r := n\_f * 0.5, tem := r]$ is the result of substituting actual parameter n_f used in the method invocation $Discount(n\_f)$ for formal parameter x used in the method definition in the original subpath $[r := x * 0.5, tem := r]$. Similarly, we can easily use testing to prove that the implication $\tilde{\ }a > 0\ and\ \tilde{\ }n\_f > 1 => \tilde{\ }a <= 12\ and\ \tilde{\ }n\_f * *2 - \tilde{\ }n\_f - \tilde{\ }n\_f * 0.5 = \tilde{\ }n\_f - \tilde{\ }n\_f * 0.5$ is false, indicating that an error is found on the path.

6   Potential Challenges

While our experience in the case study mentioned above shows that applying TBFV to practical systems is feasible and can be effective, we have also learned two major potential challenges or limitations. One is that if the expression E in the assignment $x := E$ has a side effect (e.g., in addition to returning a value, it also modifies some state or has an observable interaction with calling functions), the axiom for assignment in Hoare logic is no longer valid. TBFV inherits this limitation from Hoare logic, but how to automatically resolve the side effect without affecting the semantics of the original expression remains a topic for further research. A possible solution is to train programmers to avoid side effect in expressions, but there is no guarantee of its effect in practice. Another way to deal with this problem is to apply the inspection method to allow human to check the correctness, but this would be extremely difficult to be performed automatically in general. The other challenge is that if the program under testing invokes a method (as a call statement) of a software component (e.g., a class in Java API) whose source code is not available to the tester, TBFV may not work well. The difficulty is that automatically inserting probes (monitors) to identify traversed program paths is impossible in this case. However, since most embedded programs are small in size and independent of any existing software components, applying TBFV should encounter few problems in this aspect.

To deal with realistic programs in general, TBFV can be applied flexibly. For the programs whose source code is available and expressions do not have side effect, the technique described in this paper can be applied, but for those with the above two challenges or limitations, the functional scenario-based testing technique combined with inspection can be more exploited.

7   Related Work

Research on integration of Hoare logic and testing seems to mainly concentrate on using pre- and post-assertions in Hoare triple for test case generation and test result analysis, but none of them takes the same approach as our TBFV to solve the same problem in specification-based testing.

One of the earliest efforts is Meyer's view of Design By Contract (DBC) implemented in the programming language Eiffel [12, 13]. Eiffel's success in checking pre- and post-conditions and encouraging the DBC discipline in programming partly contributed to the development of the similar work for other languages such as the Sunit testing system for Smalltalk [14]. Cheon and Leavens describe an approach to unit testing that uses a formal specification language's run-time assertion checker to decide whether methods are working correctly with respect to a formal specification using pre- and post-conditions, and have implemented this idea using the Java Modeling Language (JML) and the JUnit testing framework [15]. Gray and Microsoft describe another approach to testing Java programs using Hoare-style specifications [16]. They show how logical test specifications with a more relaxed post-condition than existing restricted Hoare-style post-condition can be embedded within Java and how the resulting test specification language can be compiled into Java for executable validation of the program. There are many other similar results in the literature, but we have to omit them due to the space limit.

8   Conclusion and Future Research

We presented a new approach, known as testing-based formal verification (TBFV), for error detection in programs by integrating specification-based testing, Hoare logic, and specification-based inspection. The principle underlying

TBFV is first to use the functional scenario-based testing (FSBT) to achieve a (representative) path coverage in the program under testing, and then to apply the Hoare logic-based approach to formally verify the correctness of every traversed path. When the verification is impractical, inspection is adopted to replace the role of proof.

While focusing on the presentation of the essential idea of the TBFV approach and an example from the case study to show its feasibility and potential effectiveness in this paper, a controlled experiment needs to be conducted to systematically assess the effectiveness and to compare with the related testing and formal verification approaches. Further research is also needed to address the two major challenges mentioned in Sect. 6 and tool support issues.

References

1. Hoare, C.A.R., Wirth, N.: An axiomatic definition of the programming language PASCAL. Acta Inf. $2(4)$, 335–355 (1973)
2. Khurshid, S., Marinov, D.: TestEra: specification-based testing of Java programs using SAT. Autom. Softw. Eng. $11(4)$, 403–434 (2004)
3. Liu, S., Nakajima, S.: A decompositional approach to automatic test case generation based on formal specifications. In: 4th IEEE International Conference on Secure Software Integration and Reliability Improvement (SSIRI 2010), Singapore, 9–11 June 2010, pp. 147–155. IEEE CS Press (2010)
4. Liu, S.: Utilizing Hoare logic to strengthen testing for error detection in programs. In: Proceedings of the Turing Centenary Conference, June 2012. EPiC Series, Manchester, UK, pp. 229–238 (2012)
5. Parnas, D.L., Madey, J., Iglewski, M.: Precise documentation of well-structured programs. IEEE Trans. Softw. Eng. $20(12)$, 948–976 (1994)
6. Aurum, A., Petersson, H., Wohlin, C.: State-of-the-art: software inspections after 25 years. Softw. Test. Verification Reliab. $12(3)$, 133–154 (2002)
7. Liu, S., Hayashi, T., Takahashi, K., Kimura, K., Nakayama, T., Nakajima, S.: Automatic transformation from formal specifications to functional scenario forms for automatic test case generation. In: 9th International Conference on Software Methodologies, Tools and Techniques (SoMet 2010), Yokohama City, Japan, September 29–October 1 (page to appear). IOS International Publisher (2010)
8. Liu, S.: Formal Engineering for Industrial Software Development Using the SOFL Method. Springer, Heidelberg (2004). ISBN 3-540-20602-7
9. Liu, S., Chen, Y., Nagoay, F., McDermid, J.: Formal specification-based inspection for verification of programs. IEEE Trans. Softw. Eng. $38(5)$, 1100–1122 (2012)
10. Liu, S., Nakajima, S.: A "Vibration" method for automatically generating test cases based on formal specifications. In: 18th Asia-Pacific Software Engineering Conference (APSEC 2011), HCM city, Vietnam, 5–8 December 2011, pp. 73–80. IEEE CS Press (2011)
11. Liu, S., McDermid, J.A., Chen, Y.: A rigorous method for inspection of model-based formal specifications. IEEE Trans. Reliab. $59(4)$, 667–684 (2010)
12. Meyer, B.: Applying design by contract. IEEE Comput. $25(10)$, 40–51 (1992)
13. Meyer, B.: Eiffel: The Language. Object-Oriented Series. Prentice Hall, Upper Saddle River (1991)
14. Castellon, M.C., Molina, J.G., Pimentel, E., Repiso, I.: Design by contract in smalltalk. J. Object-Oriented Program. $9(7)$, 23–28 (1996)

15. Cheon, Y., Leavens, G.T.: A simple and practical approach to unit testing: the JML and JUnit way. In: Magnusson, B. (ed.) ECOOP 2002. LNCS, vol. 2374, pp. 231–234. Springer, Heidelberg (2002)
16. Gray, K.E., Mycroft, A.: Logical testing: Hoare-style specification. In: Chechik, M., Wirsing, M. (eds.) FASE 2009. LNCS, vol. 5503, pp. 186–200. Springer, Heidelberg (2009)

Theory of Test Modeling Based on Regular Expressions

Pan Liu[1,2(✉)] and Huaikou Miao[3]

[1] College of Computer Engineering and Science, Shanghai Business School,
Shanghai 201400, China
Pan1008@163.com
[2] Shanghai Key Laboratory of Computer Software Testing and Evaluating,
Shanghai 201112, China
[3] School of Computer Engineering and Science, Shanghai University,
Shanghai 200072, China

Abstract. This paper presents a theory of test modeling by using regular expressions for software behaviors. Unlike the earlier modeling theory of regular expression, the proposed theory is used to build a test model which can derive effective test sequences easily. We firstly establish an expression algebraic system by means of transition sequences and a set of operators. And we then give the modeling method for behaviors of software under test based on this algebraic system. Some examples are also given for illustrating our test modeling method. Compared with the finite state machine model, the expression model is more expressive for the concurrent system and can provide the accurate and concise description of software behaviors.

Keywords: Test modeling · Regular expression · Expression algebraic system · Concurrent operation

1 Introduction

Software testing is a critical activity to assure software quality [1]. However, earlier studies have shown that software testing can consume more than fifty percent of the development costs [2]. Therefore automating software testing as a long-term goal has been highlighted in the industry for many years. Model-based testing [3–5], as a method of automatic test, has been widely studied to generate abstract test sequences. The finite state machine (FSM [6, 7]), a formal notation for describing software behaviors, is often employed for test modeling and test generation, forming a series of test generation methods [8–10].

For a concurrent system, however, it is hard to build a model by FSM due to the limitation of the expressive power of FSM. Therefore the other modeling methods have been suggested for modeling concurrent systems. For example, Petri nets [11, 12] was used for modeling software behaviors and generating test cases for accessibility test [13]. However, Petri nets easily causes the state-space explosion problem [14] when the system is complex. Regular expressions are also used to build the model of distributed systems, such as path expressions [15], behavior expressions [16] and

S. Liu and Z. Duan (Eds.): SOFL+MSVL 2013, LNCS 8332, pp. 17–31, 2014.
DOI: 10.1007/978-3-319-04915-1_2, © Springer International Publishing Switzerland 2014

extended regular expression [17]. Garg et al. [16, 18] proposed an algebraic model called concurrent regular expressions for modeling and analysis of distributed systems. However, this algebraic model is suitable for model checking and not for test generation because it lacks of the essential path information, which consists of the initial node, the terminal node and path sequences. Ravi et al. [19] proposed a novel methodology for high-level testability analysis and optimization of register-transfer level controller/data path circuits based on regular expressions. Qian et al. [20] presented a method to generate test sequences from regular expressions describing software behaviors. This method firstly uses the FSM to build the model of software behaviors. And then the FSM is converted into a regular expression according to three construction rules. Finally, test sequences are obtained from this regular expression. However, the suggested expression model does not have the capability for describing concurrent operations because regular expressions are derived from FSM.

In this paper, we suggest constructing the test model by regular expressions for software behaviors. Referring to the modeling theories of concurrent regular expressions in [16, 18] and that of FSM in [7, 21], we set up an expression algebraic system. And some examples are employed for illustrating our modeling approaches.

The rest of this paper is organized as follows. Section 2 presents the expression algebraic system. Section 3 introduces the method of test modeling by regular expressions. Some examples of test modeling are presented in Sect. 4. Section 5 discusses the advantages and disadvantages between the traditional test generation method and our test generation method. Section 6 concludes the whole paper.

2 Expression Algebraic System

Before we introduce the expression algebraic system, the definition of FSM needs to be introduced so that we can build the bridge between the regular expression and FSM.

A finite-state machine (FSM) [22, 23] $M = <S, I, O, f, g, s_0>$ consists of a finite set S of states, a finite input alphabet I, a finite output alphabet O, a transition function f that assigns to each state and input pair a new state, an output function g that assigns to each state and input pair an output, and an initial state s_0. According to the definition of FSM, we give the definitions of both transition and transition sequence.

Definition 1 (transition): A transition of FSM is defined by $t = (s_1, i/o, s_2)$, where $f(s_1, i) = s_2, i \in I, g(s_1, i) = o, o \in O, s_1$ is the pre-state of t, s_2 is the next-state of t, i is the transition condition of t and o is the output result of t.

Definition 2 (transition sequence): For any transition a, the syntax of the transition sequence ts can be defined via Backus-Naur form:

$$ts ::= \varepsilon \mid a \mid a.ts \mid ts.a \mid ts.ts,$$

Where ε denotes the empty and ts is any transition sequence.

Let Σ be a nonempty set of transition sequences in FSM, and $\varepsilon = a^0$ for any $a \in \Sigma$. Let $\#ts$ denote the number of transitions in ts.

Definition 3 (software regular expression): A software regular expression describing software behaviors is an expression consisting of symbols from Σ and the operators |, +,., *, α (), °, and ||, which are defined as follows:

| | denotes the choice operator;
. | denotes the concatenation operator;
* | is the Kleene closure;
+ | is the positive closure;
α | is a positive integer which denotes the alpha closure;
() | denotes the range;
° | denotes the synchronization;
|| | indicates the concurrent operator

In Defintion 3, the descriptions of four operators |,., * and + refer to the statements in [16, 20]. We set the priority of operators high to low: (), *, + and α,., ° and ||, |.

Definition 4 (expression algebraic system): An expression algebraic system consists of both Σ and the operators |, +,., *, α (), °, and ||, denoted as $< Σ, |, +,., *, α (), °, || >$, and ε is the identity element of this system.

3 Test Modeling

In this section, we do not take account of the inputs and outputs on transitions and all transitions are directly labeled on the edges of the graphs.

3.1 Concatenation Operator

A software behavior model with the concatenation operator shown in Fig. 1 can be described by $t_1.t_2$, where t_1 and t_2 are two transitions, and t_2 is occurred after t_1. The concatenation operator satisfies the following properties:

(1) $\forall a, b \in Σ \bullet a.b \neq b.a \Rightarrow a \neq b \wedge a \neq ε \wedge b \neq ε$
(2) $\forall a, b, c \in Σ \bullet a.b.c = (a.b).c = a.(b.c)$
(3) $\forall a \in Σ \bullet a.ε = ε.a = a$

3.2 Choice Operator

Let the symbol | denote the choice operator. In the model shown in Fig. 2, the transitions t_3 and t_2 are alternative. So the model can be described by $t_1.(t_3|t_2)$, where t_3

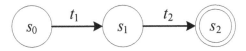

Fig. 1. The software behavior model with the concatenation operator.

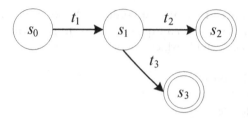

Fig. 2. The software behavior model with the choice operator.

or t_2 is executed in accordance with the different inputs on s_1. The choice operator satisfies the following properties:

(1) $\forall a, b \in \Sigma \bullet a|b \Rightarrow a \vee b$.
(2) $\forall a, b \in \Sigma \bullet a|b = b|a$ (Commutativity)
(3) $\forall a, b, c \in \Sigma \bullet a|b|c = (a|b)|c = a|(b|c)$ (Associativity)
(4) $\forall a \in \Sigma \bullet a|\varepsilon = \varepsilon|a = a$
(5) $\forall a \in \Sigma \bullet a|a = a$ (Identity)
(6) $\forall a, b_1, b_2, \ldots, b_n \in \Sigma \bullet a.(b_1|b_2|\ldots|b_n) = a.b_1|a.b_2|\ldots|a.b_n$ (Distributivity)
(7) $\forall a_1, a_2, \ldots, a_n, b \in \Sigma \bullet (a_1|a_2|\ldots|a_n).b = a_1.b|a_2.b|\ldots|a_n.b$ (Distributivity)

3.3   Kleene Closure

Let the symbol * denotes the Kleene closure. Then the model shown in Fig. 3 can be described as $t_1.t_2^*.t_3$, where t_2 can be executed repeatedly. The Kleene closure satisfies the following properties:

(1) $\forall a \in \Sigma \bullet a^* = \bigcup_{i=0,1,\ldots} a^i$
(2) $\forall a \in \Sigma \bullet (a^*)^* = a^*$ (Absorption)
(3) $a_i \in \Sigma \wedge 1 \le i \le n \bullet (a_1|a_2|\ldots|a_n)^* = a_1^*|a_2^*|\ldots|a_n^*$ (Distributivity)
(4) $\varepsilon^* = \varepsilon$

3.4   Positive Closure

Let the symbol + denote the positive closure. E.g., a^+ denotes that a is executed at least once. The model of a temperature control system is shown in Fig. 4, where

– s_0 is the initial state,
– s_2 is the terminal state,

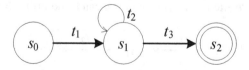

Fig. 3. The software behavior model with the Kleene closure.

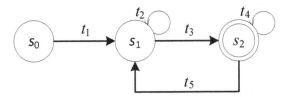

Fig. 4. The software behavior model with the positive closure.

- t_0 denotes that the engine of the temperature control system is launched,
- t_2 denotes the heating-up process when the temperature on s_1 is lower than the given threshold x,
- t_3 denoted that the engine stops working,
- t_4 denotes the cooling process when the temperature on s_2 is still greater than x,
- t_5 denoted the warming process is triggered and the system will return to s_1.

This model can be described by $t_1.\left(t_2^+.t_3.t_4^+.t_5\right)^*.t_2^+.t_3.t_4^+$. The positive closure satisfies the following properties:

(1) $\forall a \in \Sigma \bullet a^+ = \bigcup_{i=1,2,\ldots} a^i$

(2) $\forall a \in \Sigma \bullet a^+ = a.a^* = a^*.a$

(3) $\forall a \in \Sigma \bullet a.a^+ = a^+.a = a^+$

(4) $\forall a \in \Sigma \bullet (a^+)^+ = a^+$ (Absorption)

(5) $a_i \in \Sigma \land 1 \leq i \leq n \bullet (a_1|a_2|\ldots|a_n)^+ = a_1^+|a_2^+|\ldots|a_n^+$ (Distributivity)

(6) $\varepsilon^+ = \varepsilon$

3.5 Alpha-closure

Let α be the alpha-closure, which denotes a maximum cycle times. E.g., b^α denotes that the transition b is executed repeatedly α times. The model of an online bank login system is shown in Fig. 5. If the user types the wrong username or password for three

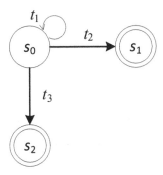

Fig. 5. The software behavior model with the alpha-closure.

times, the system will be automatically locked for 24 h. The symbols in this model denote as follows:

- s_0 denotes the login page,
- s_1 is the main page,
- s_2 denotes the locked page,
- t_1 denotes the self-check on s_0,
- t_2 denotes the login success,
- t_3 denotes the login failure.

According to the above description of system, there exists $\alpha = 3$ and this system can be described by $t_1^3.t_3|t_2|t_1.t_2|t_1^2.t_2$. The alpha-closure satisfies the following Properties:

(1) $\forall a \in \Sigma \bullet a^\alpha = \overbrace{a.a...a}^{\alpha}$
(2) $\forall a \in \Sigma \bullet a.a^\alpha = a^\alpha.a = a^\alpha$
(3) $a_i \in \Sigma \wedge 1 \le i \le n \bullet (a_1|a_2|...|a_n)^\alpha = a_1^\alpha|a_2^\alpha|...|a_n^\alpha$ (Distributivity)
(4) $\forall a \in \Sigma \bullet (a^*)^\alpha = (a^\alpha)^* = a^\alpha$ (Absorption)
(5) $\forall a \in \Sigma \bullet (a^+)^\alpha = (a^\alpha)^+ = a^\alpha$ (Absorption)
(6) $\varepsilon^\alpha = \varepsilon$

3.6 Synchronous Operator

Let the symbol $\circ$ denote the synchronous operator, which can describe the synchronization between two or more transition sequences. E.g., $a \circ b$ denotes that both a and b are synchronized in the system. A simple model of the bus scheduling system at the terminal station is shown in Fig. 6. In this system, buses entering and leaving the station are synchronous. The symbols in this model denote as follows:

- s_0 denotes the initial state of the terminal station,
- s_1 denotes the state of the terminal station after a period of time,
- t_1 denotes the sequences of the buses entering the station,
- t_2 denotes the sequences of the buses leaving the station.

This model can be described by $t_1 \circ t_2$. The synchronous operator satisfies the following Properties:

(1) $\forall a, b \in \Sigma \bullet a \circ b = b \circ a$ (Commutativity)
(2) $\forall a \in \Sigma \bullet a \circ \varepsilon = a$

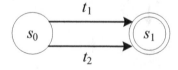

Fig. 6. The software behavior model with the synchronous operator.

(3) $\forall a, b, c \in \Sigma \bullet a \circ b \circ c = (a \circ b) \circ c = a \circ (b \circ c)$ (Associativity)

(4) $\forall a, b \in \Sigma \bullet \#a = \#b = 1 \Rightarrow a \circ b = a.b | b.a$

(5) $\forall a, b, c \in \Sigma \bullet a \circ b.c = ((a \circ b).c) | (b.(a \circ c))$

(6) $\forall a, b, c \in \Sigma \bullet a.b \circ c = ((a \circ c).b) | (a.(b \circ c))$

(7) $\forall a, b_1, \ldots, b_n \in \Sigma \bullet a \circ (b_1 | b_2 | \ldots | b_n)$

   $= (a \circ b_1) | (a \circ b_2) | \ldots | (a \circ b_n)$ (Distributivity)

Theorem 1

$\forall a, b, c, d \in \Sigma \bullet \#a = \#b = \#c = \#d = 1 \Rightarrow (a.b \circ c.d = a.b.c.d | a.c.b.d |$
  $a.c.d.b | c.a.b.d | c.a.d.b | c.d.a.b)$.

Proof. According to the Property (5) of $\circ$,

$$a.b \circ c.d = ((a.b \circ c).d) | (c.(a.b \circ d)) \tag{1}$$

By the Property (6) of $\circ$,

$$a.b \circ c = (a \circ c).b | a.(b \circ c) \tag{2}$$

By the Property (4) of $\circ$ and $\#a = \#b = \#c = \#d = 1$,

$$a \circ c = a.c | c.a \tag{3}$$

$$b \circ c = b.c | c.b \tag{4}$$

From Eqs. (2)–(4) and the Properties (3) and (7) of |,

$$
\begin{aligned}
a.b \circ c &= (a.c | c.a).b | a.(b.c | c.b) \\
&= (a.c.b | c.a.b)(a.b.c | a.b.c) \\
&= a.c.b | c.a.b | a.b.c | a.c.b
\end{aligned}
\tag{5}
$$

By the Property (6) of $\circ$,

$$a.b \circ d = (a \circ d).b | a.(b \circ d) \tag{6}$$

According to the Property (4) of $\circ$ and $\#a = \#b = \#c = \#d = 1$,

$$a \circ d = a.d | d.a \tag{7}$$

$$b \circ d = b.d | d.b \tag{8}$$

From Eqs. (6)–(8) and the Properties (3) and (7) of |,

$$
\begin{aligned}
a.b \circ d &= (a.d | d.a).b | a.(b.d | d.b) \\
&= (a.d.b | d.a.b) | (a.b.d | a.d.b) \\
&= a.d.b | d.a.b | a.b.d
\end{aligned}
\tag{9}
$$

By the Properties (3), (6) and (7) of |,

$$(a.b \circ c).d = (a.c.b|c.a.b|a.b.c|a.c.b).d$$
$$= a.c.b.d|c.a.b.d|a.b.c.d|a.c.b.d \tag{10}$$

$$c.(a.b \circ d) = c.(a.d.b|d.a.b|a.b.d|a.d.b)$$
$$= c.a.d.b|c.d.a.b|c.a.b.d \tag{11}$$

From Eqs. (1) (10) and (11),

$$a.b \circ c.d = a.c.b.d|c.a.b.d|a.b.c.d|a.c.b.d|c.a.d.b|c.d.a.b|c.a.b.d$$
$$= a.c.b.d|c.a.b.d|a.b.c.d|a.c.b.d|c.a.d.b|c.d.a.b$$

$$\square$$

Theorem 2: The synchronous operator between any two transition sequences is equal to the **C**hoice **O**perator of the **F**inite **T**ransition **S**equences, denoted as **COFTS**.

Proof. Assume that two transition sequences are $A = a_1.a_2...a_i$ and $B = b_1.b_2...b_j$, where $a_k(1 \leq k \leq i)$ and $b_l(1 \leq l \leq j)$ are two transitions. The Proof of Theorem 2 includes two phases: (1) let $i = 1$ and then prove $A \circ B = a_1 \circ (b_1.b_2...b_j)$ is **COFTS**, and (2) prove $A \circ B = (a_1.a_2...a_i) \circ (b_1.b_2...b_j)$ is **COFTS**.

Base case 1: $i = 1$ and $j = 1$.

According to the Property (4) of $\circ$ and the assumption that a_1 and b_1 are two transitions,

$$A \circ B = a_1 \circ b_1 = a_1.b_1|b_1.a_1, \tag{12}$$

which are the choice operation of two transition sequences.

Base case 2: $i = 1$ and $j = 2$.

According to the Properties (4) and (5) of $\circ$ and the Properties (3), (6) and (7) of |,

$$A \circ B = a_1 \circ b_1.b_2$$
$$= ((a_1 \circ b_1).b_2)|(b_1.(a_1 \circ b_2))$$
$$= ((a_1.b_1|b_1.a_1).b_2)|(b_1.(a_1.b_2|b_2.a_1))$$
$$= a_1.b_1.b_2|b_1.a_1.b_2|b_1.a_1.b_2|b_1.b_2.a_1 \tag{13}$$

which are the choice operation of four transition sequences.

Inductive hypothesis 1. Assume that Theorem 2 is true for $i = 1$ and $j = m-1$. That is,

$$A \circ B = C_1|C_2|...|C_k, \tag{14}$$

where $C_1...C_k$ are transition sequences and k is a finite positive integer.

We need to prove $A \circ B$ is also **COFTS** for $i = 1$ and $j = m$. Assume $B_1 = b_1.b_2...b_{m-1}$. Then according to the property (5) of $\circ$,

$$A \circ B = a_1 \circ B_1.b_m$$
$$= (a_1 \circ B_1).b_m| B_1.(a_1 \circ b_m) \tag{15}$$

According to **Inductive hypothesis 1**,

$$a_1 \circ B_1 = C_1|C_2|\ldots|C_k \tag{16}$$

By the property (4) of $\circ$, and both a_1 and b_m are two transitions,

$$a_1 \circ b_m = a_1.b_m|b_m.a_1 \tag{17}$$

which is **COFTS**.

Hence according to the Property (6) of $|$,

$$\begin{aligned}
B_1.(a_1 \circ b_m) &= B_1.(a_1.b_m|b_m.a_1) \\
&= (b_1.b_2\ldots b_{m-1}).(a_1.b_m|b_m.a_1) \\
&= b_1.b_2\ldots b_{m-1}.a_1.b_m|b_1.b_2\ldots b_{m-1}.b_m.a_1
\end{aligned} \tag{18}$$

which is **COFTS**.

From Eqs. (15), (17)–(18),

$$A \circ B = a_1.b_m|b_m.a_1|b_1.b_2\ldots b_{m-1}.a_1.b_m|b_1.b_2\ldots b_{m-1}.b_m.a_1 \tag{19}$$

which is **COFTS**.

$$\text{Hence theorem 2 is true for } i = 1 \text{ and any } j. \tag{20}$$

Inductive hypothesis 2. Assume that Theorem 2 is true for $i = n-1$ and any j. That is,

$$A \circ B = D_1|D_2|\ldots|D_l, \tag{21}$$

where $D_1\ldots D_l$ are transition sequences and l is a finite positive integer.

We need to prove $A \circ B$ is also **COFTS** for $i = n$ and any j. Assume $A_1 = a_1.a_2\ldots a_{n-1}$. Then according to the property (6) of $\circ$,

$$\begin{aligned}
A \circ B &= A_1.a_n \circ B \\
&= A_1.a_n \circ b_1.b_2\ldots b_j \\
&= (A_1 \circ b_1.b_2\ldots b_j).a_n|A_1.(a_n \circ b_1.b_2\ldots b_j)
\end{aligned} \tag{22}$$

According to **Inductive hypothesis 2**,

$$(A_1 \circ b_1.b_2\ldots b_j) = D_1|D_2|\ldots|D_l \tag{23}$$

which is **COFTS**.

From (22) and the Property (7) of $|$,

$$\begin{aligned}
(A_1 \circ b_1.b_2\ldots b_j).a_n &= (D_1|D_2|\ldots|D_l).a_n \\
&= D_1.a_n|D_2.a_n|\ldots|D_l.a_n
\end{aligned} \tag{24}$$

which is **COFTS**.

By (20), $a_n \circ b_1.b_2\ldots b_j$ is **COFTS**. Assume that

$$a_n \circ b_1.b_2\ldots b_j = K_1|K_2|\ldots|K_p \tag{25}$$

where $K_1\ldots K_p$ are transition sequences and p is a finite positive integer.

Then according to the Property (6) of |,

$$A_1.(a_n \circ b_1.b_2...b_j) = A_1.(K_1|K_2|...|K_p)$$
$$= A_1.K_1|A_1.K_2|...|A_1.K_p \quad (26)$$

which is **COFTS**.

From Eqs. (24) and (26), A∘ B is also **COFTS** for $i = n$ and any j. To sum up, Theorem 2 is proved. □

According to Theorem 2, we always make use of the choice operator of finite transition sequences to denote the synchronous operations among some transition sequences.

3.6.1   Concurrent Operator

Let the symbol ‖ denote the concurrent operator. $a \| b$ denotes a or b is a single occurrence, or the synchronous occurrence denoted as $a\circ b$. The model described as the stock trading requests is shown in Fig. 7. In the stock trading system, the trading requests that the buyers and the sellers are concurrent. The symbols in the model are described as follows:

- s_0 denotes the current state of the stock trading,
- s_1 denotes the next state of the stock trading,
- t_1 denotes the sequences of the buyer requests,
- t_2 denotes the sequences of the seller requests,
- t_3 denotes the next state is converted into the current state.

The model shown in Fig. 7 can be described by $((t_1\|t_2).t_3)^*$. The concurrent operator satisfies the following properties:

(1) $a\|b = a|b|a \circ b \forall a, b \in \Sigma$
(2) $a\|b = b\|a \forall a, b \in \Sigma$ (Commutativity)
(3) $a\|\varepsilon = \varepsilon\|a = a \forall a \in \Sigma$ (Commutativity and Identity)
(4) $a\|b\|c = (a\|b)\|c = a\|(b\|c) \forall a,b,c \in \Sigma$ (Associativity)
(5) $(a_1|a_2|...|a_n)\|b = (a_1\|b)|(a_2\|b)|...|(a_n\|b) \forall a_1,...,a_n, b \in \Sigma$ (Distribution)

Corollary 1:   The concurrent operation of any two transition sequences is **COFTS**.

Proof. Assume that two transition sequences are A and B. Then A ‖ B = A | B | A∘ B. According to Theorem 2, A∘ B is **COFTS**, hence A ‖ B is also **COFTS**. Corollary 1 is proved. □

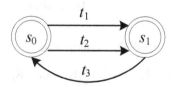

Fig. 7. The software behavior model with the concurrent operator.

Corollary 2: The concurrent operations among finite transition sequences are **COFTS**.

Proof. Assume that there are a suite of test sequences A_1, A_2, ..., and A_i, where i is a finite positive integer. Then Corollary 2 can be rewritten as $A_1 \| A_2 \| ... \| A_i$ is **COFTS**.

Base case: $i = 1$
Since A_1 is a transition sequence, Corollary 2 is true.

Base case: $i = 2$
By Corollary 1, $A_1 \| A_2$ is **COFTS**, hence Corollary 2 is true.

Inductive hypothesis. Assume that Corollary 2 is true for $i = n-1$. That is,

$$A_1 \| A_2 \| ... \| A_{n-1} = B_1 | B_2 | ... | B_k, \tag{27}$$

where B_i $(1 \leq i \leq k)$ is a transition sequence.
We need to prove $A_1 \| A_2 \| ... \| A_n$ is also **COFTS** for $i = n$.
By **Inductive hypothesis** and the property (5) of $\|$,

$$
\begin{aligned}
A_1 \| A_2 \| ... \| A_n &= (A_1 \| A_2 \| ... \| A_{n-1}) \| A_n \\
&= (B_1 | B_2 | ... | B_k) \| A_n \\
&= (B_1 \| A_n) | (B_2 \| A_n) | ... | (B_k \| A_n)
\end{aligned}
\tag{28}
$$

By Corollary 1,

$$B_i \| A_n (1 \leq i \leq n) \text{ is } \textbf{COFTS}. \tag{29}$$

From (27)–(29),

$$A_1 \| A_2 \| ... \| A_n \text{ is } \textbf{COFTS}. \tag{30}$$

To sum up, Corollary 2 is proved.   □

According to Corollary 2, any one of regular expressions with concurrent operators can be denoted as the choice operation of finite transition sequences.

4 Modeling Capability

Using the expression algebraic system, we can construct the model of the complex system. Now we consider building the expression models for two complex systems with the different software requirements.

Figure 8 shows two FSM models. Assume that there exist many different software requirements for two models shown in Fig. 8.

Case 1: Software requirements for the model shown in Fig. 8 (a) include that

- s_0 is the start state,
- s_3 is the terminal state,
- $t_1.t_3$ and $t_2.t_4$ are choice,
- t_5 is a return transition.

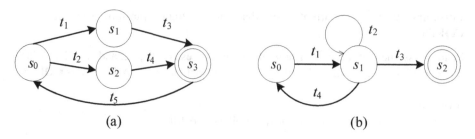

Fig. 8. Two models of the complex systems.

Therefore the system in Case 1 can be described by $(t_1.t_3 \mid t_2.t_4).(t_5.(t_1.t_3 \mid t_2.t_4))^*$.
Case 2: Software requirements for the model shown in Fig. 8 (a) include that

- s_0 is the start state,
- S_3 is the terminal state,
- $t_1.t_3$ and $t_2.t_4$ are concurrent,
- t_5 must be executed at least once.

Therefore the system in Case 2 can be described by $(t_1.t_3 \parallel t_2.t_4).(t_5.(t_1.t_3 \parallel t_2.t_4))^+$.
Case 3: Software requirements for the model shown in Fig. 8 (b) include that

- s_0 is the start state
- s_2 is the terminal state.

Therefore the system in Case 3 can be described by $t_1.(t_2^*.(t_4.t_1.t_2^*)^*).t_3$.
Case 4: Software requirements for the model shown in Fig. 8 (b) include that

- s_0 is the start state
- s_2 is the terminal state.
- t_2 and t_4 are choice.

Therefore the system in Case 4 can be described by $t_1.(t_2^* \mid (t_4.t_1)^*).t_3$.
Discussion 1: Through Cases 1–4, we find the fact that the FSM model can't distinguish the system with the nice distinctions in software requirements, while the expression model can distinguish them. Therefore the modeling capability of regular expressions is more expressive than that of the FSM.

5   Test Sequences

In the traditional test generation method, a graph (or FSM) is usually transformed to a test tree. And then all paths from the root to all leaves in this tree are produced. According to this method, we obtain two test sequences (as test paths) $t_1.t_3.t_5$ and $t_2.t_4.t_5$ from the test tree shown in Fig. 9 (b) for the model shown in Fig. 9 (a). However, $t_1.t_3.t_5$ and $t_2.t_4.t_5$ are two ineffective test segments because the last state s_0 in two sequences is not the terminal state s_3 of the system shown in Fig. 9(a).

Now we demonstrate the method of test sequence generation from regular expressions.

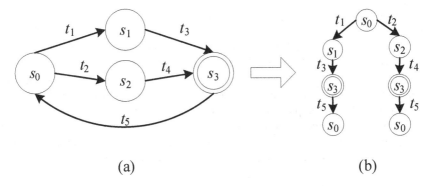

Fig. 9. The traditional test generation method.

Assume that software requirements satisfy case 1 in Sect. 4. The model shown in Fig. 9 (a) can be described by $(t_1.t_3 \mid t_2.t_4).(t_5.(t_1.t_3 \mid t_2.t_4))^*$. Then we assign 0, 1 and k for * in regular expression. Hence

$$(t_1.t_3 \mid t_2.t_4).(t_5.(t_1.t_3 \mid t_2.t_4))^* = (t_1.t_3 \mid t_2.t_4).(t_5.(t_1.t_3 \mid t_2.t_4))^0 \mid (t_1.t_3 \mid$$
$$t_2.t_4).(t_5.(t_1.t_3 \mid t_2.t_4))^1 \mid (t_1.t_3 \mid t_2.t_4).(t_5.(t_1.t_3 \mid t_2.t_4))^k$$
$$= (t_1.t_3 \mid t_2.t_4).\varepsilon \mid (t_1.t_3 \mid t_2.t_4).(t_5.(t_1.t_3 \mid t_2.t_4)) \mid (t_1.t_3 \mid t_2.t_4).(t_5.(t_1.t_3 \mid t_2.t_4))^k$$
$$= (t_1.t_3 \mid t_2.t_4) \mid (t_1.t_3 \mid t_2.t_4).(t_5.(t_1.t_3 \mid t_2.t_4)) \mid (t_1.t_3 \mid t_2.t_4).(t_5.(t_1.t_3 \mid t_2.t_4))^k \mid (t_1.t_3 \mid$$
$$t_2.t_4).(t_5.(t_1.t_3 \mid t_2.t_4))^k$$
$$= t_1.t_3 \mid t_2.t_4 \mid (t_1.t_3.(t_5.(t_1.t_3 \mid t_2.t_4)) \mid t_2.t_4.(t_5.(t_1.t_3 \mid t_2.t_4)) \mid t_1.t_3.(t_5.(t_1.t_3 \mid$$
$$t_2.t_4))^k \mid t_2.t_4.(t_5.(t_1.t_3 \mid t_2.t_4))^k$$
$$= t_1.t_3 \mid t_2.t_4 \mid t_1.t_3.t_5.t_1.t_3 \mid t_1.t_3.t_5.t_2.t_4 \mid t_2.t_4.t_5.t_1.t_3 \mid t_2.t_4.t_5.t_2.t_4 \mid t_1.t_3.$$
$$\left((t_5.t_1.t_3)^k \mid (t_5.t_2.t_4)^k\right) \mid t_2.t_4.((t_5.t_1.t_3)^k \mid (t_5.t_2.t_4)^k)$$
$$= t_1.t_3 \mid t_2.t_4 \mid t_1.t_3.t_5.t_1.t_3 \mid t_1.t_3.t_5.t_2.t_4 \mid t_2.t_4.t_5.t_1.t_3 \mid t_2.t_4.t_5.t_2.t_4 \mid$$
$$t_1.t_3.(t_5.t_1.t_3)^k \mid t_1.t_3.(t_5.t_2.t_4)^k \mid t_2.t_4.(t_5.t_1.t_3)^k \mid t_2.t_4.(t_5.t_2.t_4)^k$$

Discussion 2: (1) Sometimes, test sequences generated from the traditional method can't be taken as the effective test paths. For example, the terminal node in test path $t_1.t_3.t_5$ is s_0 which deviates from the actual software requirements. (2) Test coverage of test sequences generated from the traditional method is not complete, resulting in the low fault detection capability. (3) Based on the operations in the algebraic system, we can obtain test sequences from regular expressions. And all operations can be automatically achieved. (4) Test sequences derived from our method include all possible paths, hence they have the higher fault detection capability than those derived from the traditional method. (5) A shortcoming of our method is that the number of test sequences is too much. Therefore the redundant test sequences need to be reduced according to some techniques in Ref. [24].

6 Conclusions

In this paper, we present an expression algebraic system to support test modeling. This system consists of regular expressions denoted by transition sequences and operators, including., |, *, +, α (), ° and ||. Some examples are given to illustrate our modeling method and test generation method. Compared with the FSM model, the expression model not only is more expressive for the concurrent system, but also can generate high quality test sequences from the model. In the future, we will plan to unify test modeling and test generation into a frame by regular expressions. And we will also research the techniques for reduced-order modeling and redundant reduction.

Acknowledgments. This work is supported by National Natural Science Foundation of China (NSFC) under grant No. 61170044 and No. 61073050, Shanghai Natural Science Fund (No. 13ZR1429600), Innovation Program of Shanghai Municipal Education Commission (No. 13YZ141), and Young teacher training scheme of Shanghai Universities (No. SXY12014).

References

1. Liu, P., Miao, H.: A new approach to generating high quality test cases. In: 2010 19th IEEE Asian Test Symposium (ATS), pp. 71–76. IEEE (2010)
2. Bertolino, A.: Software testing research: achievements, challenges, dreams. In: Future of Software Engineering, FOSE'07, pp. 85–103. IEEE (2007)
3. Dalal, S.R., Jain, A., Karunanithi, N., Leaton, J., Lott, C.M., Patton, G.C., Horowitz, B.M.: Model-based testing in practice. In: Proceedings of the 21st International Conference on Software Engineering, pp. 285–294. ACM (1999)
4. Utting, M., Legeard, B.: Practical Model-Based Testing: a Tools Approach. Morgan Kaufmann, San Francisco (2010)
5. Hemmati, H., Arcuri, A., Briand, L.: Achieving scalable model-based testing through test case diversity. ACM Trans. Softw. Eng. Methodol. (TOSEM) **22**, 6 (2013)
6. Belinfante, A., Frantzen, L., Schallhart, C.: 14 tools for test case generation. In: Broy, M., Jonsson, B., Katoen, J.-P., Leucker, M., Pretschner, A. (eds.) Model-Based Testing of Reactive Systems. LNCS, vol. 3472, pp. 391–438. Springer, Heidelberg (2005)
7. Liu, P., Miao, H.-K., Zeng, H.-W., Liu, Y.: FSM-based testing: Theory, method and evaluation. Jisuanji Xuebao(Chinese J. Comput.) **34**, 965–984 (2011)
8. Fujiwara, S., Khendek, F., Amalou, M., Ghedamsi, A.: Test selection based on finite state models. IEEE Trans. Softw. Eng. **17**, 591–603 (1991)
9. Sidhu, D.P., Leung, T.-K.: Formal methods for protocol testing: a detailed study. IEEE Trans. Softw. Eng. **15**, 413–426 (1989)
10. Chow, T.S.: Testing software design modeled by finite-state machines. IEEE Trans. Softw. Eng. **4**, 178–187 (1978)
11. Lai, R.: A survey of communication protocol testing. J. Syst. Softw. **62**, 21–46 (2002)
12. Wu, N.Q., Zhou, M.: Modeling, analysis and control of dual-arm cluster tools with residency time constraint and activity time variation based on Petri nets. IEEE Trans. Autom. Sci. Eng. **9**, 446–454 (2012)
13. Notomi, M., Murata, T.: Hierarchical reachability graph of bounded Petri nets for concurrent-software analysis. IEEE Trans. Softw. Eng. **20**, 325–336 (1994)

14. Chu, F., Xie, X.-L.: Deadlock analysis of Petri nets using siphons and mathematical programming. IEEE Trans. Robot. Autom. **13**, 793–804 (1997)
15. Li, Q., Moon, B.: Indexing and querying XML data for regular path expressions. In: VLDB, pp. 361–370 (2001)
16. Garg, V.K., Ragunath, M.: Concurrent regular expressions and their relationship to Petri nets. Theoret. Comput. Sci. **96**, 285–304 (1992)
17. Sen, K., Roşu, G.: Generating optimal monitors for extended regular expressions. Electron. Notes Theoret. Comput. Sci. **89**, 226–245 (2003)
18. Garg, V.K.: Modeling of Distributed Systems by Concurrent Regular Expressions. In: FORTE, pp. 313.-327 (1989)
19. Ravi, S., Lakshminarayana, G., Jha, N.K.: TAO: regular expression-based register-transfer level testability analysis and optimization. IEEE Trans. Very Large Scale Integr. (VLSI) Syst. **9**, 824–832 (2001)
20. Qian, Z.S.: Model-based approaches to generating test cases for web applications. Ph.D. thesis, Shanghai University (2008)
21. Broy, M., Jonsson, B., Katoen, J.-P., Leucker, M., Pretschner, A. (eds.): Model-Based Testing of Reactive Systems. LNCS, vol. 3472. Springer, Heidelberg (2005)
22. Hopcroft, J.E.: Introduction to Automata Theory, Languages, and Computation, 3/E. Pearson Education India (2008)
23. Rosen, K.H., Krithivasan, K.: Discrete Mathematics and Its Applications, 5th edn. McGraw-Hill, New York (2003)
24. Miao, H.K., Liu, P., Mei, J., Zeng, H.W.: A new approach to automated redundancy reduction for test sequences. In: 15th IEEE Pacific Rim International Symposium on Dependable Computing, 2009. PRDC'09, pp. 93–98. IEEE (2009)

Simulation and Model Checking

Integrating Separation Logic with PPTL

Xu Lu[1], Zhenhua Duan[1]([✉]), Cong Tian[1], and Hongjin Liu[2]

[1] ICTT and ISN Lab, Xidian University,
Xi'an 710071, People's Republic of China
xulu@stu.mail.xidian.edu.cn, {zhhduan,ctian}@mail.xidian.edu.cn
[2] Beijing Institute of Control Engineering, Haidian, Beijing, China
lhjbuaa@hotmail.com

Abstract. In this paper, we integrate Separation Logic with propositional Projection Temporal Logic (PPTL) to obtain a two-dimensional logic, named PPTL^{SL}. The spatial dimension is realized by a decidable fragment of separation logic which can be used to describe linked lists, and the temporal dimension is expressed by PPTL. Furthermore, we prove that any PPTL^{SL} formula can be transformed into its normal form. Example are given to show how to specify temporal heap properties by this hybrid logic.

Keywords: Temporal logic · Separation logic · Heap · Many-dimensional logic

1 Introduction

Heap is an area of memory for dynamic memory allocation, pointers are references to heap cells. It is hard to detect errors of heap-manipulating programs with inappropriate management of heap. Verification of such programs is a very active research field today and has been a long history ever since the early 1970s [1]. However, it is still a big challenge because of aliasing, that is, the same heap cell can be accessed through different pointers which yields what Hoare and He call "the complexity of pointer swing" [2]. Programs become more error-prone with serious problems involving the existence of memory violation, the emergence of memory leaks, etc. In addition, reasoning about temporal properties of such programs is yet quite difficult.

Several advanced logics have been developed for verifying and analyzing heap. Alias analysis [3], as the name implies, is a point-to analysis which naively checks whether pointers can be aliased. Shape analysis [4] is another form of pointer analysis that goes beyond the shallow alias analysis. It attempts to discover the

This research is supported by the NSFC Grant Nos. 61133001, 61272118, 61272117, 61202038, 91218301, 61322202, 61373043 and National Program on Key Basic Research Project (973 Program) Grant No. 2010CB328102.

S. Liu and Z. Duan (Eds.): SOFL+MSVL 2013, LNCS 8332, pp. 35–47, 2014.
DOI: 10.1007/978-3-319-04915-1_3, © Springer International Publishing Switzerland 2014

possible shapes of pointer structures inside the heap at each program point and to prove that these structures are not misused or corrupted during the execution of a program. One of the most prominent works on shape analysis formalized by Sagiv et al. [5] exploits "shape graphs" as heap abstraction and three-valued logic as a basis that makes the successful development of Three-Valued-Logic Analyzer (TVLA) [6].

A great progress in this realm has been made at the beginning of this century by Reynolds and O'Hearn who propose a Hoare-style logic well known as separation logic [7]. More recently, separation logic is increasingly being used and extended for automated assertion checking [8] and shape analysis [9]. Separation logic is famous for its flexible, intuitionistic and modular characteristics. Intuitively speaking, it allows each component of a system to only talk about the portion of the global heap it refers to during its execution. In particular, it introduces a novel specific form of binary logical connective, separation conjunction $*$. The formula $P*Q$ specify properties hold respectively for disjoint portions of the heap, one makes P true and the other makes Q true. The strength of separation logic lies in its reasoning style rather than its expressive power [10].

Temporal logic is another highly successful formalism for verification. Interval Temporal Logic (ITL) [11] is a specific form in temporal logic families. Duan et al. [12] introduced Projection Temporal Logic (PTL) and propositional PTL (PPTL) which extended ITL with a new projection construct $(p_1, \ldots, p_m) \, prjq$, and generalized ITL to infinite time intervals. Using PTL as a basis, Duan further developed an executable subset, called the Modeling Simulation and Verification Language (MSVL) [13] which is an extension of Framed Tempura [14]. However, neither MSVL nor PPTL has the ability to reason about heaps so far. There are various temporal logics previously designed for heap verification in many literatures. Evolution Temporal Logic (ETL) [15] is a first-order Linear Temporal Logic (LTL) for the description of program behaviors that causes dynamic allocation and deallocation of heap to evolve. Based on a tableau model checking algorithm, Navigation Temporal Logic (NTL) [16] extends LTL with pointer assertions for reasoning about the evolution of heap cells during program execution. In [17], LTL and CTL (Computation Tree Logic) are combined, in time and space, to specify complex properties of programs with dynamic heap structures.

Motivation. In fact, temporal logic describes all computations (or traces) of a system in terms of time, while separation logic is a static logic and focuses on pre- and post-conditions for partial correctness of program blocks. It is useful if we can integrate the two types of logics such that heap evolutions properties over discrete time can be specified and verified in a unified manner.

The work closest to ours is LTL^{mem} [18] that introduced by Brochenina et al. However, they devised the two-dimensional logic LTL^{mem} by means of a quantifier-free fragment of separation logic as the underlying assertion language on top of which is propositional LTL (PLTL). LTL^{mem} is of very limited use because the fragment of the separation logic employed by them cannot account for reachability in some way. In this paper, we utilize a decidable fragment of separation logic including formulas for describing complex heap structures such as linked list segments. In addition, PPTL is more powerful than PLTL with regard to expressiveness since the expressiveness of PPTL is full regular. By contrast, PLTL is star free regular. The spatial-temporal logic introduced in this paper contains temporal connectives ";" for sequentially combining formulas which enable us easily to express the occurrence of sequential events, whereas "+" or "*" enables us to state loop properties. For instance, the formula $p; q$ asserts that p holds from now until some point in the future, and from that point on, q holds. p^* means that p is repeatedly executed a finite or infinite number of times. All these properties cannot be expressed in LTL, but they are very useful for verification. Moreover, we have a powerful and mature tool supporting verification of PPTL.

The remainder of this paper is organized as follows. In the following Sect. the syntax, semantics of PPTL^{SL} is presented. In Sect. 3, we give some logic laws and a straight forward example that is easy for understanding to show the expressiveness of PPTL^{SL}. In Sect. 4, the proof of a normal form of PPTL^{SL} formulas is presented. Finally, conclusions are drawn in Sect. 5.

2   The Hybrid Logic PPTL^{SL}

The decidability of the satisfiability problem for full separation logic is known undecidable [19]. Several decidable fragments of the separation logic have been intensively studied. In this subsection, we first introduce one of them [20] which succinctly consists of formulas for describing linked list structures. Then we make a temporal extension to SL by adding temporal connectives of PPTL.

2.1   A Decidable Separation Logic for Linked Lists

Syntax. We call this logic SL for short. Let $Var = \{l, l', \ldots\}$ be an infinite countable set of pointer variables; $Val = Loc \cup \{nil\}$ an infinite set of values, where Loc is the set of memory addresses while nil is a distinguished value that is non-addressable. $l, l', \ldots$, are ranged over Val.

Terms	$e ::= nil \mid x$	simple Pures	$\alpha ::= e_1 = e_2 \mid \neg\alpha$
Pures	$\beta ::= true \mid \beta \wedge \alpha$	simple Spatials	$\gamma ::= e_1 \mapsto e_2 \mid ls^n(e_1, e_2) \mid$
			$ls(e_1, e_2)$
Spatials	$\delta ::= emp \mid \delta * \gamma$	Symbolic heaps	$\varphi ::= \beta \wedge \delta$

When writing properties, we are not interested in the value of variables. Rather, we care about the heap cells to which pointed by variables or other heap cells. $e_1 = e_2$ states that e_1 and e_2 are aliases in pure formulas. The atomic formulas emp is true just in the empty heap whose defined element of its domain is $\emptyset$; for $e_1 \mapsto e_2$, we mean e_1 points to e_2, where e_1 uniquely represents an address in the heap and e_2 is the value stored in that address. The separation conjunction formula $\delta * \gamma$ means the current heap can be split into two disjoint components (two heaps with non-overlap domains) such that one component is for δ to hold and the other for γ to hold. Moreover, the two forms of ls formulas, $ls^n(e_1, e_2)$ (where $n > 0$), as well as $ls(e_1, e_2)$, formulate non-empty segments of linked lists, or potential incomplete linked lists structures in heaps. A complete linked list formula may be written as $ls(e, nil)$, which can be considered as a special case of nil-tailed list segments. $ls(e_1, e_2)$ is equivalent to a nonempty list segment containing at least one heap cell. Symbolic heaps are formulas of pairs, including heap-independent part called pure formulas connected by conjunctions $\wedge$ and heap-dependent part known as spatial formulas separated by separation conjunctions $*$.

Semantics. Following the standard semantics of the separation logic, we refer to a pair (I_s, I_h) as a memory state s, where I_s represents a stack and I_h a heap. I_s serves as valuations of variables and I_h as valuations of heap cells. It is noteworthy that nil does not exist in the domain of any heap. Notation $\rightharpoonup_{fin}$ is employed to indicate partial functions with finite domain. Heaps are not stacks. They need not define on all elements of the domain.

$$I_s \in \text{Stacks} \stackrel{\text{def}}{=} Var \rightarrow Val \quad I_h \in \text{Heaps} \stackrel{\text{def}}{=} Loc \rightharpoonup_{fin} Val$$

$$s \in \text{States} \stackrel{\text{def}}{=} \text{Stacks} \times \text{Heaps}$$

We call this logic SL for short. The semantics of SL is given as follows by a forcing relation $\models_{SL}$ equipped with a subscript SL. Terms depend only on the stack I_s and $fv(e)$ denotes the set of all free variables that appear in term e. We specify the domain of a mapping f by $dom(f)$ and write $f_1 \perp f_2$ to denote two mappings f_1 and f_2 with disjoint domains, i.e., $dom(f_1) \cap dom(f_2) = \emptyset$. Moreover, we use $f_1 * f_2$ to denote the union of two mappings $f_1 \cup f_2$ which is undefined when $f_1 \not\perp f_2$. The notation $f[x \rightarrow v]$ is introduced for describing a mapping that maps x into v and keeps all values of other members in f's domain unchanged.

$$\llbracket x \rrbracket I_s \stackrel{\text{def}}{=} I_s(x) \quad \llbracket nil \rrbracket I_s \stackrel{\text{def}}{=} nil$$

$$I_s, I_h \models_{SL} e_1 = e_2 \quad \text{iff} \quad \llbracket e_1 \rrbracket I_s = \llbracket e_2 \rrbracket I_s.$$

$$I_s, I_h \models_{SL} \neg \alpha \quad \text{iff} \quad I_s, I_h \not\models_{SL} \alpha.$$

$$I_s, I_h \models_{SL} true \quad \text{always.}$$

$$I_s, I_h \models_{SL} \beta \wedge \alpha \quad \text{iff} \quad I_s, I_h \models_{SL} \beta \text{ and } I_s, I_h \models_{SL} \alpha.$$

$$I_s, I_h \models_{SL} e_1 \mapsto e_2 \quad \text{iff} \quad I_h = \{ \llbracket e_1 \rrbracket I_s, \llbracket e_2 \rrbracket I_s \}.$$

$$I_s, I_h \models_{SL} ls^n(e_1, e_2) \quad \text{iff} \quad \begin{cases} \llbracket e_1 \rrbracket I_s \neq \llbracket e_2 \rrbracket I_s \text{ and } I_s, I_h \models_{SL} e_1 \mapsto e_2 & \text{if } n = 1, \\ \llbracket e_1 \rrbracket I_s \neq \llbracket e_2 \rrbracket I_s \text{ and there exists } v \in Val : \\ I_s[x \rightarrow v], I_h \models_{SL} e_1 \mapsto x * ls^{n-1}(x, e_2) & \text{if } n > 1. \\ \text{for } x \notin fv(e_1, e_2) \end{cases}$$

$$I_s, I_h \models_{SL} ls(e_1, e_2) \quad \text{iff} \quad \text{there exists } n : I_s, I_h \models_{SL} ls^n(e_1, e_2).$$

$$I_s, I_h \models_{SL} emp \quad \text{iff} \quad I_h = \emptyset.$$

$$I_s, I_h \models_{SL} \delta * \gamma \quad \text{iff} \quad \text{there exists } I_{h_1}, I_{h_2} : I_h = I_{h_1} * I_{h_2} \text{ and } I_s, I_{h_1} \models_{SL} \delta$$
$$\text{and } I_s, I_{h_2} \models_{SL} \gamma.$$

$$I_s, I_h \models_{SL} \beta \wedge \delta \quad \text{iff} \quad I_s, I_h \models_{SL} \beta \text{ and } I_s, I_h \models_{SL} \delta.$$

2.2 Temporal Extension to Separation Logic

Syntax. In order to express temporal properties of heap systems, we integrate SL with PPTL, and name the hybrid logic as PPTL^{SL}. The formula p of PPTL^{SL} is given by the following grammar:

Terms $e ::= nil \mid x$

State Formulas $\phi ::= e_1 = e_2 \mid emp \mid e_1 \mapsto e_2 \mid ls^n(e_1, e_2) \mid$
$$ls(e_1, e_2) \mid \phi_1 * \phi_2 \mid \neg\phi \mid \phi_1 \wedge \phi_2$$

PPTL^{SL} Formulas $p ::= \phi \mid \neg p \mid p_1 \wedge p_2 \mid \bigcirc p \mid (p_1, \ldots, p_m) \, prj \, p \mid p^+$

where $p_1, \ldots, p_m$ are all well-formed PPTL^{SL} formulas. SL is a strict subset of PPTL^{SL}. $\bigcirc$ (next), prj (projection) and $^+$ (plus) are basic temporal operators. A formula is said to be a state formula if it does not contain any temporal operators (that is, $\bigcirc$, $^+$(plus), prj), otherwise it is a temporal formula. It is easy to see that a state formula ϕ is also a SL formula.

Semantics. An interval $\sigma = \langle s_0, s_1, \ldots \rangle$ is a sequence of states, possibly finite or infinite. ϵ denotes an empty interval. The length of σ, denoted by $|\sigma|$, is ω if σ is infinite, otherwise it is the number of states minus one. To have a uniform notation for both finite and infinite intervals, we will use extended integers as indices. That is, we consider the set N_0 of non-negative integers and ω, define $N_\omega = N_0 \cup \{\omega\}$, and extend the comparison operators, $=$, $<$, $\leq$, to N_ω by considering $\omega = \omega$, and for all $i \in N_0$, $i < \omega$. Moreover, we define $\preceq$ as $\leq -\{(\omega, \omega)\}$. With such a notation, $\sigma_{(i \ldots j)}(0 \leq i \preceq j \leq |\sigma|)$ denotes the sub-interval $\langle s_i, \ldots, s_j \rangle$ and $\sigma^{(k)}(0 \leq k \preceq |\sigma|)$ denotes the suffix interval $\langle s_k, \ldots, s_{|\sigma|} \rangle$ of σ. The concatenation of σ with another interval (or empty string) σ' is denoted by $\sigma \cdot \sigma'$. To define the semantics of the projection operator we need an auxiliary operator for intervals.

Let $\sigma = \langle s_k, \ldots, s_{|\sigma|} \rangle$ be an interval and $r_1, \ldots, r_h$ be integers $(h \geq 1)$ such that $0 \leq r_1 \leq r_2 \leq \cdots \leq r_h \preceq |\sigma|$. The projection of σ onto $r_1, \ldots, r_h$ is the interval (called projected interval), is

$$\sigma \downarrow (r_1, \ldots, r_h) = \langle s_{t_1}, \ldots, s_{t_l} \rangle$$

where $t_1, \ldots, t_l$ is obtained from $r_1, \ldots, r_h$ by deleting all duplicates. That is, $t_1, \ldots, t_l$ is the longest strictly increasing subsequence of $r_1, \ldots, r_h$. For example,

$$\langle s_0, s_1, s_2, s_3, s_4 \rangle \downarrow (0, 0, 2, 2, 2, 3) = \langle s_0, s_2, s_3 \rangle$$

This is convenient to define an interval obtained by taking the endpoints (rendezvous points) of the intervals over which $p_1, \ldots, p_m$ are interpreted in the projection construct.

The binary operators interval concatenation $\cdot$ operating on intervals and yielding to a combined fresh interval is defined as follows:

—— Interval concatenation $\cdot$

$$\sigma \cdot \sigma' = \begin{cases} \sigma & \text{if } |\sigma| = \omega \text{ or } \sigma' = \epsilon, \\ \sigma' & \text{if } \sigma = \epsilon, \\ \langle s_0, \ldots, s_i, s_{i+1}, \ldots \rangle & \text{if } \sigma = \langle s_0, \ldots, s_i \rangle \text{ and } \sigma' = \langle s_{i+1}, \ldots \rangle. \end{cases}$$

An interpretation for a PPTL^{SL} formula is a quadruple $\mathcal{I} = (\sigma, i, k, j)$ where $\sigma = \langle s_0, s_1, \ldots \rangle$ is an interval, i and k are non-negative integers and j is an integer or ω such that $i \leq k \preceq j \leq |\sigma|$. We write (σ, i, k, j) to mean that a formula is interpreted over a sub-interval $\sigma_{(i \ldots j)}$ with the current state being s_k. The notation $s_k = (I_s^k, I_h^k)$ indexed by k represents the kth state of an interval σ.

Using those notions illustrated above, it follows that the satisfaction correlation for PPTL^{SL} formulas $\models$ is inductively defined as follows.

$\mathcal{I} \models \phi$	iff	$I_s^k, I_h^k \models_{SL} \phi$.
$\mathcal{I} \models \neg p$	iff	$\mathcal{I} \not\models p$.
$\mathcal{I} \models p_1 \wedge p_2$	iff	$\mathcal{I} \models p_1$ and $\mathcal{I} \models p_2$.
$\mathcal{I} \models \bigcirc p$	iff	$k < j$ and $(\sigma, i, k+1, j) \models p$.
$\mathcal{I} \models (p_1, \ldots, p_m) \, \text{prj} \, p$	iff	there exists integers $k = r_0 \leq r_1 \leq \cdots \leq r_m \preceq j$

such that $(\sigma, i, r_0, r_1) \models p_1$, $(\sigma, r_{l-1}, r_{l-1}, r_l) \models p_l$
(for $1 < l \leq m$), and $(\sigma', 0, 0, |\sigma'|) \models p$
for one of the following σ' :
(a) $r_m < j$ and $\sigma' = \sigma \downarrow (r_0, \ldots, r_m) \cdot \sigma_{(r_m+1 \ldots j)}$
(b) $r_m = j$ and $\sigma' = \sigma \downarrow (r_0, \ldots, r_h)$
for some $0 \leq h \leq m$.

$\mathcal{I} \models p^+$ iff   there are finitely many $r_0, \ldots, r_n \in N_\omega$ such that
$k = r_0 \leq r_1 \leq \cdots \leq r_{n-1} \preceq r_n = j (n \geq 1)$ and
$(\sigma, i, r_0, r_1) \models p$ and for all $1 < l \leq n$
$(\sigma, r_{l-1}, r_{l-1}, r_l) \models p$;
or there are infinitely many integers
$k = r_0 \leq r_1 \leq r_2 \leq \cdots$ such that $\lim_{i \to \infty} r_i = \omega$ and
$(\sigma, i, r_0, r_1) \models p$ and for all $l > 1$
$(\sigma, r_{l-1}, r_{l-1}, r_l) \models p$.

With the convention, a formula p is satisfied by an interval σ, denoted by $\sigma \models p$, if $(\sigma, 0, 0, |\sigma|) \models p$ holds. When $\sigma \models p$ holds for some interval σ, we say that formula p is satisfiable. A formula p is valid, denoted by $\models p$, if $\sigma \models p$ holds for all σ. In principle, we can define other connectives $true, false, \wedge, \rightarrow, \leftrightarrow$ in the standard way. Also we have the following derived formulas:

$$\varepsilon \overset{def}{=} \neg \bigcirc true \qquad\qquad more \overset{def}{=} \neg \varepsilon$$

$$len(0) \overset{def}{=} \varepsilon \qquad\qquad len(n) \overset{def}{=} \bigcirc len(n-1), n \geq 1$$

$$skip \overset{def}{=} len(1) \qquad\qquad \odot p \overset{def}{=} \varepsilon \vee \bigcirc p$$

$$p; q \overset{def}{=} (p,q) \text{ prj } \varepsilon \qquad\qquad \Diamond p \overset{def}{=} true; p$$

$$\Box p \overset{def}{=} \neg \Diamond \neg p \qquad\qquad p^* \overset{def}{=} \varepsilon \vee p^+$$

$$\bigcirc^0 p \overset{def}{=} p \qquad\qquad \bigcirc^n p \overset{def}{=} \bigcirc(\bigcirc^{n-1} p), n \geq 1$$

where $\odot$ (weak next), $\Box$ (always), $\Diamond$ (sometimes) and ; (chop) are derived temporal operators, ε (empty) denotes an interval with zero length, and $more$ means the current state is not the final one over an interval. In order to avoid an excessive number of parentheses, the precedence rules is shown in Table 1, where 1 is the highest and 6 the lowest.

Table 1. Precedence rules

Precedence	Operators	Precedence	Operators
1	$\neg$	4	$\vee$
2	$\bigcirc, \Diamond, \Box, {}^+, {}^*$	5	$\rightarrow, \leftrightarrow$
3	$*, \wedge$	6	$;, prj$

Example 1. PPTL^{SL} does not allow arbitrary nesting of connectives in SL and PPTL. For instance, $\Diamond p_1 * \Box p_2$ is illegal according to the syntax of PPTL^{SL} since $*$ can only appear in state formulas. Hence it cannot connect two temporal formulas. Further, $\Diamond(\phi_1 * \phi_2)$ is a legal formula.

Example 2. As another example, formula $ls(x, nil); \Diamond emp$ means that now in the heap, there exists a complete linked list $ls(x, nil)$ whose head pointer is x, and after some time units in the future, the heap becomes empty. This property enable us to characterize the sequential behavior of a list disposal program which accepts a linked list as input and deletes all elements of the list in the end.

Example 3. $(\bigcirc^2(ls(x, nil) \wedge \varepsilon))^+$ states that $\bigcirc^2(ls(x, nil) \wedge \varepsilon)$ repeatedly holds for a finite or infinite number of times (more than once). Besides, $\bigcirc^2(ls(x, nil) \wedge \varepsilon)$ asserts that $ls(x, nil)$ holds in the 3-rd state from now on and specifies exactly two units of time over an interval. We can see that * or $^+$ is suitable for describing loop properties, e.g., loop invariants in programs.

3 Logic Laws Of PPTL^{SL} Formulas

Sometimes, we denote $\models \Box(p \leftrightarrow q)$ by $p \equiv q$ which is called "strong equivalence". Similarly, we denote $\models \Box(p \to q)$ by $p \supset q$ which is called "strong implication". The former means that p and q have the same truth value in all states of every model. Similar explanations can be given for the strong implication. Table 2 shows some useful logic laws. $\phi, \phi_i, \phi_p, \phi_s$ are state formulas and also SL formulas. We say a state formula is pure, it means that formula only has the form ϕ_p, whereas a state formula is spatial when it has the form ϕ_s. Other laws associated with temporal connectives are the same as those in PPTL. See [22] for more details.

Pure Formulas $\phi_p ::= e_1 = e_2 \mid \neg\phi_p \mid \phi_{p_1} \wedge \phi_{p_2}$
Spatial Formulas $\phi_s ::= emp \mid e_1 \mapsto e_2 \mid ls^n(e_1, e_2) \mid ls(e_1, e_2) \mid \phi_{s_1} * \phi_{s_2}$

Table 2. Logic laws for PPTL^{SL}

L_1	$\phi * emp \equiv \phi$
L_2	$\phi_1 * \phi_2 \equiv \phi_2 * \phi_1$
L_3	$(\phi_1 * \phi_2) * \phi_3 \equiv \phi_1 * (\phi_2 * \phi_3)$
L_4	$(\phi_1 \vee \phi_2) * \phi \equiv (\phi_1 * \phi) \vee (\phi_2 * \phi)$
L_5	$(\phi_1 \wedge \phi_2) * \phi \supset (\phi_1 * \phi) \wedge (\phi_2 * \phi)$
L_6	$(\phi_1 \wedge \phi_2) * \phi \equiv (\phi_1 * \phi) \wedge (\phi_2 * \phi)$ when ϕ is spatial
L_7	$\phi_1 \wedge \phi_2 \supset \phi_1 * \phi_2$ when ϕ_1 or ϕ_2 is pure
L_8	$\phi_1 * \phi_2 \supset \phi_1 \wedge \phi_2$ when ϕ_1 and ϕ_2 are pure
L_9	$\dfrac{\phi_0 \supset \phi_1 \quad \phi_2 \supset \phi_3}{\phi_0 * \phi_2 \supset \phi_1 * \phi_3}$
L_{10}	$(\phi_1 \wedge \phi_2) * \phi_3 \supset (\phi_1 * \phi_3) \wedge \phi_2$ when ϕ_2 is pure

Proof. We only prove L_1, L_4, L_5, L_6 of the laws. In the proofs, we use some interpretation rules, abbreviations, and proved logic laws without declaration. Let σ be an interval, and i, j, k integers, $0 \leq k \preceq |\sigma|$ and (I_s^k, I_h^k) be the k-th state of σ.

The proof of $L_1 : \phi * emp \equiv \phi$

$$
\begin{aligned}
&(\sigma, 0, k, |\sigma|) \models \phi * emp \\
\Longleftrightarrow\ &(I_s^k, I_h^k) \models_{SL} \phi * emp \\
\Longleftrightarrow\ &(I_s^k, I_h^k) \models_{SL} \phi \\
\Longleftrightarrow\ &(\sigma, 0, k, |\sigma|) \models \phi
\end{aligned}
$$

The proof of L_4 : $(\phi_1 \vee \phi_2) * \phi \equiv (\phi_1 * \phi) \vee (\phi_2 * \phi)$

$$
\begin{aligned}
&(\sigma, 0, k, |\sigma|) &&\models &&(\phi_1 \vee \phi_2) * \phi \\
\Longleftrightarrow &(I_s^k, I_h^k) &&\models_{SL} &&(\phi_1 \vee \phi_2) * \phi \\
\Longleftrightarrow &(I_s^k, I_{h_1}^k) &&\models_{SL} &&\phi_1 \vee \phi_2 \text{ and } (I_s^k, I_{h_2}^k) \models_{SL} \phi \text{ for some } I_{h_1}^k, I_{h_2}^k, I_{h_1}^k * I_{h_2}^k \\
& && &&= I_h^k \\
\Longleftrightarrow &((I_s^k, I_{h_1}^k) &&\models_{SL} &&\phi_1 \text{ or } (I_s^k, I_{h_1}^k) \models_{SL} \phi_2) \\
&\text{and} \\
&(I_s^k, I_{h_2}^k) &&\models_{SL} &&\phi \text{ for some } I_{h_1}^k, I_{h_2}^k, I_{h_1}^k * I_{h_2}^k = I_h^k \\
\Longleftrightarrow &(I_s^k, I_{h_1}^k) &&\models_{SL} &&\phi_1 \text{ and } (I_s^k, I_{h_2}^k) \models_{SL} \phi \\
&\text{or} \\
&(I_s^k, I_{h_1}^k) &&\models_{SL} &&\phi_2 \text{ and } (I_s^k, I_{h_2}^k) \models_{SL} \phi \text{ for some } I_{h_1}^k, I_{h_2}^k, I_{h_1}^k * I_{h_2}^k = I_h^k \\
\Longleftrightarrow &(I_s^k, I_{h_1}^k * I_{h_2}^k) &&\models_{SL} &&\phi_1 * \phi \text{ or } (I_s^k, I_{h_1}^k * I_{h_2}^k) \models_{SL} \phi_2 * \phi \\
\Longleftrightarrow &(I_s^k, I_h^k) &&\models_{SL} &&(\phi_1 * \phi) \vee (\phi_2 * \phi) \\
\Longleftrightarrow &(\sigma, 0, k, |\sigma|) &&\models &&(\phi_1 * \phi) \vee (\phi_2 * \phi)
\end{aligned}
$$

The proof of L_5 : $(\phi_1 \wedge \phi_2) * \phi \supset (\phi_1 * \phi) \wedge (\phi_2 * \phi)$.

$$
\begin{aligned}
&(\sigma, 0, k, |\sigma|) &&\models &&(\phi_1 \wedge \phi_2) * \phi \\
\Longleftrightarrow &(I_s^k, I_h^k) &&\models_{SL} &&(\phi_1 \wedge \phi_2) * \phi \\
\Longleftrightarrow &(I_s^k, I_{h_1}^k) &&\models_{SL} &&\phi_1 \wedge \phi_2 \text{ and } (I_s^k, I_{h_2}^k) \models_{SL} \phi \text{ for some } I_{h_1}^k, I_{h_2}^k, I_{h_1}^k * I_{h_2}^k \\
& && &&= I_h^k \\
\Longleftrightarrow &((I_s^k, I_{h_1}^k) &&\models_{SL} &&\phi_1 \text{ and } (I_s^k, I_{h_1}^k) \models_{SL} \phi_2) \\
&\text{and} \\
&(I_s^k, I_{h_2}^k) &&\models_{SL} &&\phi \text{ for some } I_{h_1}^k, I_{h_2}^k, I_{h_1}^k * I_{h_2}^k = I_h^k \\
\Longrightarrow &(I_s^k, I_{h_1}^k) &&\models_{SL} &&\phi_1 \text{ and } (I_s^k, I_{h_2}^k) \models_{SL} \phi \text{ for some } I_{h_1}^k, I_{h_2}^k, I_{h_1}^k * I_{h_2}^k = I_h^k \\
&\text{and} \\
&(I_s^k, I_{h_1}^k) &&\models_{SL} &&\phi_2 \text{ and } (I_s^k, I_{h_2}^k) \models_{SL} \phi \text{ for some } I_{h_1}^k, I_{h_2}^k, I_{h_1}^k * I_{h_2}^k = I_h^k \\
\Longleftrightarrow &(I_s^k, I_{h_1}^k * I_{h_2}^k) &&\models_{SL} &&\phi_1 * \phi \text{ and } (I_s^k, I_{h_1}^k * I_{h_2}^k) \models_{SL} \phi_2 * \phi \\
\Longleftrightarrow &(I_s^k, I_h^k) &&\models_{SL} &&(\phi_1 * \phi) \wedge (\phi_2 * \phi) \\
\Longleftrightarrow &(\sigma, 0, k, |\sigma|) &&\models &&(\phi_1 * \phi) \wedge (\phi_2 * \phi)
\end{aligned}
$$

However, its converse are not valid for all state formulas. For example, suppose $x \neq y$, the formula

$$(x \mapsto z * (x \mapsto z \vee y \mapsto z)) \wedge (y \mapsto z * (x \mapsto z \vee y \mapsto z))$$

is true, but

$$(x \mapsto z \wedge y \mapsto z) * (x \mapsto z \vee y \mapsto z)$$

is obviously false. However, the converse is valid when ϕ is spatial. Hence, we can prove L_6.

The proof of L_6 : $(\phi_1 \wedge \phi_2) * \phi \equiv (\phi_1 * \phi) \wedge (\phi_2 * \phi)$ when ϕ is spatial

case 2: if q or r is a temporal formula, then the proof is

$$q \wedge r \equiv (q_e \wedge \varepsilon \vee \bigvee_{i=1}^{n} q_i \wedge \bigcirc q_i') \wedge (r_e \wedge \varepsilon \vee \bigvee_{j=1}^{n'} r_j \wedge \bigcirc r_j')$$

$$\equiv (q_e \wedge r_e \wedge \varepsilon) \vee \bigvee_{i=1}^{n} \bigvee_{j=1}^{n'} q_i \wedge r_j \wedge \bigcirc(q_i' \wedge r_j')$$

If $p \equiv \neg q$,

case 1: if q is a state formula, then $\neg q$ is a state formula, the proof is

$$\neg q \equiv (\neg q \wedge \varepsilon) \vee (\neg q \wedge \bigcirc true)$$

case 2: if q is a temporal formula, then we can reused the proof method in [22, 23].

If $p \equiv (p_1, \ldots, p_m)$ prj q or $p \equiv q^+$, we can also reused the proof method in [22, 23].

Therefore, we can finally conclude that any PPTL^{SL} formula p can be written into its normal form. □

5   Conclusion

This paper integrates a decidable fragment of Separation Logic (SL) with Propositional Projection Temporal Logic (PPTL) to obtain a two-dimensional (spatial and temporal) logic PPTL^{SL}. The state formulas of PPTL^{SL} are SL assertions, on top of which are the outer temporal connectives taken from PPTL. Some examples are given to show its applications. It is useful to specify temporal properties of heaps. We also prove a series of logic laws and a useful conclusion that any PPTL^{SL} formula can be transformed into its normal form. A normal form can be divided into two parts, one is the present component and the other is the future component. In the future, the decidability of PPTL^{SL} will be investigated. Then a model checking approach using PPTL^{SL} as the specification language will also be studied. In addition, we will develop a model checker based on our approach, and do case studies to evaluate the approach.

References

1. Burstall, R.M.: Some techniques for proving correctness of programs which alter data structures. J. Mach. Intell. **7**, 23–50 (1972)
2. Hoare, C.A.R., He, J.: A trace model for pointers and objects. In: Guerraoui, R. (ed.) ECCOP 1999. LNCS, vol. 1628, pp. 1–17. Springer, Heidelberg (1999)
3. Chase, D.R., Wegman, M., Zadeck, F.K.: Analysis of pointers and structures. In: PLDI, pp. 296–310. ACM Press, New York (1990)
4. Wilhelm, R., Sagiv, S., Reps, T.W.: Shape analysis. In: Watt, D.A. (ed.) CC/ETAPS 2000. LNCS, vol. 1781, pp. 1–17. Springer, Heidelberg (2000)

5. Sagiv, M., Reps, T., Wilhelm, R.: Parametric shape analysis via 3-valued logic. J. ACM Trans. Program. Lang. Syst. **24**, 217–298 (2002)
6. Lev-Ami, T., Sagiv, M.: TVLA: A system for implementing static analyses. In: Palsberg, J. (ed.) SAS 2000. LNCS, vol. 1824, pp. 280–302. Springer, Heidelberg (2000)
7. Reynolds, J.C.: Separation logic: a logic for shared mutable data structures. In: 17th IEEE Symp. on Logic in Comput. Sci., pp. 55–74. IEEE Press, New York (2002)
8. Berdine, J., Calcagno, C., O'Hearn, P.W.: Symbolic execution with separation logic. In: Yi, K. (ed.) ALAPS 2005. LNCS, vol. 3780, pp. 52–68. Springer, Heidelberg (2005)
9. Distefano, D., O'Hearn, P.W., Yang, H.: A local shape analysis based on separation logic. In: Hermanns, H., Palsberg, J. (eds.) TACAS 2006. LNCS, vol. 3920, pp. 287–302. Springer, Heidelberg (2006)
10. Calcagno, C., Gardner, P., Hague, M.: From separation logic to first-order logic. In: Sassone, V. (ed.) FoSSaCS 2005. LNCS, vol. 3441, pp. 395–409. Springer, Heidelberg (2005)
11. Moszkowski, B.C.: Reasoning about digital circuits. Ph.D. thesis, Stanford University (1983)
12. Duan, Z.: An extended interval temporal logic and a framing technique for temporal logic programming. Ph.D. thesis, University of Newcastle Upon Tyne (1996)
13. Duan, Z., Koutny, M.: A framed temporal logic programming language. J. Comput. Sci. Technol. **19**, 341–351 (2004)
14. Duan, Z., Yang, X., Koutny, M.: Framed temporal logic programming. J. Sci. Comput. Program. **70**, 31–61 (2008)
15. Yahav, E., Reps, T., Sagiv, M., Wilhelm, R.: Verifying temporal heap properties specified via evolution logic. In: Degano, P. (ed.) ESOP 2003. LNCS, vol. 2618, pp. 204–222. Springer, Heidelberg (2003)
16. Distefano, D., Katoen, J.-P., Rensink, A.: Safety and liveness in concurrent pointer programs. In: de Boer, F.S., Bonsangue, M.M., Graf, S., de Roever, W.-P. (eds.) FMCO 2005. LNCS, vol. 4111, pp. 280–312. Springer, Heidelberg (2006)
17. del Mar Gallardo, M., Merino, P., Sanán, D.: Model checking dynamic memory allocation in operating systems. J. Autom. Reason. **42**, 229–264 (2009)
18. Brochenin, R., Demri, S., Lozes, E.: Reasoning about sequences of memory states. J. Ann. Pure Appl. Logic **161**, 305–323 (2009)
19. Calcagno, C., Yang, H., O'Hearn, P.W.: Computability and complexity results for a spatial assertion language for data structures. In: Hariharan, R., Mukund, M., Vinay, V. (eds.) FSTTCS 2001. LNCS, vol. 2245, pp. 108–119. Springer, Heidelberg (2001)
20. Berdine, J., Calcagno, C., O'Hearn, P.W.: A decidable fragment of separation logic. In: Lodaya, K., Mahajan, M. (eds.) FSTTCS 2004. LNCS, vol. 3328, pp. 97–109. Springer, Heidelberg (2004)
21. Duan, Z., Tian, C.: A unified model checking approach with projection temporal logic. In: Liu, S., Maibaum, T., Araki, K. (eds.) ICFEM 2008. LNCS, vol. 5256, pp. 167–186. Springer, Heidelberg (2008)
22. Duan, Z., Tian, C., Zhang, L.: A decision procedure for propositional projection temporal logic with infinite models. J. Acta Inform. **45**, 43–78 (2008)
23. Tian, C., Duan, Z.: Complexity of propositional projection temporal logic with star. J. Math. Struct. Comput. Sci. **19**, 73–100 (2009)

Improved Net Reductions
for LTL\X Model Checking

Ya Shi[1], Zhenhua Duan[1(✉)], Cong Tian[1], and Hua Yang[2]

[1] ICTT and ISN Lab, Xidian University,
Xi'an 710071, China
y.shi@stu.xidian.edu.cn,
{zhhduan,ctian}@mail.xidian.edu.cn
[2] Beijing Institute of Control Engineering, Beijing 100000, China
yangh@bice.org.cn

Abstract. A set of reduction rules for LTL\X model checking of 1-safe Petri nets are presented in this paper. Compared with the rules available, more original transitions and places could be removed from the synchronization of Büchi automata obtained from LTL\X formulae and 1-safe Petri nets with the new proposed rules. As a result, a compact synchronization is generated. This is useful in improving efficiency of LTL\X model checking of 1-safe Petri nets.

Keywords: 1-safe Petri nets · LTL\X · Model checking · Synchronization · Reduction rules

1 Introduction

Unfolding method is a partial order technique, introduced in [15,16], to attack state space explosion problem in model checking of Petri nets by constructing a complete prefix of the unfolding rather than generating a reachability graph. The complete prefix of the unfolding encodes global states of a net system with local places, while the reachability graph explicitly presents these states as nodes of a graph. It is useful in reducing the state space significantly especially when a great number of concurrent transitions are involved in the net system.

Unfolding method has been successfully applied in deadlock detection, reachability analysis and invariant checking [6,8,11,14–17]. It is also employed in LTL\X (short for LTL without next operators) model checking of 1-safe Petri nets [3,4,19]. To check whether a net system satisfies a desirable property described by a LTL\X formula, it is required to (1) translate the negation of the formula as a Büchi automaton that accepts exactly the language defined by

This research is supported by the NSFC Grant Nos. 61133001, 61272118, 61272117, 61202038, 91218301, 61322202, 61373043, and National Program on Key Basic Research Project (973 Program) Grant No. 2010CB328102.

S. Liu and Z. Duan (Eds.): SOFL+MSVL 2013, LNCS 8332, pp. 48–61, 2014.
DOI: 10.1007/978-3-319-04915-1_4, ⓒ Springer International Publishing Switzerland 2014

the negation of the formula [9,13]; (2) construct a combined system, i.e. synchronization, from the net system and Büchi automaton such that the net system satisfies the property iff the synchronization does not contain infinite transition sequences: illegal ω-traces and livelocks; and (3) check whether the synchronization contains illegal ω-traces or illegal livelocks by constructing unfolding of the synchronization. However, the construction of unfolding is inefficient especially the sub-process for building extensions of prefixes is NP-complete [11]. Further, it is possible that the unfolding of the synchronization grows exponentially along with the process for looking for illegal ω-traces and livelocks.

To overcome the above shortages, it is important to reduce the synchronization as a compact one. In [1,2,10,12,14], several reduction rules are proposed for various subclasses of Petri nets that preserve different interesting properties such as deadlock and liveness. Also, a few of reduction rules are proposed for the synchronization in [7]. However, the synchronization is still very large. Motivated by this, this paper improves the reducing rules in [7] by improving some of the rules existing and introducing new rules. By the improved rules, more original transitions and places can be removed from the synchronization of 1-safe Petri nets and Büchi automata.

The rest of the paper is organized as follows. Section 2 presents preliminaries of 1-safe Petri nets and LTL\X. LTL\X model checking of 1-safe Petri nets is introduced in Sect. 3. In Sect. 4, a set of reduction rules for the synchronization are proposed. Correctness of the reduction rules is proved in Sect. 5. Finally, conclusions are drawn and the future research directions are pointed out in Sect. 6.

2   Preliminaries

This section briefly presents 1-safe Petri nets and LTL\X.

2.1   1-safe Petri Nets

A *net* is a 3-tuple $N = (P, T, F)$, where P and T are disjoint sets of *places* and *transitions*, respectively, and $F \subseteq (P \times T) \cup (T \times P)$ is a set of *arcs* (*flow relation*). For a node $z \in P \cup T$, $^\bullet z = \{y \in P \cup T | (y, z) \in F\}$ and $z^\bullet = \{y \in P \cup T | (z, y) \in F\}$ are the *input set* and *output set* of z, respectively. For a set of nodes $Z \subseteq P \cup T$, $^\bullet Z = \bigcup_{z \in Z} {}^\bullet z$ and $Z^\bullet = \bigcup_{z \in Z} z^\bullet$. The *marking* of a net is a multiset of places M. A place p is *marked* by a marking M with $M(p)$ tokens if $M(p) > 0$. A marking M *enables* a transition t if for each place $p \in {}^\bullet t$, it has $M(p) > 0$. In case t is enabled by M, it can *occur*, and its occurrence leads to a new marking $M' = M - {}^\bullet t + t^\bullet$, denoted by $M \xrightarrow{t} M'$. Two places p_1 and p_2 complement each other if $^\bullet p_1 = p_2^\bullet$ and $p_1^\bullet = {}^\bullet p_2$.

A *net system* is a 4-tuple $\Sigma = (P, T, F, M_0)$, where (P, T, F) is a net, and M_0 is the *initial marking*. A sequence of transitions $\sigma = t_1 t_2 \ldots t_n$ is an *occurrence sequence* from M if there exist markings $M_1, M_2, \ldots,$ and M_n such that $M \xrightarrow{t_1} M_1 \xrightarrow{t_2} \ldots \xrightarrow{t_n} M_n$. An occurrence sequence $\sigma = t_1 t_2 \ldots t_n$ is finite (infinite) if

n is a natural number (infinity). $M \xrightarrow{\sigma} M'$ means that a marking M' is reached from M through a finite occurrence sequence σ. Meanwhile, $M \xrightarrow{\sigma}$ denotes that σ is an infinite occurrence sequence. A marking M is a *reachable marking* if there exists a finite occurrence sequence σ with $M_0 \xrightarrow{\sigma} M$. We assume that net systems presented in the rest of the paper are *1-safe*, i.e. every reachable marking marks each place with at most one token. An ω-word induced by Σ is a marking sequence $M_0 M_1 \ldots$ such that there exists an infinite occurrence sequence $t_1 t_2 \ldots$ where $M_0 \xrightarrow{t_1} M_1 \xrightarrow{t_2} \ldots$ is satisfied.

2.2   LTL\X

LTL\X is LTL [18] with next operators X removed. Given a finite set *Prop* of atomic propositions, the syntax of LTL\X is defined as follows, where $p \in Prop$:

$$\varphi ::= p \mid \neg\varphi \mid \varphi_1 \wedge \varphi_2 \mid \varphi_1 U \varphi_2$$

An interpretation of a LTL\X formula is an ω-word over alphabet 2^{Prop}. $\xi \models \phi$ is used to indicate the truth of a LTL\X formula ϕ for an ω-word $\xi \in (2^{Prop})^\omega$. ξ_i is the ith element in ξ, and ξ^k is the tail of ξ starting from ξ_k. The relation $\models$ is defined inductively as follows:

1. $\xi \models p$ if $p \in \xi_0$
2. $\xi \models \neg\phi$ if $p \not\models \phi$
3. $\xi \models \phi_1 \vee \phi_2$ if $\xi \models \phi_1$ or $\xi \models \phi_2$
4. $\xi \models \phi_1 U \phi_2$ if $\exists i \geq 0 : \xi^i \models \phi_2$ and $\forall j < i : \xi_j \models \phi_1$

In this paper, LTL\X is used to describe properties of a net system $\Sigma = (P, T, F, M_0)$, hence *Prop* is identified with P. Since the state of Σ is presented as a reachable marking M, a proposition p is true at M iff the place p is marked by M. Let $\Sigma = (P, T, F, M_0)$ be a net system, and φ a LTL\X formula over the set P of atomic propositions. A place $p \in P$ is *observable* for φ if the proposition $p \in \langle\varphi\rangle$, where $\langle\varphi\rangle$ is a set of atomic propositions appearing in φ. A transition $t \in T$ is *visible* for φ if the occurrence of t changes the markings of observable places, i.e. $(({}^\bullet t \backslash t^\bullet) \cup (t^\bullet \backslash {}^\bullet t)) \cap \langle\varphi\rangle \neq \emptyset$. An infinite occurrence sequence $\sigma = t_1 t_2 \ldots$, with $M_0 \xrightarrow{t_1} M_1 \xrightarrow{t_2} \ldots$, of Σ satisfies φ, denoted by $\sigma \models \varphi$, if ω-word $M_0 M_1 \ldots$ satisfies φ. Σ satisfies φ, denoted by $\Sigma \models \varphi$, if every infinite occurrence sequence from M_0 of Σ satisfies φ. Infinite occurrence sequences from M_0 of Σ violating φ are split into two classes: infinite occurrence sequences of type I that contain infinitely many occurrences of visible original transitions, and infinite occurrence sequences of type II that contain finitely many.

A *Büchi automaton* is a 5-tuple $BA = (Q, \Gamma, q_0, \delta, Final)$, where Q is a finite non-empty set of *states*, Γ an *alphabet*, $q_0 \in Q$ the *initial state*, $\delta \subseteq Q \times \Gamma \times Q$ the *transition relation*, and *Final* $\subseteq Q$ the set of *accepting states*. BA accepts an ω-word ξ if there exists some accepting state that appears infinitely often in some run of BA on ξ. A Büchi automaton BA_φ can be obtained from a LTL\X formula φ such that an ω-word ξ is accepted by BA_φ if and only if ξ satisfies φ [9,13].

3   LTL\X Model Checking of 1-safe Petri Nets

Let $\Sigma = (P, T, F, M_0)$ be a net system, and φ a LTL\X formula over the set of atomic propositions P. The model checking approach [4] for checking whether Σ satisfies φ consists of three steps. First, translate formula $\neg\varphi$ into the corresponding *Büchi automaton* $BA_{\neg\varphi}$ with q_0 as the initial state. Second, a synchronization $\Sigma_{\neg\varphi}$ is constructed from Σ and $BA_{\neg\varphi}$ as follows:

1. Translate $BA_{\neg\varphi}$ into a net system $\Omega_{\neg\varphi}$ by treating each state $q \in Q$ as a place, and each transition $d = (q, x, q') \in \delta$ as a net transition. It is pointed that only q_0 is marked initially. For a net transition $d = (q, x, q')$, the input and output sets are $\{q\}$ and $\{q'\}$, respectively. The set of propositions x is the *observation* of d, denoted by $Obs(d)$.
2. For each observable place p of Σ, add a complementary place $\bar{p}$ to Σ such that by every reachable marking, either p or $\bar{p}$ is marked. Obviously, place p stands for proposition p, while its complementary place $\bar{p}$ denotes proposition $\neg p$.
3. Put $\Omega_{\neg\varphi}$ and Σ side by side. For convenience, we call the places (transitions) of $\Omega_{\neg\varphi}$ *Büchi places* (*transitions*), and the places (transitions) belonging to Σ *original places* (*transitions*).
4. The input and output sets of each Büchi transition $d = (q, x, q')$ are both extended with places in $Obs(d)$ and complementary places $\bar{p}$ such that $p \in \langle\varphi\rangle\backslash Obs(d)$. As a result, d can be enabled if the observable propositions it cares about are true, and the others are false.
5. Add two schedule places s_s and s_f where only s_f is marked initially. The input and output sets of each visible original transition are extended with s_s and s_f, respectively, while the input and output sets of each Büchi transition are extended with s_f and s_s, respectively. This step guarantees that, initially, $\Omega_{\neg\varphi}$ can fire a transition, and all visible transitions of Σ are disabled. After an occurrence of some transition of $\Omega_{\neg\varphi}$, only Σ can fire transitions. When Σ fires a visible transition, $\Omega_{\neg\varphi}$ can fire a transition again and again until neither $\Omega_{\neg\varphi}$ nor Σ can fire any transition in its turn.
6. For each Büchi transition $t = (q, x, q')$, add a new transition t' such that $^\bullet t' = {}^\bullet t$ and $t'^\bullet = t^\bullet\backslash\{s_s\}$, where $^\bullet t$ and $t^\bullet$ are the input and output sets of t after the previous steps. L is the set of the added transitions. I is the set of Büchi transitions d with $d^\bullet \cap Final \neq \emptyset$.

An *illegal ω-trace* of $\Sigma_{\neg\varphi}$ is an infinite occurrence sequence from the initial marking, where some transition in I occurs infinitely often. An *illegal livelock* of $\Sigma_{\neg\varphi}$ is an infinite occurrence sequence from the initial marking, in the form $\sigma_1 d\sigma_2$, where σ_1 is a finite occurrence sequence from M_0, d belongs to L and ω-word $(Obs(d))^\omega$ is accepted by $BA_{\neg\varphi}$ with a Büchi place in $^\bullet d$ being the initial state, and σ_2 consists of invisible original transitions. Let $\Sigma_{\neg\varphi} = (P, T, F, M_0, I, L)$ be the synchronization constructed from a net system Σ and a Büchi Automaton $BA_{\neg\varphi}$. It has been proved in [4] that Σ satisfies φ if and only if $\Sigma_{\neg\varphi}$ has neither illegal ω-traces nor illegal livelocks.

Finally, an unfolding method is utilized to check whether $\Sigma_{\neg\varphi}$ has any illegal ω-trace or illegal livelock. Usually, unfolding of the synchronization grows exponentially and the construction of the unfolding is inefficient [11].

4   Reductions Rules for Synchronization

In this section we propose a set of reduction rules for the synchronization. Several reduction rules for the synchronization have been presented in [7]. Among them, there are two Linear Programming Rules, named Dead Transition and Implicit Place Rule. The aim of Dead Transition Rule is to remove places, which never get any tokens, and their output transitions. Obviously, such transitions can never be enabled. Implicit Place Rule tries to remove places which never restrict the firing of their output transitions.

4.1   T-Reduction Rule

T-Reduction Rule is illustrated in Fig. 1. Since transitions t_1 and t_2 have the same input and output set, both t_1 and t_2 belong to $L\ (I)$, or neither. Further, for every occurrence sequence σ containing t_2, there exits an occurrence sequence $\sigma_{t_1\backslash t_2}$ obtained from σ by replacing t_2 with t_1. Therefore, t_2 is a redundant transition which can be removed by T-Reduction Rule.

Let $\Sigma_{\neg\varphi} = (P, T, F, M_0, I, L)$ be the synchronization constructed from a net system Σ and a Büchi Automaton $BA_{\neg\varphi}$. If $\Sigma_{\neg\varphi}$ has two distinct transitions t_1 and t_2 with $^\bullet t_1 = {}^\bullet t_2$ and $t_1{}^\bullet = t_2{}^\bullet$, then T-Reduction Rule will remove t_2, and generate the resulting synchronization $\Sigma'_{\neg\varphi} = (P, T', F', M_0, I, L)$, where $T' = T'\backslash\{t_2\}$ and $F' = F \cap ((T' \times P') \cup (P' \times T'))$.

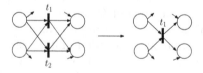

Fig. 1. T-Reduction Rule

4.2   Post-Reduction Rule

Post-Reduction Rule is shown in Fig. 2. Transition t is enabled after the occurrence of transition u, and cannot be disabled by the occurrences of any other transitions. Therefore, every occurrence sequence σ containing u and t can be reordered into an occurrence sequence σ' such that every occurrence of u is immediately followed by an occurrence of t. This rule aims to hide occurrences of t after occurrences of u by making u produce tokens immediately into $t^\bullet$ rather than $^\bullet t$.

Let $\Sigma_{\neg\varphi} = (P, T, F, M_0, I, L)$ be the synchronization constructed from a net system Σ and a Büchi Automaton $BA_{\neg\varphi}$. If $\Sigma_{\neg\varphi}$ has two distinct transitions u and t such that ${}^\bullet t \neq t^\bullet$, ${}^\bullet t \subseteq u^\bullet$, and $\forall p \in {}^\bullet t$, $p^\bullet = \{t\}$, then by Post-Reduction Rule, we can obtain the resulting synchronization $\Sigma'_{\neg\varphi} = (P, T, F', M_0, I, L)$, where $F' = (F \backslash (\{u\} \times {}^\bullet t)) \cup (\{u\} \times t^\bullet)$.

Post-Reduction Rule is derived from A-Reduction Rule in [1] by removing conditions $|{}^\bullet t| > 1$, $\not\exists p \in {}^\bullet t$ such that ${}^\bullet p = \{u\}$, and adding restrictions ${}^\bullet t \neq t^\bullet$ and for all $p \in {}^\bullet t$, it has $p^\bullet = \{t\}$. The synchronization remains unchanged if t has the same input and output sets. If $\forall p \in {}^\bullet t$, $p^\bullet = \{t\}$ is ignored, the occurrence of u cannot make transitions of $({}^\bullet t)^\bullet \backslash \{t\}$ enabled in $\Sigma'_{\neg\varphi}$.

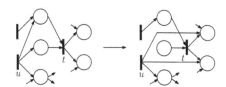

Fig. 2. Post-Reduction Rule

4.3 Pre-Reduction Rule

This rule is described in Fig. 3. Transition t is enabled only after occurrences of transitions u_1 and u_2, and cannot be disabled by the occurrences of any other transitions. Occurrences of u_1 and u_2 do not affect each other. Thereby, every occurrence sequence σ containing u_1, u_2, and t can be reordered into an occurrence sequence σ' containing sub-sequence $u_1 u_2 t$. This rule aims to hide occurrences of u_1 and u_2 by merging them with t.

Before introducing Pre-Reduction Rule formally, we present several functions *PreTran*, *PreSet*, *Seq*, and *dec*. *PreTran* is a function $T \rightarrow 2^T$ with $PreTran(t) = \{u \in T | u^\bullet \cap {}^\bullet t \neq \emptyset\}$. *PreSet* is a function $T \rightarrow 2^{2^T}$ satisfying $PreSet(t) = \{U \subseteq PreTran(t) | U^\bullet = {}^\bullet t, \forall u_1, u_2 \in U, ({}^\bullet u_1 \cap {}^\bullet u_2) \cup (u_1^\bullet \cap u_2^\bullet) = \emptyset\}$. *Seq* is a function $2^T \rightarrow T^*$ such that $Seq(U)$ is a transition sequence where each element of U appears exactly once. *dec* is a function $T^* \rightarrow 2^T$ where $dec(s)$ is the set of transitions appearing in transition sequence s.

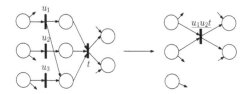

Fig. 3. Pre-Reduction Rule

Let $\Sigma_{\neg\varphi} = (P, T, F, M_0, I, L)$ be the synchronization constructed from a net system Σ and a Büchi Automaton $BA_{\neg\varphi}$ with q_0 being the initial state. If $\Sigma_{\neg\varphi}$ has a transition t such that ${}^\bullet t \cap t^\bullet = \emptyset$, $\forall u \in PreTran(t)$, $u^\bullet \subset {}^\bullet t$, $\forall p \in {}^\bullet t$, ${}^\bullet p \neq \emptyset$, $p^\bullet = \{t\}$, and $M(p) = 0$, then by Pre-Reduction Rule, we can obtain the resulting synchronization $\Sigma'_{\neg\varphi} = (P', T', F', M_0, I, L)$, where $P' = P \backslash {}^\bullet t$, $T' = (T \backslash (PreTran(t) \cup \{t\})) \cup D$ with $D = \{\underline{st}|U \in PreSet(t), s = Seq(U)\}$, $F' = (F \cap ((T' \times P') \cup (P' \times T'))) \cup (\bigcup_{\underline{u} \in D}({}^\bullet(dec(\underline{u}) \backslash \{t\}) \times \{\underline{u}\})) \cup (D \times t^\bullet)$. To distinguish the new produced transitions from the ones in the ordinary transition sequences, $u_1 u_2 t$ in Fig. 3 is presented with underline.

4.4   Post-A Rule

This rule is demonstrated in Fig. 4. Both transitions t_1 and t_2 are enabled after the occurrence of transition u, since they have only one input place $p \in u^\bullet$. Therefore, every occurrence sequence σ containing u can be reordered into an occurrence sequence σ' such that every occurrence of u is immediately followed by an occurrence of t_1 or t_2. This rule aims to hide occurrences of transition t_1 (t_2) by merging t_1 (t_2) with u.

Let $\Sigma_{\neg\varphi} = (P, T, F, M_0, I, L)$ be the synchronization constructed from a net system Σ and a Büchi Automaton $BA_{\neg\varphi}$. If $\Sigma_{\neg\varphi}$ has a place p such that ${}^\bullet p \neq \emptyset$, $p^\bullet \neq \emptyset$, $\forall t \in p^\bullet$, ${}^\bullet t = \{p\}$ and $p \notin t^\bullet$, then by Post-A rule, we can obtain the resulting synchronization $\Sigma'_{\neg\varphi} = (P, T', F', M_0, I, L)$, where

- $T' = (T \backslash {}^\bullet p) \cup ({}^\bullet p \times p^\bullet)$,
- $\forall q \in P$, $\forall t \in T \backslash {}^\bullet p$, $F'(q, t) = F(q, t)$, $F'(t, q) = F(t, q)$;
  $\forall q \in P$, $\forall \underline{t_1 t_2} \in ({}^\bullet p \times p^\bullet)$, $F'(q, \underline{t_1 t_2}) = F(q, t_1)$, $F'(\underline{t_1 t_2}, q) = F(t_1, q) + F(t_2, q)$.

Elements in ${}^\bullet p \times p^\bullet$ with underline are used to denote new transitions.

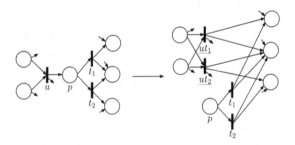

Fig. 4. Post-A Rule

Post-A Rule is extended from Post-Agglomeration Rule in [7] by removing condition $M_0(p) = 0$, and adding restriction $\forall t \in p^\bullet$, $p \notin t^\bullet$. Additionally, the rule preserves p and its output transitions $p^\bullet$. This makes condition $M_0(p) = 0$ unnecessary in the rule. It seems that preservation of p and transitions of $p^\bullet$

makes the synchronization worse for unfolding. Actually, p and transitions of $p^\bullet$ can be preserved after the whole reduction process if p is marked initially. Otherwise, they will be removed by Dead Transition Rule. Although p and transitions of $p^\bullet$ are preserved eventually, transitions of $p^\bullet$ are only considered for the possible extensions in the first run during the construction of unfolding. This is because the construction algorithm of unfolding is breadth-first [5]. Thus, preservation of p and transitions of $p^\bullet$ has little affect on the construction of unfolding.

4.5 Pre-A Rule

Pre-A Rule is shown in Fig. 5. Transition u can be enabled only after the occurrence of transition t_1 or t_2. Here both t_1 and t_2 have only one output place p. Thus, every occurrence sequence σ containing u must contain t_1 or t_2, and can be reordered into an occurrence sequence σ' such that every occurrence of t_1 or t_2 is immediately followed by an occurrence of u. This rule aims to hide occurrences of u by merging u with t_1 (t_2).

Let $\Sigma_{\neg\varphi} = (P, T, F, M_0, I, L)$ be the synchronization constructed from a net system Σ and a Büchi Automaton $BA_{\neg\varphi}$. If $\Sigma_{\neg\varphi}$ has a place p such that $^\bullet p \neq \emptyset$, $p^\bullet \neq \emptyset$, $\forall t \in {}^\bullet p$, $t^\bullet = \{p\}$ and $p \notin {}^\bullet t$, then by Pre-A Rule, we can obtain the resulting synchronization $\Sigma'_{\neg\varphi} = (P, T', F', M_0, I)$, where

- $T' = (T \backslash {}^\bullet p) \cup ({}^\bullet p \times p^\bullet)$,
- $\forall q \in P'$, $\forall t \in T \backslash {}^\bullet p$: $F'(q, t) = F(q, t)$, $F'(t, q) = F(t, q)$;
  $\forall q \in P'$, $\forall \underline{t_1 t_2} \in ({}^\bullet p \times p^\bullet)$: $F'(q, \underline{t_1 t_2}) = F(q, t_1) + F(q, t_2)$, $F'(\underline{t_1 t_2}, q) = F(t_2, q)$.

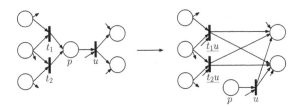

Fig. 5. Pre-A Rule

Transitions reduced by Abstract Rule and Pre-Agglomeration Rule in [7] can be dealt with by this rule. Restriction $\forall t \in {}^\bullet p$, $p \notin {}^\bullet t$ is necessary for Abstract Rule and Pre-Agglomeration Rule but ignored in [7]. Note that p and transitions of $p^\bullet$ are preserved by this rule. But they are possible to be removed by Dead Transition Rule if p is not marked by the initial marking M_0.

5 Correctness of Reduction Rules

In this section we show that the reduction rules do not affect the result of LTL\X model checking of 1-safe Petri nets. We first present a Theorem proved in [7].

Theorem 1. *Let $\Sigma_{\neg\varphi} = (P, T, F, M_0, I, L)$ be the synchronization constructed from a net system Σ and a Büchi Automaton $BA_{\neg\varphi}$. Σ satisfies φ if and only if at least one of the following conditions hold for $\Sigma_{\neg\varphi}$:*

1. *there exists an illegal ω-trace σ in $\Sigma_{\neg\varphi}$, or*
2. *there exists a finite occurrence sequence $M_0 \xrightarrow{\sigma_0} M$ in $\Sigma_{\neg\varphi}$ such that*
   (a) *there exists an infinite occurrence sequence $M|_B \xrightarrow{\sigma_1}$ containing infinitely many transitions of I in $\Sigma_{\neg\varphi}|_B$, and*
   (b) *there exists an infinite occurrence sequence $M|_N \xrightarrow{\sigma_2}$ containing only invisible original transitions in $\Sigma_{\neg\varphi}|_N$,*

where $\Sigma_{\neg\varphi}|_B$ ($\Sigma_{\neg\varphi}|_N$) is the subnet of $\Sigma_{\neg\varphi}$ corresponding to $BA_{\neg\varphi}$ (Σ), and $M|_B$ ($M|_N$) is the part of M belonging to $\Sigma_{\neg\varphi}|_B$ ($\Sigma_{\neg\varphi}|_N$). □

Let $\Sigma_{\neg\varphi}$ be a synchronization, and $\Sigma'_{\neg\varphi}$ the synchronization obtained by applying a reduction rule on $\Sigma_{\neg\varphi}$. The reduction rule is *correct* if each condition of Theorem 1 holds for both $\Sigma_{\neg\varphi}$ and $\Sigma'_{\neg\varphi}$, or neither.

Theorem 2. *T-Reduction Rule is correct.*

Proof. Let t_1 and t_2 be two transitions in $\Sigma_{\neg\varphi}$ satisfying conditions of T-Reduction Rule, and $\Sigma'_{\neg\varphi}$ the synchronization obtained from $\Sigma_{\neg\varphi}$ by removing t_2 by T-Reduction Rule. We prove that condition 1 (2) of Theorem 1 holds for $\Sigma_{\neg\varphi}$ if and only if it holds for $\Sigma'_{\neg\varphi}$. Unless stated otherwise, σ means an occurrence sequence of $\Sigma_{\neg\varphi}$, while σ' denotes an occurrence sequence belonging to $\Sigma'_{\neg\varphi}$.

$\Rightarrow$ 1. Suppose condition 1 of Theorem 1 holds for $\Sigma_{\neg\varphi}$. Since ${}^\bullet t_1 = {}^\bullet t_2$ and $t_1^\bullet = t_2^\bullet$, we have that both t_1 and t_2 belong to $L(I)$, or neither. It follows that in $\Sigma_{\neg\varphi}$ there exists an illegal ω-trace $\sigma_{t_1\backslash t_2}$, which is obtained from σ by replacing t_2 with t_1. Because of $M'_0 = M_0$ and none of transitions in $\sigma_{t_1\backslash t_2}$ is affected by T-Reduction Rule, we have that there exists an illegal ω-trace $\sigma_{t_1\backslash t_2}$ in $\Sigma'_{\neg\varphi}$. Therefore, condition 1 of Theorem 1 holds for $\Sigma'_{\neg\varphi}$.

   2. Suppose condition 2 of Theorem 1 holds for $\Sigma_{\neg\varphi}$. By ($\Rightarrow$ 1), we have that there exists a finite occurrence sequence $M_0 \xrightarrow{\sigma_0 \, t_1\backslash t_2} M$ in $\Sigma'_{\neg\varphi}$. Since ${}^\bullet t_1 = {}^\bullet t_2$ and $t_1^\bullet = t_2^\bullet$, we have that both t_1 and t_2 belong to either $\Sigma_{\neg\varphi}|_N$ or $\Sigma_{\neg\varphi}|_B$. Further, t_1 and t_2 still have the same input and output sets, respectively, in $\Sigma_{\neg\varphi}|_N$ or $\Sigma_{\neg\varphi}|_B$. It follows that (a) there exists an infinite occurrence sequence $M|_B \xrightarrow{\sigma_1 \, t_1\backslash t_2}$ containing infinitely many transitions of I in $\Sigma'_{\neg\varphi}|_B$, and (b) there exists an infinite occurrence sequence $M|_N \xrightarrow{\sigma_2 \, t_1\backslash t_2}$ containing only invisible original transitions in $\Sigma'_{\neg\varphi}|_N$. Therefore, condition 2 of Theorem 1 holds for $\Sigma'_{\neg\varphi}$.

$\Leftarrow$ 1. Suppose condition 1 of Theorem 1 holds for $\Sigma'_{\neg\varphi}$. Since t_2 does not belong to $\Sigma'_{\neg\varphi}$, we have that σ' does not contain any t_2, and then none of the transitions in σ' has been affected by T-Reduction Rule. Because of $M'_0 = M_0$, there exists an illegal ω-trace σ' in $\Sigma_{\neg\varphi}$. Thus, condition 1 of Theorem 1 holds for $\Sigma_{\neg\varphi}$.

2. Suppose condition 2 of Theorem 1 holds for $\Sigma'_{\neg\varphi}$. Since t_2 does not belong to $\Sigma'_{\neg\varphi}$, we have that σ'_0, σ'_1, and σ'_2 do not contain any t_2, and then none of transitions in them has been affected by T-Reduction Rule. Since $M'_0 = M_0$, it has that condition 2 of Theorem 1 holds for $\Sigma_{\neg\varphi}$. □

Theorem 3. *Let u and t be a pair of transitions in $\Sigma_{\neg\varphi}$ satisfying Post-Reduction Rule. For a finite occurrence sequence $M_0 \xrightarrow{\sigma_1 u \sigma_2 t \sigma_3} M$ in $\Sigma_{\neg\varphi}$, if σ_2 does not contain any t, then σ_2 does not contain any u either, and there exists an occurrence sequence $M_0 \xrightarrow{\sigma_1 u t \sigma_2 \sigma_3} M$.*

Proof. Assume that $M_0 \xrightarrow{\sigma_1 u} M_1 \xrightarrow{\sigma_2} M_2 \xrightarrow{t} M_3 \xrightarrow{\sigma_3} M$ is a finite occurrence sequence of $\Sigma_{\neg\varphi}$ where σ_2 does not contain any t. From $\forall p \in {}^{\bullet}t$, $p^{\bullet} = \{t\}$, it has that only t consumes tokens in places of ${}^{\bullet}t$. Because of ${}^{\bullet}t \subseteq u^{\bullet}$, σ_2 does not contain any t, and $\Sigma_{\neg\varphi}$ is 1-safe, it can be obtained that σ_2 does not contain any u. Since ${}^{\bullet}t \subseteq u^{\bullet}$, we have $M_0 \xrightarrow{\sigma_1 u} M_1 \xrightarrow{t} M'_1$ where $M'_1 = (M_1 \backslash {}^{\bullet}t) \cup t^{\bullet}$. Since only t consumes tokens in places of ${}^{\bullet}t$, and σ_2 does not contain any t, it has that none of transitions in σ_2 consumes tokens in places of ${}^{\bullet}t$, and then $M_0 \xrightarrow{\sigma_1 u} M_1 \xrightarrow{t} M'_1 \xrightarrow{\sigma_2} M'_2$ where $M'_2 = M_3$. Therefore, $M_0 \xrightarrow{\sigma_1 u} M_1 \xrightarrow{t} M'_1 \xrightarrow{\sigma_2} M_3 \xrightarrow{\sigma_3} M$. □

Lemma 4. *Let u and t be a pair of transitions touched by Post-Reduction Rule. u and t are original transitions.*

Proof.

1. Suppose that t is a Büchi transition. It has $s_f \in {}^{\bullet}t$ and there exists one Büchi place $q \in {}^{\bullet}t$. Since ${}^{\bullet}t \subseteq u^{\bullet}$, we have $\{s_f, q\} \subseteq u^{\bullet}$. Further $q \in u^{\bullet}$, it follows that u is also a Büchi transition. This contradicts with $s_f \in u^{\bullet}$. Therefore, t is an original transition.
2. Suppose that u is a Büchi transition. Since t is an original transition, we have that t has at least one original place p in its input set. Because of ${}^{\bullet}t \subseteq u^{\bullet}$, it has $p \in u^{\bullet}$. Since p is an original place, and u is a Büchi transition, we have $p \in {}^{\bullet}u \cap u^{\bullet}$. This contradicts with condition $\forall p \in {}^{\bullet}t$, $p^{\bullet} = \{t\}$. Therefore, u is also an original transition. □

Theorem 5. *Post-Reduction Rule is correct.*

Proof. Let u and t be a pair of transitions in $\Sigma_{\neg\varphi}$ satisfying conditions of Post-Reduction Rule, $\Sigma'_{\neg\varphi}$ the synchronization obtained from $\Sigma_{\neg\varphi}$ by dealing with u and t by Post-Reduction Rule. We prove that condition 1 (2) of Theorem 1 holds for $\Sigma_{\neg\varphi}$ if and only if it holds for $\Sigma'_{\neg\varphi}$. Note that u' presents transition u in the new synchronization $\Sigma'_{\neg\varphi}$.

$\Rightarrow$ 1. Suppose condition 1 of Theorem 1 holds for $\Sigma_{\neg\varphi}$. From Theorem 3, it follows that σ can be reordered into an illegal ω-trace ρ of $\Sigma_{\neg\varphi}$ such that every occurrence of u is immediately followed by an occurrence of t. Since $F' = (F \backslash (\{u\} \times {}^{\bullet}t)) \cup (\{u\} \times t^{\bullet})$, we have ${}^{\bullet}u' = {}^{\bullet}u$ and $u'^{\bullet} = (u^{\bullet} \backslash {}^{\bullet}t) \cup t^{\bullet}$.

Because of $M_0' = M_0$, there exists an infinite occurrence sequence σ' from M_0' in $\Sigma'_{\neg\varphi}$, where σ' is obtained from ρ by replacing ut with u'. By Lemma 4, it has that u and t are original transitions, and thus none of Büchi transitions in σ' has been affected by Post-Reduction Rule. Thus, σ' contains infinitely many transitions of I leading it to be an illegal ω-trace. Therefore, condition 1 of Theorem 1 holds for $\Sigma'_{\neg\varphi}$.

2. Suppose condition 2 of Theorem 1 holds for $\Sigma_{\neg\varphi}$ and $\sigma_0 = \sigma_3 v$. From the proof of Theorem 1 in [7], we have $v \in L$ and then v is a Büchi transition. Therefore, Post-Reduction Rule can affect occurrence sequence σ_3 in $M_0 \xrightarrow{\sigma_3 v} M$. By ($\Rightarrow$ 1), it has that there exists an occurrence sequence $M_0 \xrightarrow{\sigma_3' v} M$ in $\Sigma'_{\neg\varphi}$, where σ_3' is obtained from σ_3 by replacing every u with u', and removing the first t after this u. Since transitions of $\Sigma_{\neg\varphi}|_B$ are Büchi transitions, infinite occurrence sequence σ_1 of $\Sigma_{\neg\varphi}|_B$ consists of only Büchi transitions. Thus, none of transitions in σ_1 is affected by Post-Reduction Rule, and thus there exists an infinite occurrence sequence $M|_B \xrightarrow{\sigma_1}$ containing infinitely many transitions of I in $\Sigma'_{\neg\varphi}|_B$. By ($\Rightarrow$ 1), we have that there exists an infinite occurrence sequence $M|_N \xrightarrow{\sigma_2'}$ in $\Sigma'_{\neg\varphi}|_N$, where σ_2' is obtained from σ_2 by replacing every u with u', and removing the first t after this u. Therefore, condition 2 of Theorem 1 holds for $\Sigma'_{\neg\varphi}$.

$\Leftarrow$ 1. Suppose condition 1 of Theorem 1 holds for $\Sigma'_{\neg\varphi}$. By ${}^\bullet u' = {}^\bullet u$, $u'{}^\bullet = (u^\bullet \backslash {}^\bullet t) \cup t^\bullet$, and $M_0' = M_0$, it follows that in $\Sigma_{\neg\varphi}$ there exists an infinite occurrence sequence σ from M_0 which is obtained from σ' by replacing u' with ut. Since u' is not a Büchi transition, we have that σ contains infinitely many transitions of I, and then it is an illegal ω-trace. Thus, condition 1 of Theorem 1 holds for $\Sigma_{\neg\varphi}$.

2. Suppose condition 2 of Theorem 1 holds for $\Sigma'_{\neg\varphi}$. From ($\Rightarrow$ 2), it follows that transitions in σ_0 and σ_2 might have been affected by Post-Reduction Rule. By ($\Leftarrow$ 1), we have that there exists an occurrence sequence $M_0' \xrightarrow{\sigma_0} M'$ in $\Sigma_{\neg\varphi}$ ($M'|_N \xrightarrow{\sigma_2}$ in $\Sigma_{\neg\varphi}|_N$), where σ_0 (σ_2) is obtained from σ_0' (σ_2') by replacing u' with ut. Since σ_1' consists of only Büchi transitions, none of transitions in σ_1' has been affected by Post-Reduction Rule. Thus, there exists a finite occurrence sequence $M'|_B \xrightarrow{\sigma_1'}$ in $\Sigma_{\neg\varphi}|_B$ where σ_1' contains infinitely many transitions of I. Therefore, condition 2 of Theorem 1 holds for $\Sigma_{\neg\varphi}$. $\qquad\square$

Lemma 6. *Let t be a transition satisfying conditions of Pre-Reduction Rule. For a finite occurrence sequence $M_1 \xrightarrow{\sigma t} M_2$ of $\Sigma_{\neg\varphi}$, where M_1 is a reachable marking, $M_1 \cap {}^\bullet t = \emptyset$, and σ does not contain any t, it has that there exits a finite occurrence sequence $M_1 \xrightarrow{\sigma' u_1 \ldots u_m t} M_2$ in $\Sigma_{\neg\varphi}$, where σ' is the finite occurrence sequence obtained from σ by removing transitions of PreSet(t) and $U = \{u_1, u_2, \ldots u_m\} \in$ PreSet(t).*

Proof. Let $\sigma = \sigma_1 u_m \sigma_2$, where σ_2 does not contain any transition of $PreTran(t)$. Since $\forall u \in PreTran(t)$, $u^\bullet \subset {}^\bullet t$, and $\forall p \in {}^\bullet t$, $p^\bullet = \{t\}$, we have that only t consumes tokens produced by transitions of $PreTran(t)$. Since σ does not contain any t, none of transitions in σ_2 consumes any tokens produced by u_m. Thus, we have $M_1 \xrightarrow{\sigma_1 \sigma_2} M \xrightarrow{u_m t} M_2$. It follows that $M \xrightarrow{\sigma' u_1 \dots u_m t} M_t$, where σ' is the transition sequence obtained from σ by removing transitions of $PreTran(t)$, and $U = \{u_1, u_2, \dots u_m\}$ are the set of transitions of $PreTran(t)$ in σ. From $M_1 \cap {}^\bullet t = \emptyset$, we have that ${}^\bullet t \subseteq U^\bullet$. Since $\forall u \in PreTran(t)$, $u^\bullet \subset {}^\bullet t$, it has $U^\bullet \subseteq {}^\bullet t$ and thus $U^\bullet = {}^\bullet t$. Since $\Sigma_{\neg\varphi}$ is 1-safe, $\forall u_i, u_j \in U, ({}^\bullet u_i \cap {}^\bullet u_j) \cup (u_i^\bullet \cap u_j^\bullet) = \emptyset$ and then $U \in PreSet(t)$. $\square$

Lemma 7. *Let t be a transition of $\Sigma_{\neg\varphi}$ satisfying conditions of Pre-Reduction Rule. Transitions of $PreTran(t)$ and t are original transitions.*

Proof.

1. Suppose t is a Büchi transition. It has that $s_f \in {}^\bullet t$ and there exists one Büchi place $q \in {}^\bullet t$. Since $\forall p \in {}^\bullet t$, ${}^\bullet p \neq \emptyset$, there exists a transition u with $q \in u^\bullet$. It follows that u is a Büchi transition and then $s_s \in u^\bullet$. Since $u^\bullet \subset {}^\bullet t$, it has $s_s \in {}^\bullet t$. This contradicts with the fact that t is a Büchi transition. Thus, t is an original transition.
2. Suppose there exists a Büchi transition $u \in PreTran(t)$. It has that $s_s \in u^\bullet$ and there exists one Büchi place $s \in u^\bullet$. Since $u^\bullet \subset {}^\bullet t$, it has $s \in {}^\bullet t$ and t is a Büchi transition. This contradicts with the fact that t is an original transition. Therefore, transitions of $PreTran(t)$ are original transitions. $\square$

Theorem 8. *Pre-Reduction Rule is correct.*

Proof. Let t be a transition in $\Sigma_{\neg\varphi}$ satisfying conditions of Pre-Reduction Rule, $\Sigma'_{\neg\varphi}$ the synchronization obtained from $\Sigma_{\neg\varphi}$ by dealing with t and $PreSet(t)$ with Pre-Reduction Rule. We prove that condition 1 (2) of Theorem 1 holds for $\Sigma_{\neg\varphi}$ if and only if it holds for $\Sigma'_{\neg\varphi}$.

$\Rightarrow$ 1. Suppose condition 1 of Theorem 1 holds for $\Sigma_{\neg\varphi}$. By Lemma 6, it follows that σ can be reordered into an illegal ω-trace ρ of $\Sigma_{\neg\varphi}$ such that every occurrence of t is immediately preceded by a transition sequence γ with $dec(\gamma) \in PreSet(t)$. Since $F' = (F \cap ((T' \times P') \cup (P' \times T'))) \cup (\bigcup_{\underline{u} \in D} ({}^\bullet(dec(\underline{u}) \backslash \{t\}) \times \{\underline{u}\})) \cup (D \times t^\bullet)$, it has that ${}^\bullet \underline{\gamma t} = {}^\bullet(dec(\gamma))$ and $\underline{\gamma t}^\bullet = t^\bullet$. Because of $M_0' = M_0$, there exists an infinite occurrence sequence σ' from M_0' in $\Sigma'_{\neg\varphi}$, where σ' is obtained from ρ by replacing transition sequence γt with transition $\underline{\gamma t}$. By Lemma 7, it has that transitions of $PreTran(t)$ and t are original transitions, and then none of Büchi transitions in σ' has been affected by Pre-Reduction Rule. Thus, σ' is an illegal ω-trace. Therefore, condition 1 of Theorem 1 holds for $\Sigma'_{\neg\varphi}$.
    2. The proof is similar to that of Theorem 5.

$\Leftarrow$ 1. Suppose condition 2 of Theorem 1 holds for $\Sigma_{\neg\varphi}$. From $^\bullet\gamma t = {}^\bullet(dec(\gamma))$
and $\gamma t^\bullet = t^\bullet$, it follows that in $\Sigma_{\neg\varphi}$ there exists an illegal ω-trace σ, which is obtained from σ' by replacing every transition $\gamma t \in D$ with the transition sequence γt. Since γt is not a Büchi transition, σ is an illegal ω-trace. Thus, condition 1 of Theorem 1 holds for $\Sigma_{\neg\varphi}$.

2. The proof is similar to that of Theorem 5. $\square$

Correctness of Post-A Rule and Pre-A Rule can be proved similarly to Local Reduction Rules in [7].

6   Conclusion

Five correct reduction rules for reducing synchronization of 1-safe Petri nets and Büchi automata are presented in this paper. Among them, Post-A Rule and Pre-A Rule can deal with all transitions and places reduced by Local Reduction Rules in [7]. Thus, compared with the existing work, a compact synchronization can be generated by our method. In the near further, all the rules will be implemented and utilized in reducing synchronization of 1-safe Petri nets and Büchi automata in practise.

References

1. Desel, J.: Reduction and design of well-behaved concurrent systems. In: Baeten, J.C.M., Klop, J.W. (eds.) CONCUR 1990. LNCS, vol. 458, pp. 166–181. Springer, Heidelberg (1990)
2. Esparza, J.: Reduction and synthesis of live and bounded free choice petri nets. Inf. Comput. **114**(1), 50–87 (1994)
3. Esparza, J., Heljanko, K.: A new unfolding approach to LTL model checking. In: Montanari, U., Rolim, J.D.P., Welzl, E. (eds.) ICALP 2000. LNCS, vol. 1853, pp. 475–486. Springer, Heidelberg (2000)
4. Esparza, J., Heljanko, K.: Implementing LTL model checking with net unfoldings. In: Dwyer, M. (ed.) SPIN 2001. LNCS, vol. 2057, pp. 37–56. Springer, Heidelberg (2001)
5. Esparza, J., Kanade, P., Schwoon, S.: A negative result on depth-first net unfoldings. Softw. Tools Technol. Transfer **10**(2), 161–166 (2008)
6. Esparza, J., Römer, S., Vogler, W.: An improvement of Mcmillan's unfolding algorithm. Formal Methods Syst. Des. **20**(3), 285–310 (2002)
7. Esparza, J., Schröter, C.: Net reductions for LTL model-checking. In: Margaria, T., Melham, T. (eds.) CHARME 2001. LNCS, vol. 2144, pp. 310–324. Springer, Heidelberg (2001)
8. Esparza, J., Schröter, C.: Unfolding based algorithms for the reachability problem. Fundamenta Informaticae **47**(3), 231–245 (2001)
9. Gastin, P., Oddoux, D.: Fast LTL to büchi automata translation. In: Berry, G., Comon, H., Finkel, A. (eds.) CAV 2001. LNCS, vol. 2102, pp. 53–65. Springer, Heidelberg (2001)
10. Haddad, S., Pradat-Peyre, J.F.: New efficient petri nets reductions for parallel programs verification. Parallel Process. Lett. **16**(1), 101–116 (2006)

11. Heljanko, K.: Deadlock and reachability checking with finite complete prefixes. Research Report A56, Helsinki University of Technology, Laboratory for Theoretical Computer Science, Espoo (1999)
12. Hyung, L., Favrel, J., Baptiste, P.: Generalized petri net reduction method. IEEE Trans. Syst. Man Cybern. SMC **17**(2), 297–303 (1987)
13. Katoen, J.P.: Concepts, Algorithms, and Tools for Model Checking. IMMD, Erlangen (1999)
14. Khomenko, V., Koutny, M.: Verification of bounded petri nets using integer programming. Formal Methods Syst. Des. **30**(2), 143–176 (2007)
15. McMillan, K.L.: Symbolic Model Checking. Springer, New York (1993)
16. McMillan, K.L.: Using unfoldings to avoid the state explosion problem in the verification of asynchronous circuits. In: von Bochmann, G., Probst, D.K. (eds.) CAV 1992. LNCS, vol. 663, pp. 164–177. Springer, Heidelberg (1993)
17. Melzer, S., Römer, S.: Deadlock checking using net unfoldings. In: Grumberg, O. (ed.) CAV 1997. LNCS, vol. 1254, pp. 352–363. Springer, Heidelberg (1997)
18. Pnueli, A.: Applications of temporal logic to the specification and verification of reactive systems: a survey of current trends. In: Rozenberg, G., de Bakker, J.W., de Roever, W.-P. (eds.) Current Trends in Concurrency. LNCS, vol. 224, pp. 510–584. Springer, Heidelberg (1986)
19. Wallner, F.: Model checking LTL using net unforldings. In: Hu, A.J., Vardi, M.Y. (eds.) CAV 1998. LNCS, vol. 1427, pp. 207–218. Springer, Heidelberg (1998)

Formalizing and Implementing Types in MSVL

Xiaobing Wang, Zhenhua Duan[✉], and Liang Zhao

Institute of Computing Theory and Technology and ISN Laboratory,
Xidian University, Xian 710071, People's Republic of China
xbwang@mail.xidian.edu.cn, zhenhua_duan@126.com, lzhao@xidian.edu.cn

Abstract. This paper investigates techniques for formalizing and implementing types in the temporal logic programming language MSVL, which is an executable subset of Projection Temporal Logic. To this end, the data domain of MSVL is extended to include typed values, and then typed functions and predicates concerning the extended data domain are defined. Based on these definitions, the statement for type declaration of program variables is formalized. The implementation mechanisms of the type declaration statement in the MSVL interpreter are also discussed, which is based on the notion of normal form of MSVL programs. To illustrate how to program with types, an example of in-place reversing an integer list is given.

Keywords: Type · Temporal logic programming · MSVL · Projection Temporal Logic

1 Introduction

In many formal verification fields ranging from digit circuit design to software engineering, temporal logics have been widely used as an efficient tool for describing and reasoning about properties of concurrent systems [1–3]. Projection Temporal Logic (PTL) extends Interval Temporal Logic (ITL) and is widely applied to system specification and verification [4]. In most cases the system modeling techniques have nothing to do with temporal logics while the desired properties are described by temporal logic formulas, thus verification has suffered from a defect that different formal methods have different denotations and semantics. To improve this situation, one way is to use the same language for modeling systems and describing properties. Modeling, Simulation and Verification Language (MSVL) is a temporal logic programming language developed as an executable subset of PTL, where concurrent systems can be modeled, simulated and verified [5]. In this method, a concurrent system is modeled by an MSVL program while properties of this system are specified by Propositional Projection Temporal Logic (PPTL) formulas [6]. By model checking within the same temporal logic

This research is supported by the NSFC Grant Nos. 61272118, 61272117, 61133001, 61202038, 61373043, 973 Program Grant No. 2010CB328102, and the Fundamental Research Funds for the Central Universities Nos. K5051203014, K5051303020.

S. Liu and Z. Duan (Eds.): SOFL+MSVL 2013, LNCS 8332, pp. 62–75, 2014.
DOI: 10.1007/978-3-319-04915-1_5, ©Springer International Publishing Switzerland 2014

framework, whether or not a concurrent system satisfies the desired properties can be verified.

Introducing types into a programming languages is important, which enables us to write more sound and practical programs. As we known, most conventional programming languages such as C, C++ and Java have their own data types, including integer, array, list, etc. However, most temporal logic programming languages, e.g. MSVL, Tempura [7], XYZ/E [8], TLA [9] and METATEM [10], have not implemented types yet. To bridge the gap between temporal logic programming and conventional programming, we are motivated to investigate techniques for formalzing and implementing types in MSVL.

In [11], there are two basic built-in types, integer and bool, which can be given pure set-theoretic definitions in Tempura. Further types can be built from these basic types by means of the $\times$ operator and the power set operator. Also, they defined a statement $type(x, T)$ to introduce a variable x of a type T. But so far as we know, no further formalization and implementation details have been published to clarify a proper way to implement types in Tempura, neither does the Tempura interpreter consider the execution of type statements.

The main contributions of this paper are as follows. (1) The data domain D of MSVL is formalized to describe types including integer, float, character, array, list, etc. (2) Typed functions and predicates, and the type declaration statement are defined. (3) The normal form for those statements are given and they are implemented in the MSVL interpreter. With these contributions, the language MSVL can be used to model, simulate and verify typed programs.

The rest of the paper is organized as follows. Section 2 briefly introduces PTL and MSVL. In Sect. 3, the data domain, typed functions and predicates, and the type declaration statement are formalized. Then, Sect. 4 provides the MSVL interpreter implementation mechanisms based on the notion of the normal form. In Sect. 5, the MSVL interpreter is used to model and verify an in-place reversal of an integer list. Finally, conclusions are drawn in Sect. 6.

2   Preliminaries

2.1   Projection Temporal Logic

Let $\mathcal{P}$ be a countable set of propositions, and $\mathcal{V}$ be a countable set of typed static and dynamic variables. PTL terms e and formulas p are given by the following grammar [4].

$$e ::= x \mid \bigcirc e \mid \ominus e \mid f(e_1, \ldots, e_m)$$
$$p ::= r \mid e_1 = e_2 \mid P(e_1, \ldots, e_m) \mid \neg p \mid p_1 \wedge p_2 \mid \exists v : p \mid$$
$$\bigcirc p \mid (p_1, \ldots, p_m)\, \mathsf{prj}\, p$$

where $r \in \mathcal{P}$ is a proposition, and $x \in \mathcal{V}$ is a dynamic or static variable. In $f(e_1, \ldots, e_m)$ and $P(e_1, \ldots, e_m)$, f is a function and P is a predicate. Each function and predicate has a fixed arity. A formula (term) is called a *state* formula (term) if it does not contain any temporal operators (i.e. $\bigcirc$ or prj); otherwise it is a *temporal* formula (term).

A state s is a pair of assignments (I_v, I_p) where for each variable x defines $s[x] = I_v[x]$, and for each proposition r defines $s[r] = I_p[r]$. $I_v[x]$ is a value in the data domain $\mathcal{D}$ or nil which means "undefined", and $I_p[r]$ is a value in $\mathbb{B} = \{\mathsf{true}, \mathsf{false}\}$. An interval $\sigma = \langle s_0, s_1, \ldots \rangle$ is a non-empty (possibly infinite) sequence of states. The length of σ, denoted by $|\sigma|$, is defined as ω if σ is infinite; otherwise it is the number of states in σ minus one. To have a uniform notation for both finite and infinite intervals, we will use extended integers as indices. That is, we consider the set $\mathbb{N}$ of natural numbers and ω, $\mathbb{N}_\omega = \mathbb{N} \cup \{\omega\}$, and extend the comparison operators, $=, <, \leq$, to $\mathbb{N}_\omega$ by considering $\omega = \omega$, and for all $i \in \mathbb{N}$, $i < \omega$. Moreover, we define $\preceq$ as $\leq -\{(\omega, \omega)\}$. With such a notation, $\sigma_{(i..j)}(0 \leq i \preceq j \leq |\sigma|)$ denotes the sub-interval $\langle s_i, \ldots, s_j \rangle$ and $\sigma(k)(0 \leq k \preceq |\sigma|)$ denotes $\langle s_k, \ldots, s_{|\sigma|} \rangle$. The concatenation of σ with another interval (or empty string) σ' is denoted by $\sigma \bullet \sigma'$. To define the semantics of the projection operator we need an auxiliary operator for intervals. Let $\sigma = \langle s_0, s_1, \ldots \rangle$ be an interval and $n_1, \ldots, n_h$ be integers $(h \geq 1)$ such that $0 \leq n_1 \leq n_2 \leq \ldots \leq n_h \preceq |\sigma|$. The projection of σ onto $n_1, \ldots, n_h$ is the interval (called projected interval), $\sigma \downarrow (n_1, \ldots, n_h) = \langle s_{m_1}, s_{m_2}, \ldots, s_{m_l} \rangle$, where $m_1, \ldots, m_l$ is obtained from $n_1, \ldots, n_h$ by deleting all duplicates. For example,

$$\langle s_0, s_1, s_2, s_3, s_4 \rangle \downarrow (0, 0, 2, 2, 2, 3) = \langle s_0, s_2, s_3 \rangle$$

An interpretation for a PTL term or formula is a tuple $\mathcal{I} = (\sigma, i, k, j)$, where $\sigma = \langle s_0, s_1, \ldots \rangle$ is an interval, i and k are non-negative integers, and j is an integer or ω, such that $i \leq k \preceq j \leq |\sigma|$. We use (σ, i, k, j) to mean that a term or formula is interpreted over a subinterval $\sigma_{(i..j)}$ with the current state being s_k. For every term e, the evaluation of e relative to interpretation $\mathcal{I} = (\sigma, i, k, j)$, denoted as $\mathcal{I}[e]$, is a value in $\mathcal{D}$ or nil. It is defined by structural induction, shown in Fig .1.

$$\mathcal{I}[x] = s_k[x] = I_v^k[x]$$

$$\mathcal{I}[\bigcirc e] = \begin{cases} (\sigma, i, k+1, j)[e] & \text{if } k < j \\ nil & \text{otherwise} \end{cases}$$

$$\mathcal{I}[\ominus e] = \begin{cases} (\sigma, i, k-1, j)[e] & \text{if } i < k \\ nil & \text{otherwise} \end{cases}$$

$$\mathcal{I}[f(e_1, \ldots, e_m)] = \begin{cases} \mathcal{I}[f](\mathcal{I}[e_1], \ldots, \mathcal{I}[e_m]) & \text{if } \mathcal{I}[e_h] \neq nil \text{ for all } h \\ nil & \text{otherwise} \end{cases}$$

Fig. 1. Interpretation of PTL terms

The satisfaction relation for formulas $\models$ is inductively defined as follows.

1. $\mathcal{I} \models r$ if $s_k[r] = I_p^k[r] = \mathsf{true}$.
2. $\mathcal{I} \models e_1 = e_2$ if $\mathcal{I}[e_1] = \mathcal{I}[e_2]$.

3. $\mathcal{I} \models P(e_1, \ldots, e_m)$ if $\mathcal{I}[e_h] \neq nil$ for $1 \leq h \leq m$ and $\mathcal{I}[P](\mathcal{I}[e_1], \ldots, \mathcal{I}[e_m]) =$ true.
4. $\mathcal{I} \models \neg p$ if $\mathcal{I} \not\models p$.
5. $\mathcal{I} \models p_1 \wedge p_2$ if $\mathcal{I} \models p_1$ and $\mathcal{I} \models p_2$.
6. $\mathcal{I} \models \exists v : p$ if for some interval σ' which has the same length as σ, $(\sigma', i, k, j) \models p$ and the only difference between σ and σ' can be the values of the variable v at the state k.
7. $\mathcal{I} \models \bigcirc p$ if $k < j$ and $(\sigma, i, k+1, j) \models p$.
8. $\mathcal{I} \models (p_1, \ldots, p_m)\, \mathrm{prj}\, q$ if there exist integers $k = k_0 \leq k_1 \leq \ldots \leq k_m \leq j$ such that $(\sigma, i, k_0, k_1) \models p_1$, $(\sigma, k_{l-1}, k_{l-1}, k_l) \models p_l$ (for $1 < l \leq m$), and $(\sigma', 0, 0, |\sigma'|) \models q$ for one of the following σ':
   (a) $k_m < j$ and $\sigma' = \sigma \downarrow (k_0, \ldots, k_m) \bullet \sigma_{(k_m+1..j)}$
   (b) $k_m = j$ and $\sigma' = \sigma \downarrow (k_0, \ldots, k_h)$ for some $0 \leq h \leq m$.

A formula p is said to be:

1. *satisfied* by an interval σ, denoted as $\sigma \models p$, if $(\sigma, 0, 0, |\sigma|) \models p$.
2. *satisfiable* if $\sigma \models p$ for some σ.
3. *valid*, denoted as $\models p$, if $\sigma \models p$ for all σ.
4. *equivalent* to another formula q, denoted as $p \equiv q$, if $\models \Box(p \leftrightarrow q)$.

The connectors $\vee$, $\rightarrow$ and $\leftrightarrow$ are defined as usual. In particular, the abbreviations true $\overset{\text{def}}{=} p \vee \neg p$ and false $\overset{\text{def}}{=} p \wedge \neg p$ for any formula p. In Fig. 2 derived formulas and composite predicates are shown.

empty $\overset{\text{def}}{=} \neg \bigcirc$ true		more $\overset{\text{def}}{=} \neg$empty	
$p; q$ $\overset{\text{def}}{=} (p, q)\, \mathrm{prj}\, $empty		$\Diamond p$ $\overset{\text{def}}{=}$ true; p	
$\Box p$ $\overset{\text{def}}{=} \neg\Diamond\neg p$		halt(p) $\overset{\text{def}}{=} \Box($empty $\leftrightarrow p)$	
keep(p) $\overset{\text{def}}{=} \Box(\neg$empty $\rightarrow p)$		fin(p) $\overset{\text{def}}{=} \Box($empty $\rightarrow p)$	
skip $\overset{\text{def}}{=} \bigcirc$empty		len(n) $\overset{\text{def}}{=} \bigcirc$len$(n-1)$ for $n > 0$	
len(0) $\overset{\text{def}}{=}$ empty			
p^* $\overset{\text{def}}{=}$ empty $\vee (p; p^*) \vee p \wedge \Box$more			

Fig. 2. Derived formulas and composite predicates

In order to avoid an excessive number of parentheses, the following precedence rules are used as shown in Table 1. An operator with a smaller number has a higher precedence, while operators with the same number have the same precedence.

Table 1. Precedence rules of PTL

1	$\neg$	2 $\bigcirc \ominus \Diamond \Box$	3 $\wedge$	4 $\vee$
5	$:== $	6 $\rightarrow \leftrightarrow$	7 prj	8 ;

2.2 MSVL

Let n range over integers and x range over variables. MSVL arithmetic expressions e and boolean expressions b are PTL terms and formulas, respectively [5]. They are given by the following grammar:

$$e ::= n \mid x \mid \bigcirc x \mid \ominus x \mid e_1 + e_2 \mid e_1 - e_2 \mid e_1 * e_2 \mid e_1/e_2 \mid e_1 \bmod e_2$$
$$b ::= \mathsf{true} \mid \mathsf{false} \mid e_1 = e_2 \mid e_1 > e_2 \mid e_1 \geq e_2 \mid e_1 < e_2 \mid e_1 \leq e_2 \mid \neg b \mid b_1 \wedge b_2$$

The elementary statements p, q of MSVL are PTL formulas and defined as follows.

Assignment:	$x = e$
P-I-Assignment:	$x \Leftarrow e \overset{\text{def}}{=} x = e \wedge r_x$
Unit Assignment:	$x := e \overset{\text{def}}{=} \mathsf{skip} \wedge \bigcirc x \Leftarrow e$
Sequential Composition:	$p; q$
Conditional Choice:	$\mathsf{if}\ b\ \mathsf{then}\ p\ \mathsf{else}\ q \overset{\text{def}}{=} (b \to p) \wedge (\neg b \to q)$
While Loop:	$\mathsf{while}\ b\ \mathsf{do}\ p \overset{\text{def}}{=} (b \wedge p)^* \wedge \square(\mathsf{empty} \to \neg b)$
Conjunction:	$p \wedge q$
Selection:	$p \vee q$
Parallel Composition:	$p \parallel q \overset{\text{def}}{=} p \wedge (q; \mathsf{true}) \vee q \wedge (p; \mathsf{true})$
Next:	$\bigcirc p$
Always:	$\square p$
Termination:	empty
Local variable:	$\exists x : p$
State Frame:	$\mathsf{lbf}(x) \overset{\text{def}}{=} \neg r_x \to \exists z : (\ominus x = z \wedge x = z)$
Interval Frame:	$\mathsf{frame}(x) \overset{\text{def}}{=} \square(\mathsf{more} \to \bigcirc\mathsf{lbf}(x))$
Projection:	$(p_1, \ldots, p_m)\ \mathsf{prj}\ q$
Await:	$\mathsf{await}(b) \overset{\text{def}}{=} (\mathsf{frame}(x_1) \wedge \ldots \wedge \mathsf{frame}(x_h)) \wedge$ $\square(\mathsf{empty} \leftrightarrow b)$, where $x_1, \ldots, x_h$ are the variables that occur in b

Among the statements, $x = e$, $x := e$, $x \Leftarrow e$, empty, $\mathsf{lbf}(x)$, and $\mathsf{frame}(x)$ are basic statements, while the others are composite statements. An assignment $x = e$ means that the value of x equals the value of e, while a unit assignment $x := e$ specifies the value of x by e and the length of the interval by 1. A positive immediate assignment (P-I-Assignment) $x \Leftarrow e$ indicates that the value of x equals the value of e and that the assignment flag r_x for x is true. A sequential composition $p; q$ indicates that p is executed from the current state until its termination when q is executed from. Statements of conditional choice $\mathsf{if}\ b\ \mathsf{then}\ p\ \mathsf{else}\ q$ and while loop $\mathsf{while}\ b\ \mathsf{do}\ p$ are the same as they are in conventional imperative languages. A conjunction $p \wedge q$ means that p and q are executed concurrently and share all the variables during the mutual execution, while a selection $p \vee q$ means either p or q is executed. Different from a conjunction, a parallel composition allows both processes to specify their own intervals, e.g. $\mathsf{len}(3) \parallel \mathsf{len}(4)$ can be satisfied but $\mathsf{len}(3) \wedge \mathsf{len}(4)$ is always false. A next statement $\bigcirc p$ means that p holds at the next state, while an always statement

$\Box p$ means that p holds at all states over the current interval. The termination statement empty means that the current state is the final state of the interval. An existential quantification $\exists x : p$ intends to hide x within p. A state frame $\mathsf{lbf}(x)$ means the value of x in the current state equals the value of x in the previous state if no assignment to x is encountered, while $\mathsf{frame}(x)$ indicates that the value of variable x always keeps its old value over an interval if no assignment to x is encountered. A projection statement can be thought of as a special parallel execution that is performed on different time scales. Specifically, $(p_1, \ldots, p_m)\,\mathsf{prj}\,q$ means that q is executed in parallel with $p_1, \ldots, p_m$ over an interval obtained by taking the endpoints of the intervals over which the p_i's are executed. In particular, the sequence of p_i's and q may terminate at different time points. Finally, an await statement $\mathsf{await}(b)$ simply waits until b becomes true, without changing any variables.

The precedence rules of MSVL statements are listed in Table 2, where 1 means highest and 12 means lowest.

Table 2. Precedence rules of MSVL

1	$\neg$	2	$\bigcirc\,\ominus\,\Box$	3	$*\;/\;mod$	4	$+\;-$	5	$>\geq<\leq$	6	$\exists$
7	$=\Leftarrow\;:=$	8	$\wedge$	9	$\vee\;\|$	10	$\rightarrow\;\leftrightarrow$	11	prj	12	;

3   Typed MSVL

3.1   Data Domain

In Sect. 2, for a state $s = (I_v, I_p)$ and a variable x defined in s, $I_v[x] \in \mathcal{D}$. If a variable y is irrelevant to (i.e. undefined in) s, we write $I_v[y] = nil$. So, for any interpretation $\mathcal{I}$ and variable x, $\mathcal{I}[x] \in \mathcal{D} \cup \{nil\}$. In order to extend the interpretation I_v of variables to typed values, we need to enlarge the data domain $\mathcal{D}$. We introduce into MSVL a set $\mathcal{T}$ of types, including

- basic types: int, float, char,
- list types: int$\langle\rangle$, float$\langle\rangle$, char$\langle\rangle$,
- array types: int$[\,]$, float$[\,]$, char$[\,]$.

The set of values of each basic type are defined as follows.

- int: $\mathbb{Z}$
- float: $\mathbb{F} \stackrel{\text{def}}{=} \{n.d_1 d_2 \cdots d_m \mid m \in \mathbb{N}, n \in \mathbb{Z}, d_i \in \{0, \ldots, 9\}\,for\,1 \leq i \leq m\}$
- char: $\mathbb{C} \stackrel{\text{def}}{=} \{'a', \ldots, 'z', 'A', \ldots, 'Z', '0', \ldots, '9', '\,', '!', '@', '\#', '\$', \ldots\}$

Consider typed values (v, T), i.e. values labeled by their types, where $T \in \mathcal{T}$. We define the set of typed values for each type. For a set S, S^n denotes the set of lists of length n on S ($n \in \mathbb{N}$), and S^* denotes the set of lists on S.

- Int $\overset{\text{def}}{=} \mathbb{Z} \times \{\text{int}\}$,   Int$\langle\rangle \overset{\text{def}}{=} \mathbb{Z}^* \times \{\text{int}\langle\rangle\}$,

  Int$[n] \overset{\text{def}}{=} \mathbb{Z}^n \times \{\text{int}[\,]\}$ for $n \geq 1$,   Int$[\,] \overset{\text{def}}{=} \bigcup_{n\geq 1} \text{Int}[n]$

- Float $\overset{\text{def}}{=} \mathbb{F} \times \{\text{float}\}$,   Float$\langle\rangle \overset{\text{def}}{=} \mathbb{F}^* \times \{\text{float}\langle\rangle\}$,

  Float$[n] \overset{\text{def}}{=} \mathbb{F}^n \times \{\text{float}[\,]\}$ for $n \geq 1$,   Float$[\,] \overset{\text{def}}{=} \bigcup_{n\geq 1} \text{Float}[n]$

- Char $\overset{\text{def}}{=} \mathbb{C} \times \{\text{char}\}$,   Char$\langle\rangle \overset{\text{def}}{=} \mathbb{C}^* \times \{\text{char}\langle\rangle\}$,

  Char$[n] \overset{\text{def}}{=} \mathbb{C}^n \times \{\text{char}[\,]\}$ for $n \geq 1$,   Char$[\,] \overset{\text{def}}{=} \bigcup_{n\geq 1} \text{Char}[n]$

The data domain D of variables is the union of these sets.

$$\mathcal{D} \overset{\text{def}}{=} \text{Int} \cup \text{Int}\langle\rangle \cup \text{Int}[\,] \cup \text{Float} \cup \text{Float}\langle\rangle \cup \text{Float}[\,] \cup \text{Char} \cup \text{Char}\langle\rangle \cup \text{Char}[\,]$$

3.2 Typed Functions and Predicates

Each function and predicate has not only a fixed arity but also a fixed typed. Specifically, a function f of arity m has a type $T_1 \times \ldots \times T_m \to T$, and a predicate of arity n has a type $T_1 \times \ldots \times T_n \to \mathbb{B}$, where each T_i and T is a type in $\mathcal{T}$. For example, the original MSVL function $\cdot + \cdot$ and predicate $\cdot > \cdot$ are applied to integers, and their types are denoted as $\cdot + \cdot : \text{int} \times \text{int} \to \text{int}$ and $\cdot > \cdot : \text{int} \times \text{int} \to \mathbb{B}$, respectively.

Since we extend the interpretation I_v of variables to typed values, we also need to extend the application of functions and predicates to typed values. The extension is straightforward. For a function $f : T_1 \times \ldots \times T_m \to T$ with $f(v_1, \ldots, v_m) = v$, we now have $f((v_1, T_1), \ldots, (v_m, T_m)) = (v, T)$, and for a predicate $P : T_1 \times \ldots \times T_m \to \mathbb{B}$ with $P(v_1, \ldots, v_m) = \mathsf{true}$ (or false), we now have $P((v_1, T_1), \ldots, (v_m, T_m)) = \mathsf{true}$ (or false). Implicitly, a function with ill-typed parameters evaluates to nil, and a predicate with ill-typed parameters is interpreted as false. As a result, $\mathcal{I}[e] \in \mathcal{D} \cup \{nil\}$ for any expression e and interpretation $\mathcal{I}$, according to the evaluation rules defined in Fig. 1. Notice that even for type-correct and defined parameters, the result of a function can be undefined. For example, $(3, \text{int})/(0, \text{int}) = nil$, $hd((\langle\rangle, \text{int}\langle\rangle)) = nil$. However, this will not cause any problem.

A constant c is regarded as a 0-arity function. The kinds of constants allowed in MSVL programs are listed below, together with their interpretations.

- Integers, float numbers and characters, e.g. $\mathcal{I}[8] = (8, \text{int})$, $\mathcal{I}[3.1] = (3.1, \text{float})$ and $\mathcal{I}['a'] = ('a', \text{char})$.
- Non-empty lists, e.g. $\mathcal{I}[\langle'x','y'\rangle] = (\langle'x','y'\rangle, \text{char}\langle\rangle)$.
- Empty lists, $\mathcal{I}[\langle\rangle_i] = (\langle\rangle, \text{int}\langle\rangle)$, $\mathcal{I}[\langle\rangle_f] = (\langle\rangle, \text{float}\langle\rangle)$ and $\mathcal{I}[\langle\rangle_c] = (\langle\rangle, \text{char}\langle\rangle)$.

Notice that we discriminate empty lists of integers ($\langle\rangle_i$), float numbers ($\langle\rangle_f$) and characters ($\langle\rangle_c$). This is to ensure that every expression has a fixed type.

The original functions $+, -, *, /, mod$ and predicates $>, \geq, <, \leq$ are all for the integer type. We need to define operations for new types. First, we define $+$ (and then $-$, $*$ and $/$) of float numbers. One way is to define a specific function

$$\cdot +_f \cdot : \text{float} \times \text{float} \to \text{float}$$

for the float type. A more convenient approach is to unify the two addition operations into one.

$$\cdot + \cdot : (\text{int} \times \text{int} \to \text{int}) \cup (\text{float} \times \text{float} \to \text{float})$$

That is, we allow a function f (or predicate P) to have a union of more than one fixed types. Each application of f (or P) takes one of these types.

Arithmetic operators. Besides $+$, we do the same extension on $-$, $*$ and $/$ so that

$$\cdot + \cdot, \cdot - \cdot, \cdot * \cdot, \cdot / \cdot : (\text{int} \times \text{int} \to \text{int}) \cup (\text{float} \times \text{float} \to \text{float})$$

We keep the function $mod : \text{int} \times \text{int} \to \text{int}$. We also extend the predicates $>, \geq, <, \leq$ to both integer of float types.

$$\cdot > \cdot, \cdot \geq \cdot, \cdot < \cdot, \cdot \leq \cdot : (\text{int} \times \text{int} \to \mathbb{B}) \cup (\text{float} \times \text{float} \to \mathbb{B})$$

Type cast. We define two functions for type cast between float numbers and integers.

$$(\text{int}) \cdot : \text{float} \to \text{int} \quad (n.d_1 d_2 \cdots d_m, \text{float}) \mapsto (n, \text{int})$$
$$(\text{float}) \cdot : \text{int} \to \text{float} \quad (n, \text{int}) \mapsto (n., \text{float})$$

Array and list operations. We define a set of standard operations for arrays and lists. For an array a, the operation $a[i]$ returns its ith element.

$$\cdot[\cdot] : (\text{int}[\,] \times \text{int} \to \text{int}) \cup (\text{float}[\,] \times \text{int} \to \text{float}) \cup (\text{char}[\,] \times \text{int} \to \text{char})$$
$$(\langle c_0, \ldots, c_k \rangle, T[\,]), (i, \text{int}) \mapsto (c_i, T) \quad i \in \{0, \ldots, k\}$$
$$(\langle c_0, \ldots, c_k \rangle, T[\,]), (i, \text{int}) \mapsto nil \quad i \notin \{0, \ldots, k\}$$
$$k \in \mathbb{N}, T \in \{\text{int}, \text{float}, \text{char}\}$$

For a list l, the operation $|l|$ returns the length of l.

$$|\cdot| : (\text{int}\langle\rangle \to \text{int}) \cup (\text{float}\langle\rangle \to \text{int}) \cup (\text{char}\langle\rangle \to \text{int})$$
$$(\langle c_1, \ldots, c_k \rangle, T) \mapsto (k, \text{int}) \quad k \in \mathbb{N}, T \in \{\text{int}\langle\rangle, \text{float}\langle\rangle, \text{char}\langle\rangle\}$$

Besides, the operations $hd(l)$ and $tl(l)$ return the head and tail of l, respectively.

$$hd : (\text{int}\langle\rangle \to \text{int}) \cup (\text{float}\langle\rangle \to \text{float}) \cup (\text{char}\langle\rangle \to \text{char})$$
$$(\langle\rangle, T\langle\rangle) \mapsto nil$$
$$(\langle c_0, c_1, \ldots, c_k \rangle, T\langle\rangle) \mapsto (c_0, T) \quad k \in \mathbb{N}, T \in \{\text{int}, \text{float}, \text{char}\}$$
$$tl : (\text{int}\langle\rangle \to \text{int}\langle\rangle) \cup (\text{float}\langle\rangle \to \text{float}\langle\rangle) \cup (\text{char}\langle\rangle \to \text{char}\langle\rangle)$$
$$(\langle\rangle, T) \mapsto nil$$
$$(\langle c_0, c_1, \ldots, c_k \rangle, T) \mapsto (\langle c_1, \ldots, c_k \rangle, T) \quad k \in \mathbb{N}, T \in \{\text{int}\langle\rangle, \text{float}\langle\rangle, \text{char}\langle\rangle\}$$

For two lists l_1 and l_2 of the same type, the operations $l_1 \bullet l_2$ and $l_1 \circ l_2$ calculates the concatenation and fusion of l_1 and l_2, respectively. They are defined as follows.

$$\cdot \bullet \cdot : (\text{int}\langle\rangle \times \text{int}\langle\rangle \to \text{int}\langle\rangle) \cup (\text{float}\langle\rangle \times \text{float}\langle\rangle \to \text{float}\langle\rangle)$$
$$\cup (\text{char}\langle\rangle \times \text{char}\langle\rangle \to \text{char}\langle\rangle)$$
$$(\langle c_1, \ldots, c_j \rangle, T), (\langle d_1, \ldots, d_k \rangle, T) \mapsto (\langle c_1, \ldots, c_j, d_1, \ldots, d_k \rangle, T)$$
$$j, k \in \mathbb{N}, T \in \{\text{int}\langle\rangle, \text{float}\langle\rangle, \text{char}\langle\rangle\}$$

$$\cdot \circ \cdot : (\text{int}\langle\rangle \times \text{int}\langle\rangle \to \text{int}\langle\rangle) \cup (\text{float}\langle\rangle \times \text{float}\langle\rangle \to \text{float}\langle\rangle)$$
$$\cup(\text{char}\langle\rangle \times \text{char}\langle\rangle \to \text{char}\langle\rangle)$$
$$(\langle\rangle, T), (\langle d_1, \ldots, d_k\rangle, T) \mapsto (\langle d_1, \ldots, d_k\rangle, T)$$
$$(\langle c_1, \ldots, c_j, c\rangle, T), (\langle\rangle, T) \mapsto (\langle c_1, \ldots, c_j, c\rangle, T)$$
$$(\langle c_1, \ldots, c_j, c\rangle, T), (\langle c, d_1, \ldots, d_k\rangle, T) \mapsto (\langle c_1, \ldots, c_j, c, d_1, \ldots, d_k\rangle, T)$$
$$(\langle c_1, \ldots, c_j, c\rangle, T), (\langle d, d_1, \ldots, d_k\rangle, T) \mapsto nil \qquad d \neq c$$
$$j, k \in \mathbb{N}, T \in \{\text{int}\langle\rangle, \text{float}\langle\rangle, \text{char}\langle\rangle\}$$

Other. Besides the above operations, we define an auxiliary predicate Def(). For an expression e, Def(e) means e is defined, i.e., the value of e is not *nil*.

$$\text{Def} : (\text{int} \to \mathbb{B}) \cup (\text{float} \to \mathbb{B}) \cup (\text{char} \to \mathbb{B}) \cup (\text{int}\langle\rangle \to \mathbb{B}) \cup (\text{float}\langle\rangle \to \mathbb{B})$$
$$\cup(\text{char}\langle\rangle \to \mathbb{B})$$
$$(c, T) \mapsto \text{true} \qquad T \in \{\text{int}, \text{float}, \text{char}, \text{int}\langle\rangle, \text{float}\langle\rangle, \text{char}\langle\rangle\}$$

Because an expression can evaluate to *nil*, the meaning of some predicates or formulas may not precisely reflect our intuition. For example, $e_1 \leq e_2 \equiv \neg(e_1 > e_2)$ is not valid in MSVL. Instead, $e_1 \leq e_2 \equiv \text{Def}(e_1) \wedge \text{Def}(e_2) \wedge \neg(e_1 > e_2)$. This is why the predicate Def() is useful. With the predicate, another equivalent characterization of $e_1 \leq e_2$ is $\text{Def}(e_1) \wedge \text{Def}(e_2) \wedge (e_1 < e_2 \vee e_1 = e_2)$.

3.3   Type Declaration Statement

Notice that when declaring an array we need to give the specific number of elements of the array, e.g. int[5] a. So the set of types $\mathcal{T}_d$ that are used in type declarations is slightly different from the set $\mathcal{T}$:

$$\mathcal{T}_d \stackrel{\text{def}}{=} \{\text{int}, \text{float}, \text{char}, \text{int}\langle\rangle, \text{float}\langle\rangle, \text{char}\langle\rangle,$$
$$\text{int}[1], \text{int}[2], \ldots, \text{float}[1], \text{float}[2], \ldots, \text{char}[1], \text{char}[2], \ldots\}.$$

We define predicates $\text{is}_T(\cdot)$, which means "is of type T", for each type $T \in \mathcal{T}_d$.

1. For each basic type $T \in \{\text{int}, \text{float}, \text{char}\}$, $\text{is}_T : T \to \mathbb{B}$ with $(c, T) \mapsto \text{true}$,
2. for each list type $T\langle\rangle \in \{\text{int}\langle\rangle, \text{float}\langle\rangle, \text{char}\langle\rangle\}$, $\text{is}_{T\langle\rangle} : T\langle\rangle \to \mathbb{B}$ with $(c, T\langle\rangle) \mapsto \text{true}$, and
3. for each array type $T[n] \in \{\text{int}[1], \text{int}[2], \ldots, \text{float}[1], \ldots, \text{char}[1], \ldots\}$, $\text{is}_{T[n]} : T[] \to \mathbb{B}$ with $(c, T[]) \mapsto \text{true}$ iff $|c| = n$.

Using these predicates, we define the type declaration statement as a derived PTL formula.
$$T x \stackrel{\text{def}}{=} \Box \text{is}_T(x)$$

4   Implementation Mechanisms

This section focuses on the implementation mechanisms for the type declaration statement which plays an important role in program execution in the MSVL interpreter. In order to carry out the formal verification and analysis of programs in a rigorous way, an operational semantics for the type declaration statement are needed. For reducing (executing) MSVL programs, we divide the reduction process into two phases [14]: one for state reduction and the other for interval reduction. The state reduction is mainly on how to transform a program into its normal form [5]. The interval reduction is concerned with a program from one state to another. The state reduction has to change the normal form of programs after the introduction of the type declaration statement, while the interval reduction remains unchanged.

4.1   Normal Form of Programs

Definition 1. *A typed MSVL program q is in normal form if*

$$q \overset{\text{def}}{=} (\bigvee_{i=1}^{k} q_{ei} \wedge \text{empty}) \vee (\bigvee_{j=1}^{h} q_{cj} \wedge \bigcirc q_{fj})$$

where $k + h \geq 1$ and the following hold:

1. *each q_{ei} and q_{cj} is either true or a state formula of the form $p_1 \wedge \ldots \wedge p_m$ ($m \geq 1$) such that each p_l ($1 \leq l \leq m$) is either $\text{is}_T(x)$ with $x \in V$, $T \in \mathcal{T}_d$, or $x = e$ with $e \in D$, or r_x, or $\neg r_x$.*
2. *q_{fj} is an internal program, that is, one in which variables may refer to the previous states but not beyond the first state of the current interval over which the program is executed.*

When a typed MSVL program q is deterministic $k + h = 1$ holds, otherwise $k + h > 1$ does. We call conjuncts, $\bigvee_{i=1}^{k} q_{ei} \wedge empty$, $\bigvee_{j=1}^{h} q_{cj} \wedge \bigcirc q_{fj}$ basic products: the former is called terminal products whereas the latter is called future products. Further we call q_{ei} and q_{cj} present components which are executed at the current state, and $\bigcirc q_{fj}$ future components executed in the subsequent states. An important conclusion is that any typed MSVL program including type declaration statements can be reduced to its normal form. Therefore, execute programs in MSVL is to transform them logically equivalent to their normal forms.

Let p be an MSVL program augmented with type declarations. There is a program q in normal form such that $p \equiv q$.

The proof proceeds by induction on the structure of statements. The proof of MSVL statements without type declarations can be found in [12,13].

The proof of the type declaration statement $T\,x$ is given as follows.

$$
\begin{aligned}
T\,x &\equiv \Box \text{is}_T(x) \\
&\equiv \Box \text{is}_T(x) \wedge (\text{empty} \vee \neg \text{empty}) &(i) \\
&\equiv \Box \text{is}_T(x) \wedge \text{empty} \vee \Box \text{is}_T(x) \wedge \neg \text{empty} &(ii) \\
&\equiv \text{is}_T(x) \wedge \text{empty} \vee \Box \text{is}_T(x) \wedge \neg \text{empty} &(iii) \\
&\equiv \text{is}_T(x) \wedge \text{empty} \vee \Box \text{is}_T(x) \wedge \text{more} &(iv) \\
&\equiv \text{is}_T(x) \wedge \text{empty} \vee \text{is}_T(x) \wedge \bigcirc \Box \text{is}_T(x) &(v)
\end{aligned}
$$

In the above: (i) follows from T1 in [14]; (ii) from Theorem 2.1 in [13]; (iii) from Law7 in [14]; (iv) from the definition of more; and (v) from Law8 in [14].

4.2   MSVL Interpreter

Microsoft Visual C++ has been used to implement an MSVL interpreter. The flow chart of the interpreter is shown in Fig. 3. The lexical analyzer and parser are implemented with flex and bison. In the state reduction based on the normal form an MSVL program can be rewritten by the reducer module to a logically equivalent formula $Present \wedge Remains$. The formula $Present$ is executed at the current state. It consists of true, false, empty, immediate variable assignments or variable input/output. In the interval reduction the formula $Remains$ is executed in the succeeding state if it exists. The program editor, data input, output view modules are used to deal with input and output. An MSVL program is inputted into the interpreter and executed in a sequence of states to try to find its model. If the program is transformed to true at the final state, its model is found and it is satisfiable, otherwise it has no model and is unsatisfiable.

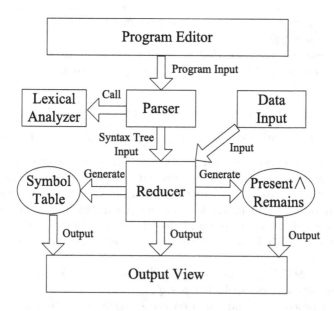

Fig. 3. Interpreter structure

The MSVL interpreter is able to work in an modeling, simulation or verification mode. In the first mode, an MSVL program is used to describe a system and executed in the interpreter. All the models of the system are presented as an Normal Form Graph (NFG) [12]. As show in Fig. 4(a) a path in the NFG ends with a bicyclic node is a model of the system. The simulation mode is a little different with the modeling mode, and the interpreter outputs only one

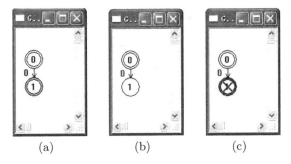

(a)   (b)   (c)

Fig. 4. Three types of nodes. (a)modeling: a path. (b)verification: a satisfiable path. (c)verification: an unsatisfiable path.

path in the NFG according to the MSVL's minimal model semantics [12]. The interpreter can also work in the verification mode. Given an MSVL program to describe a system, and a PPTL formula to describe its property, the interpreter can automatically verify whether or not the system satisfies the property. If the system is unsatisfied with the property, the interpreter will point out a counterexample. As shown in Fig. 4(b) a satisfiable path in the NFG ends with a circular node, while as shown in Fig. 4(c) an unsatisfiable path in the NFG ends with a terminative node. It is worth pointing out that the formalization of types only extends the data domain to typed values. It does not change the structures of MSVL programs or the finiteness of program states. Therefore, we can still translate a model checking problem into a satisfiability problem in PPTL since finite-state MSVL programs are equivalent to PPTL formulas [5].

5   An Application

In Fig. 5, two integer linked list both include three nodes. The integers in the first list from the head to the tail are 10, 20 and 30, and the integers in the second one are in the opposite direction. The following MSVL program executes an in-place reversal of the first integer list and gets the second one. The pointer operations & and * are defined in [15].

```
frame(node1, node2, node3, p, q, r, head, tail) and (
    int[2] node1, node2, node3;
    pointer p,q,r;
    node1[0] = 10 and node1[1] := -1;
    node2[0] = node1[0] + 10 and node2[1] := -1;
    node3[0] = (int)30.0 and node3[1] := -1;
    node2[1] := &node3;     node1[1] := &node2;
    q :=& node1;    head := *q[0];
    while(q != -1){ tail := *q[0];      q := *q[1]  };
    p :=& node1;    q := -1;
```

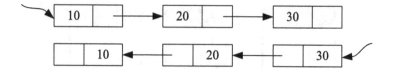

Fig. 5. In-place reversal of an integer list

```
while(p != -1){ r := *p[1]; *p[1] := q; q := p; p := r   };
head := *q[0];
while(q != -1){ tail := *q[0];      q := *q[1]  }
)
```

As showed in Fig. 6(a), the program executes successfully in the modeling mode and outputs 37 states. Before verifying the program, its properties have been formalized as follows. The proposition `prop1` is head = 10 indicates the list head is 10, and `prop2` is `tail` = 30 indicates the list tail is 30. The meanings of `prop3` and `prop4` are similar. The desirable property of the former program is described by a PPTL formula $\Diamond(prop1 \wedge prop2) \wedge \Box(empty \rightarrow prop3 \wedge prop4)$. The property is coded as follows.

```
</
    define prop1: head = 10;     define prop2: tail = 30;
    define prop3: head = 30;     define prop4: tail = 10;
    som(prop1 and prop2) and always(empty -> prop3 and prop4)
/>
```

The MSVL interpreter executes the program with properties in the verification mode and the results are showed in Fig. 6(b). The final node of the execution path is not a bicyclic node, and it shows that the desirable property is satisfied.

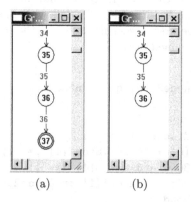

(a)   (b)

Fig. 6. Program execution. (a) modeling result. (b) verification result.

6   Conclusions

In this paper, we provide a formalization and implementation of types in the temporal logic programming language MSVL. The data domain of MSVL is enlarged to include typed values. Typed functions and predicates, and the type declaration statement are defined. The MSVL interpreter implementation mechanisms based on the notion of normal form are also given. In the near future, much research work is to be done to investigate the operational and axiomatic semantics of types in MSVL. In addition, we will also try to model and verify some larger examples within our approach.

References

1. Allen Emerson, E.: Temporal and modal logic. In: Handbook of Theoretical Computer Science, pp. 995–1072. Elsevier, Amsterdam (1995)
2. Clarke, E.M., Grumberg, O., Peled, D.: Model Checking. MIT Press, Cambridge (1999)
3. Baier, C., Katoen, J.-P.: Principles of Model Checking. MIT Press, Cambridge (2008)
4. Duan, Z., Maciej, K.: A framed temporal logic programming language. J. Comput. Sci. Technol. **19**, 341–351 (2004)
5. Duan, Z., Tian, C.: A unified model checking approach with projection temporal logic. In: Liu, S., Maibaum, T., Araki, K. (eds.) ICFEM 2008. LNCS, vol. 5256, pp. 167–186. Springer, Heidelberg (2008)
6. Tian, C., Duan, Z.: Expressiveness of propositional projection temporal logic with star. Theor. Comput. Sci. **412**, 1729–1744 (2011)
7. Cau, A., Moszkowski, B., Zedan, H.: Itl and tempura home page on the web. http://www.cse.dmu.ac.uk/STRL/ITL/ (2013)
8. Tang, Z.: Temporal Logic Program Designing and Engineering. Science Press, Beijing (1999)
9. Lamport, L.: The TLA Home Page. http://research.microsoft.com/en-us/um/people/lamport/tla/tla.html (2013)
10. Fisher, M.: METATEM: the story so far. In: Bordini, R.H., Dastani, M.M., Dix, J., El Fallah Seghrouchni, A. (eds.) PROMAS 2005. LNCS (LNAI), vol. 3862, pp. 3–22. Springer, Heidelberg (2006)
11. Zhou, S., Zedan, H., Cau, A.: Run-time analysis of time-critical systems. J. Syst. Archit. **51**, 331–345 (2005)
12. Duan, Z., Yang, X., Koutny, M.: Framed temporal logic programming. Sci. Comput. Program. **70**, 31–61 (2008)
13. Duan, Z.: Temporal Logic and Temporal Logic Programming. Science Press, Beijing (2006)
14. Yang, X., Duan, Z.: Operational semantics of framed tempura. J. Logic Algebraic Program. **78**, 22–51 (2008)
15. Duan, Z., Wang, X.: Implementing pointer in temporal logic programming languages. In: Proceedings of SBMF 2006, pp. 171–184 (2006)

Present-Future Form of Linear Time μ-Calculus

Yao Liu[1], Zhenhua Duan[1(✉)], Cong Tian[1], and Bo Liu[2]

[1] ICTT and ISN Lab, Xidian University,
Xi'an 710071, China
yao_liu@stu.xidian.edu.cn,
{zhhduan,ctian}@mail.xidian.edu.cn
[2] Beijing Institute of Control Engineering, Beijing 100000, China
liubo@bice.org.cn

Abstract. This paper presents the notion of Present-Future form (PF form) for linear time μ-calculus (νTL) formulas consisting of the present and future parts: the present part is the conjunction of atomic propositions or their negations while the future part is a closed νTL formula under the next operator. We show every closed νTL formula can be rewritten into its corresponding PF form. Finally, based on PF form, the idea of constructing a graph that describing models of a νTL formula is discussed.

Keywords: Linear time μ-calculus · Present-Future form · Present-Future form graph · Models

1 Introduction

Modal μ-calculus introduced by Kozen [1] is an extension of propositional modal logic with the least and greatest fixpoint operators and it has received ever growing interest in the past three decades. It is a formalism of great expressiveness and succinctness which allows a wide range of properties to be expressed, including liveness, safety, and fairness properties. Linear time μ-calculus (νTL) [2,3] is the linear time counterpart of modal μ-calculus whose expressive power is ω-regular. νTL has become widely used since though its syntax and semantics are simple it has enhanced expressive power compared to LTL. It is known that LTL cannot express counting properties like "q holds in every second position of a word" [4] since this is an ω-regular property. From an application point of view, it is of great significance to establish a decision procedure for checking the satisfiability of νTL formulas. However, the work is not easy due to the nestings and alternations of fixpoint operators.

Satisfiability and validity of formulas are fundamental issues in the model theory of a logic. Moreover, satisfiability plays an important role in the model

This research is supported by the NSFC Grant Nos. 61133001, 61272118, 61272117, 61202038, 91218301, 61322202, 61373043, and National Program on Key Basic Research Project (973 Program) Grant No. 2010CB328102.

S. Liu and Z. Duan (Eds.): SOFL+MSVL 2013, LNCS 8332, pp. 76–85, 2014.
DOI: 10.1007/978-3-319-04915-1_6, © Springer International Publishing Switzerland 2014

checking approach. The decision problem of satisfiability for νTL formulas has PSPACE-complete complexity [3] and is about how to find a decision procedure which determines whether a formula is satisfiable. The major milestone of the decision procedure for μ-calculus is made by Streett and Emerson [5] who introduces the notion of well-founded pre-models and applies the automata theory to check satisfiability. Related methods [6,7] translate a formula into an equivalent alternating tree automaton and then check for emptiness. In [8], Banieqbal and Barringer show that if a formula ϕ has a model, then ϕ can generate a good Hintikka structure and this can be further transformed into a good path search problem from a graph. Stirling and Walker propose a tableau system for νTL in [9] and a system for the modal μ-calculus can be found in [10]. Later, [11,12] improve the system of Stirling and Walker by simplifying the success condition for a tableau. In their systems, success for a leaf is determined by the path leading to it, whereas Stirling and Walker's method requires the examination of a potentially infinite number of paths extending over the whole tableau. However, all these methods are extremely intricate and concerned with theoretical aspects rather than practical applications. Therefore, we are motivated to investigate a simpler and more intuitive method.

To this end, Present-Future form (PF form) of νTL formulas is presented in this paper that consists of present and future parts of the formulas: the present part is the conjunction of atomic propositions or their negations while the future part is a closed νTL formula under the next operator. We prove that every closed νTL formula can be transformed into its corresponding PF form. In order to complete the proof, we first need to convert a formula into an equivalent formula in the guarded positive normal form. Finally, based on PF form, the idea of constructing Present-Future form graph (PFG) is introduced, which can be utilized to describe models of a νTL formula. It is worth noting that PFG can be further used to achieve a new decision procedure for checking the satisfiability of νTL formulas as well as a corresponding model checking approach. The idea of this paper is inspired by the normal form of Propositional Projection Temporal Logic (PPTL) [13,14]. Normal form and normal form graph have played a vital role in achieving a decision procedure for checking the satisfiability of PPTL formulas [15–18]. The occurrence of PF form opens up a new direction to the study of νTL.

The rest of this paper is structured as follows. The syntax and semantics of νTL and some basic notions are introduced in Sect. 2. The guarded positive normal form of νTL formulas is presented in Sect. 3. Section 4 defines the PF form of νTL formulas and proves that every closed νTL formula can be transformed into its corresponding PF form. Section 5 concludes the paper.

2   Preliminaries

2.1   Syntax of νTL

Let $\mathcal{P}$ be a set of atomic propositions, and $\mathcal{V}$ a set of variables. νTL formulas can be defined by the following syntax [2]:

$$\phi ::= p \mid X \mid \neg\phi \mid \bigcirc\phi \mid \phi \vee \phi \mid \mu X.\phi$$

where p ranges over $\mathcal{P}$ and X over $\mathcal{V}$. A variable is called *free* when it is not bounded by any fixpoint operators. A formula is called *closed* when there exists no free occurrence of variables in that formula. One restriction on $\mu X.\phi$ is that each free occurrence of X in ϕ lies within the scope of an even number of negations. Derived operators are defined in the usual way: $\phi \wedge \phi$ is $\neg(\neg\phi \vee \neg\phi)$; $\nu X.\phi$ is $\neg\mu X.\neg\phi[\neg X/X]$, where $\phi[\neg X/X]$ is the result of substituting $\neg X$ for each free occurrence of X in ϕ. We use σ to denote μ or ν ordinarily. X is called a μ-*variable* if $\sigma X = \mu X.\phi$ and a ν-*variable* if $\sigma X = \nu X.\phi$.

If X is a bound variable of formula ϕ, there is a unique μ- or ν-subformula $\sigma X.\varphi$ of ϕ in which X is quantified.

2.2   Semantics of νTL

νTL formulas are interpreted over linear time structures. A *linear time structure* over $\mathcal{P}$ is a function $\mathcal{K}\colon \mathbb{N} \to 2^{\mathcal{P}}$.

The semantics of a νTL formula ϕ, relative to $\mathcal{K}$ and an environment $e : \mathcal{V} \to 2^{\mathbb{N}}$, is inductively defined as follows:

$$\llbracket p \rrbracket_e^{\mathcal{K}} := \{i \in \mathbb{N} \mid p \in \mathcal{K}(i)\}$$
$$\llbracket X \rrbracket_e^{\mathcal{K}} := e(X)$$
$$\llbracket \neg\varphi \rrbracket_e^{\mathcal{K}} := \mathbb{N} \setminus \llbracket \varphi \rrbracket_e^{\mathcal{K}}$$
$$\llbracket \varphi \vee \psi \rrbracket_e^{\mathcal{K}} := \llbracket \varphi \rrbracket_e^{\mathcal{K}} \cup \llbracket \psi \rrbracket_e^{\mathcal{K}}$$
$$\llbracket \bigcirc\varphi \rrbracket_e^{\mathcal{K}} := \{i \in \mathbb{N} \mid i+1 \in \llbracket \varphi \rrbracket_e^{\mathcal{K}}\}$$
$$\llbracket \mu X.\varphi \rrbracket_e^{\mathcal{K}} := \cap \{W \subseteq \mathbb{N} \mid \llbracket \varphi \rrbracket_{e[X \mapsto W]}^{\mathcal{K}} \subseteq W\}$$

A formula ϕ is true at state i of $\mathcal{K}$, denoted by $\mathcal{K}, i \models \phi$, iff $i \in \llbracket \phi \rrbracket_e^{\mathcal{K}}$. The environment e is used to evaluate free variables and it can be dropped when ϕ is closed.

2.3   Validity and Satisfiability of νTL Formulas

A formula ϕ is *valid*, denoted by $\models \phi$, iff $\mathcal{K}, j \models \phi$ for all linear time structures $\mathcal{K}$ and all states j of $\mathcal{K}$. A formula ϕ is *satisfiable* iff there exists a linear time structure $\mathcal{K}$ and a state j of $\mathcal{K}$ such that $\mathcal{K}, j \models \phi$.

Example 1. *The validity and satisfiability of νTL formulas.*

(a) Formula $\bigcirc(p \vee \neg p)$ is valid since $\mathcal{K}, i \models \bigcirc(p \vee \neg p)$ for all linear time structures $\mathcal{K}$ and all states i of $\mathcal{K}$.
(b) Formula $\mu X.(p \vee \bigcirc X)$ is satisfiable because there exists a linear time structure $\mathcal{K}$ and a state j of $\mathcal{K}$ with $p \in \mathcal{K}(j)$ such that $\mathcal{K}, j \models \mu X.(p \vee \bigcirc X)$.

3   Guarded Positive Normal Form

In order to prove that any closed νTL formula ϕ can be rewritten into its PF form, first of all we need to prove ϕ can be transformed into a closed formula in the guarded positive normal form (GPNF).

Definition 1. *A closed νTL formula ϕ is* normal *if every occurrence of a quantifier μX or νX in ϕ binds a distinct variable.*

It is obvious that every closed νTL formula can be easily converted into an equivalent normal formula by renaming bound variables. If a formula ϕ is normal, then every variable X of ϕ identifies a unique subformula $\mu X.\varphi$ or $\nu X.\varphi$.

Example 2. *Converting formula ϕ: $\nu X.(\mu Y.(\bigcirc Y \vee \nu X.(q \wedge \bigcirc X)) \wedge \bigcirc X)$ into the equivalent normal formula.*

By renaming variable X in the subformula $\nu X.(q \wedge \bigcirc X)$ to variable Z, we can obtain the following formula:

$$\nu X.(\mu Y.(\bigcirc Y \vee \nu Z.(q \wedge \bigcirc Z)) \wedge \bigcirc X)$$

As we can see, every variable in the formula above identifies a unique subformula of ϕ.

Definition 2. *A closed νTL formula ϕ is in* positive normal form *[19] if ϕ is normal and negations appearing in ϕ can only be applied to atomic propositions.*

Positive normal form can be obtained by pushing negations inwards using DeMorgan's laws and the rules $\neg \bigcirc \phi = \bigcirc \neg \phi$, $\neg \mu X.\phi = \nu X.\neg \phi[\neg X/X]$ and $\neg \nu X.\phi = \mu X.\neg \phi[\neg X/X]$.

Example 3. *Translating formula ϕ: $\neg \nu X.(\mu Y.(\bigcirc Y \vee \nu X.(q \wedge \bigcirc X)) \wedge \bigcirc X)$ into positive normal form.*

$$\neg \nu X.(\mu Y.(\bigcirc Y \vee \nu Z.(q \wedge \bigcirc Z)) \wedge \bigcirc X)$$
$$\equiv \mu X.(\neg \mu Y.(\bigcirc Y \vee \nu Z.(q \wedge \bigcirc Z)) \vee \bigcirc X)$$
$$\equiv \mu X.(\nu Y.(\bigcirc Y \wedge \neg \nu Z.(q \wedge \bigcirc Z)) \vee \bigcirc X)$$
$$\equiv \mu X.(\nu Y.(\bigcirc Y \wedge \mu Z.(\neg q \vee \bigcirc Z)) \vee \bigcirc X)$$

Therefore, we know that formula $\mu X.(\nu Y.(\bigcirc Y \wedge \mu Z.(\neg q \vee \bigcirc Z)) \vee \bigcirc X)$ is the corresponding positive normal form of ϕ.

Subsequently, we present the definition of *guarded form* and this notion is of great significance for the latter section.

Definition 3. *A closed νTL formula is in* guarded form *if every occurrence of a bound variable X is in the scope of a $\bigcirc$ operator.*

Example 4. *Translating formula ϕ: $\nu X.(p \wedge X \wedge \mu Y.(q \vee Y \vee X \wedge \bigcirc Y))$ into its corresponding guarded form.*

$$\nu X.(p \wedge X \wedge \mu Y.(q \vee Y \vee X \wedge \bigcirc Y))$$
$$\equiv \nu X.(p \wedge \mu Y.(q \vee X \wedge \bigcirc Y))$$
$$\equiv \nu X.(p \wedge (q \vee X \wedge \bigcirc \mu Y.(q \vee X \wedge \bigcirc Y)))$$
$$\equiv \nu X.(p \wedge q \vee p \wedge \bigcirc \mu Y.(q \vee X \wedge \bigcirc Y))$$

As we can see, formula $\nu X.(p \wedge q \vee p \wedge \bigcirc \mu Y.(q \vee X \wedge \bigcirc Y))$ is the guarded form of formula ϕ.

According to [20], we have the following proposition.

Proposition 1. *Every closed νTL formula is equivalent to a formula in GPNF.*

4   PF Form of νTL Formulas

In this section, we define the PF form for a closed νTL formula ϕ consisting of the present and future parts: the present part is the conjunction of atomic propositions or their negations appearing in ϕ while the future part is a closed formula under the next operator. We prove that every closed νTL formula in GPNF can be rewritten into its corresponding PF form.

4.1   Definition of PF Form

Definition 4. *Let ϕ be a closed νTL formula, $\mathcal{P}_\phi$ the set of atomic propositions appearing in ϕ, and C the cardinality of $\mathcal{P}_\phi$. PF form of formula ϕ is defined as follows:*

$$\phi \equiv \bigvee_{i=1}^{n}(\phi_{p_i} \wedge \bigcirc \phi_{f_i})$$

where $\phi_{p_i} \equiv \bigwedge_{h=1}^{n_1} \dot{p}_{ih}$, $p_{ih} \in \mathcal{P}_\phi$, $1 \leq n_1 \leq C$; for any $r \in \mathcal{P}_\phi$, $\dot{r}$ denotes r or $\neg r$; ϕ_{f_i} is a closed νTL formula.

4.2   Rewriting a νTL Formula into PF Form

Regarding PF form of a formula, we have the following theorem:

Theorem 1. *Given a closed νTL formula φ, we have*
(1) φ can be rewritten into its PF form: $\varphi \equiv \bigvee_{i=1}^{n}(\varphi_{p_i} \wedge \bigcirc \varphi_{f_i})$; and
(2) each φ_{f_i} is a closed νTL formula.

Proof. Let φ be a closed νTL formula in GPNF. The proof proceeds by induction on the structure of φ with GPNF.

- **Base Case:**

  - $\varphi = p$: p can be written as
    $$p \equiv p \wedge \bigcirc true$$
    which satisfies the form of Definition 4 and $true$ is indeed a closed νTL formula. Thus, φ can be rewritten into PF form in this case.
  - $\varphi = \neg p$: $\neg p$ can be written as
    $$\neg p \equiv \neg p \wedge \bigcirc true$$
    which meets the form of Definition 4 and $true$ is indeed a closed νTL formula. Therefore, φ can be rewritten into PF form in this case.

- **Induction:**

  - $\varphi = \bigcirc \phi$: by induction hypothesis, ϕ can be transformed into its corresponding PF form:
    $$\phi \equiv \bigvee_{i=1}^{n}(\phi_{p_i} \wedge \bigcirc \phi_{f_i})$$
    We can see that each ϕ_{f_i} is a closed νTL formula. Further, φ can be written as
    $$\varphi \equiv \bigcirc \phi \equiv \bigcirc \bigvee_{i=1}^{n}(\phi_{p_i} \wedge \bigcirc \phi_{f_i}) \equiv \bigvee_{i=1}^{n} \bigcirc(\phi_{p_i} \wedge \bigcirc \phi_{f_i})$$
    Each ϕ_{p_i} is the conjunction of atomic propositions or their negations in ϕ, then ϕ_{p_i} is a closed νTL formula. Since each ϕ_{f_i} is a closed νTL formula, we know that each $\bigcirc \phi_{f_i}$ is also a closed νTL formula. Hence, each $\phi_{p_i} \wedge \bigcirc \phi_{f_i}$ is a closed νTL formula and φ can be transformed into PF form.
  - $\varphi = \phi_1 \vee \phi_2$: by induction hypothesis, both ϕ_1 and ϕ_2 can be rewritten into their PF forms:
    $$\phi_1 \equiv \bigvee_{i=1}^{n}(\phi_{1p_i} \wedge \bigcirc \phi_{1f_i}), \ \phi_2 \equiv \bigvee_{j=1}^{m}(\phi_{2p_j} \wedge \bigcirc \phi_{2f_j})$$
    and we have each ϕ_{1f_i} and ϕ_{2f_j} are closed νTL formulas. Subsequently, φ can be written as
    $$\varphi \equiv \phi_1 \vee \phi_2 \equiv \bigvee_{i=1}^{n}(\phi_{1p_i} \wedge \bigcirc \phi_{1f_i}) \vee \bigvee_{j=1}^{m}(\phi_{2p_j} \wedge \bigcirc \phi_{2f_j})$$
    Since each ϕ_{1f_i} and ϕ_{2f_j} are closed νTL formulas, φ can be transformed into PF form in this case.
  - $\varphi = \phi_1 \wedge \phi_2$: by induction hypothesis, both ϕ_1 and ϕ_2 can be rewritten into their PF forms:
    $$\phi_1 \equiv \bigvee_{i=1}^{n}(\phi_{1p_i} \wedge \bigcirc \phi_{1f_i}), \ \phi_2 \equiv \bigvee_{j=1}^{m}(\phi_{2p_j} \wedge \bigcirc \phi_{2f_j})$$

and we have each ϕ_{1f_i} and ϕ_{2f_j} are closed νTL formulas. Accordingly, φ can be written as

$$\varphi \equiv \phi_1 \wedge \phi_2 \equiv (\bigvee_{i=1}^n (\phi_{1p_i} \wedge \bigcirc \phi_{1f_i})) \wedge (\bigvee_{j=1}^m (\phi_{2p_j} \wedge \bigcirc \phi_{2f_j}))$$

$$\equiv \bigvee_{i=1}^n \bigvee_{j=1}^m (\phi_{1p_i} \wedge \phi_{2p_j} \wedge \bigcirc(\phi_{1f_i} \wedge \phi_{2f_j}))$$

As each ϕ_{1p_i} is a conjunction of atomic propositions or their negations in ϕ_1 and each ϕ_{2p_j} is a conjunction of atomic propositions or their negations in ϕ_2, each $\phi_{1p_i} \wedge \phi_{2p_j}$ is a conjunction of atomic propositions or their negations in φ. Since both ϕ_{1f_i} and ϕ_{2f_j} are closed νTL formulas, each $\phi_{1f_i} \wedge \phi_{2f_j}$ is still a closed νTL formula. Therefore, φ can be rewritten into PF form.

$-$ $\varphi = \mu X.\phi$: by induction hypothesis, ϕ can be transformed into its corresponding PF form:

$$\phi \equiv \bigvee_{i=1}^n (\phi_{p_i} \wedge \bigcirc \phi_{f_i})$$

and we can see each ϕ_{f_i} is a closed νTL formula. Thus, φ can be written as

$$\varphi \equiv \mu X.(\bigvee_{i=1}^n (\phi_{p_i} \wedge \bigcirc \phi_{f_i}))$$

Due to the definition of PF form, the fixpoint variable X can only appear in some ϕ_{f_i}. Subsequently, the equivalence $\mu X.\psi = \psi[\mu X.\psi/X]$ is employed to substitute the least fixpoint formula $\mu X.\phi$ for X which occurs in some ϕ_{f_i} and after that we can obtain the following formula

$$\varphi \equiv \bigvee_{i=1}^n (\phi_{p_i} \wedge \bigcirc \phi_{f_i}[\mu X. \bigvee_{i=1}^n (\phi_{p_i} \wedge \bigcirc \phi_{f_i})/X])$$

Since each ϕ_{f_i} is still a closed νTL formula after the substitution, φ can be rewritten into PF form.

$-$ $\varphi = \nu X.\phi$: by induction hypothesis, ϕ can be transformed into its corresponding PF form:

$$\phi \equiv \bigvee_{i=1}^n (\phi_{p_i} \wedge \bigcirc \phi_{f_i})$$

and we can find each ϕ_{f_i} is a closed νTL formula. Further, φ can be written as

$$\varphi \equiv \nu X.(\bigvee_{i=1}^n (\phi_{p_i} \wedge \bigcirc \phi_{f_i}))$$

Similarly, due to the definition of PF form, the fixpoint variable X can only appear in some ϕ_{f_i}. Then, the equivalence $\nu X.\psi = \psi[\nu X.\psi/X]$ is employed to substitute the greatest fixpoint formula $\nu X.\phi$ for X which occurs in some ϕ_{f_i} and after that we can obtain the following formula

$$\varphi \equiv \bigvee_{i=1}^n (\phi_{p_i} \wedge \bigcirc \phi_{f_i}[\nu X. \bigvee_{i=1}^n (\phi_{p_i} \wedge \bigcirc \phi_{f_i})/X])$$

Since each ϕ_{f_i} is still a closed νTL formula after the substitution, φ can be rewritten into PF form.

Thus, it can be concluded that every closed νTL formula in GPNF can be rewritten into its corresponding PF form.

Example 5. *Rewriting the following νTL formulas into their PF forms.*

  I. $\mu X.(p \vee \bigcirc X) \wedge \nu Y.(q \wedge \bigcirc Y)$
 II. $\nu Z.(\mu X.(p \wedge \bigcirc q \vee \bigcirc X) \wedge \bigcirc Z)$

For formula I we have

$$
\begin{aligned}
&\mu X.(p \vee \bigcirc X) \wedge \nu Y.(q \wedge \bigcirc Y) \\
\equiv\; &(p \vee \bigcirc \mu X.(p \vee \bigcirc X)) \wedge \nu Y.(q \wedge \bigcirc Y) \\
\equiv\; &(p \vee \bigcirc \mu X.(p \vee \bigcirc X)) \wedge q \wedge \bigcirc \nu Y.(q \wedge \bigcirc Y) \\
\equiv\; &p \wedge q \wedge \bigcirc \nu Y.(q \wedge \bigcirc Y) \vee q \wedge \bigcirc(\mu X.(p \vee \bigcirc X) \wedge \nu Y.(q \wedge \bigcirc Y))
\end{aligned}
$$

As we can see, both $\nu Y.(q \wedge \bigcirc Y)$ and $\mu X.(p \vee \bigcirc X) \wedge \nu Y.(q \wedge \bigcirc Y)$ appearing in the future parts of the PF form are closed νTL formulas.

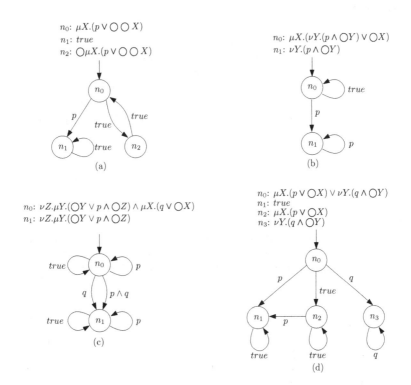

Fig. 1. Examples of PFGs

For formula II we have

$$\nu Z.(\mu X.(p \wedge \bigcirc q \vee \bigcirc X) \wedge \bigcirc Z)$$
$$\equiv \mu X.(p \wedge \bigcirc q \vee \bigcirc X) \wedge \bigcirc \nu Z.(\mu X.(p \wedge \bigcirc q \vee \bigcirc X) \wedge \bigcirc Z)$$
$$\equiv (p \wedge \bigcirc q \vee \bigcirc \mu X.(p \wedge \bigcirc q \vee \bigcirc X)) \wedge \bigcirc \nu Z.(\mu X.(p \wedge \bigcirc q \vee \bigcirc X) \wedge \bigcirc Z)$$
$$\equiv p \wedge \bigcirc(q \wedge \nu Z.(\mu X.(p \wedge \bigcirc q \vee \bigcirc X) \wedge \bigcirc Z)) \vee$$
$$\bigcirc(\mu X.(p \wedge \bigcirc q \vee \bigcirc X) \wedge \nu Z.(\mu X.(p \wedge \bigcirc q \vee \bigcirc X) \wedge \bigcirc Z))$$

As we can see, both $q \wedge \nu Z.(\mu X.(p \wedge \bigcirc q \vee \bigcirc X) \wedge \bigcirc Z)$ and $\mu X.(p \wedge \bigcirc q \vee \bigcirc X) \wedge \nu Z.(\mu X.(p \wedge \bigcirc q \vee \bigcirc X) \wedge \bigcirc Z)$ appearing in the future parts of the PF form are closed νTL formulas.

For a given closed νTL formula ϕ, we can further construct the PFG G_ϕ of ϕ according to PF form. First, ϕ is rewritten into its PF form: $\phi \equiv \bigvee_{i=1}^{n}(\phi_{p_i} \wedge \bigcirc \phi_{f_i})$. After that, we can regard ϕ, ϕ_{f_i} as nodes and ϕ_{p_i} as labels on edges in G_ϕ. Next, we can transform each ϕ_{f_i} into its PF form and obtain new nodes and edges again.

In this way, the PFG of ϕ can be constructed. A couple of examples of PFGs are depicted in Fig. 1. As PFG can be utilized to describe models of a νTL formula, it has become our main work in the future.

5   Conclusion

In this paper, we present PF form for νTL formulas and prove that every closed νTL formula can be rewritten into its corresponding PF form. The idea of constructing PFG, which is useful in describing models of a νTL formula, based on PF form is presented. In the near future we will define PFG formally and study algorithm for constructing PFG of νTL formulas. Based on PFG, a new decision procedure for checking the satisfiability of νTL formulas is hopefully to be achieved.

References

1. Kozen, D.: Results on the propositional μ-calculus. Theoret. Comput. Sci. **27**(3), 333–354 (1983)
2. Barringer, H., Kuiper, R., Pnueli, A.: A really abstract concurrent model and its temporal logic. In: Conference Record of the 13th Annual ACM Symposium on Principles of Programming Languages, pp. 173–183. ACM (1986)
3. Vardi, M.Y.: A temporal fixpoint calculus. In: Conference Record of the 15th Annual ACM Symposium on Principles of Programming Languages, pp. 250–259. ACM (1988)
4. Wolper, P.: Temporal logic can be more expressive. Inf. Control **56**(1), 72–99 (1983)
5. Streett, R.S., Emerson, E.A.: An automata theoretic decision procedure for the propositional mu-calculus. Inf. Comput. **81**(3), 249–264 (1989)
6. Emerson, E.A., Jutla, C.S., Sistla, A.P.: On model-checking for fragments of μ-calculus. In: Courcoubetis, C. (ed.) CAV 1993. LNCS, vol. 697, pp. 385–396. Springer, Heidelberg (1993)

7. Kupferman, O., Vardi, M.Y., Wolper, P.: An automata-theoretic approach to branching-time model checking. J. ACM **47**(2), 312–360 (2000)
8. Banieqbal, B., Barringer, H.: Temporal logic with fixed points. In: Banieqbal, B., Pnueli, A., Barringer, H. (eds.) Temporal Logic in Specification. LNCS, vol. 398, pp. 62–74. Springer, Heidelberg (1989)
9. Stirling, C., Walker, D.: CCS, liveness, and local model checking in the linear time mu-calculus. In: Sifakis, J. (ed.) CAV 1989. LNCS, vol. 407, pp. 166–178. Springer, Heidelberg (1990)
10. Stirling, C., Walker, D.: Local model checking in the modal mu-calculus. Theoret. Comput. Sci. **89**(1), 161–177 (1991)
11. Kaivola, R.: A simple decision method for the linear time mu-calculus. In: Proceedings of the International Workshop on Structures in Concurrency Theory, pp. 190–204. Springer (1995)
12. Bradfield, J., Esparza, J., Mader, A.: An effective tableau system for the linear time μ-calculus. In: Meyer auf der Heide, F., Monien, B. (eds.) ICALP 1996. LNCS, vol. 1099, pp. 98–109. Springer, Heidelberg (1996)
13. Duan, Z.: An extended interval temporal logic and a framing technique for temporal logic programming. Ph.D. thesis, University of Newcastle Upon Tyne (1996)
14. Duan, Z.: Temporal Logic and Temporal Logic Programming. Science Press, Beijing (2006)
15. Duan, Z., Tian, C.: Decidability of propositional projection temporal logic with infinite models. In: Cai, J.-Y., Cooper, S.B., Zhu, H. (eds.) TAMC 2007. LNCS, vol. 4484, pp. 521–532. Springer, Heidelberg (2007)
16. Duan, Z., Tian, C., Zhang, L.: A decision procedure for propositional projection temporal logic with infinite models. Acta Inf. **45**(1), 43–78 (2008)
17. Tian, C., Duan, Z.: Complexity of propositional projection temporal logic with star. Math. Struct. Comput. Sci. **19**(1), 73–100 (2009)
18. Duan, Z., Tian, C.: An improved decision procedure for propositional projection temporal logic. In: Dong, J.S., Zhu, H. (eds.) ICFEM 2010. LNCS, vol. 6447, pp. 90–105. Springer, Heidelberg (2010)
19. Stirling, C.: Modal and temporal logics. LFCS, Department of Computer Science, University of Edinburgh (1991)
20. Walukiewicz, I.: Completeness of Kozen's axiomatisation of the propositional μ-calculus. Inf. Comput. **157**(1), 142–182 (2000)

SOFL Tools

Prototype Tool for Supporting a Formal Engineering Approach to Service-Based Software Modeling

Weikai Miao[1]([✉]) and Shaoying Liu[2]

[1] Shanghai Key Laboratory of Trustworthy Computing,
Software Engineering Institute, East China Normal University, Shanghai, China
wkmiao@sei.ecnu.edu.cn
[2] Department of Computer Science, Hosei University, Tokyo, Japan
sliu@hosei.ac.jp

Abstract. Despite the advances in service-based software modeling, few existing approaches and tools support a systematic engineering process in which precise specification construction and accurate web service selection are integrated coherently. Due to this reality, how to carry out service-based software modeling so that existing services can be accurately discovered, selected, and effectively reused in the system under development is still a challenge. To solve this problem, this paper describes a prototype tool that supports a formal engineering framework for service-based software modeling. Formal specification can be constructed in an evolutionary manner; meanwhile, appropriate services are discovered and selected through the specification evolution. We illustrate the basic principle underlying the tool. The tool design and its implementation are also described. An example is presented to demonstrate major features of this tool.

1 Introduction

Research on engineering methods for constructing high quality service-based software (*service-based software*) is attracting a growing attention of both research and industry communities in recent years [13,16]. Constructing formal specifications, including both formal requirements and design specifications, based on correct understanding of requirements contributes significantly to software quality [15]. To effectively support the service-based software modeling, this fundamental principle needs to be extended.

One major problem with existing service-based software modeling is how to carry out the modeling so that existing services can be accurately discovered, selected, and effectively reused in the system under development. To tackle this challenge, effective engineering methods are demanded. An effective engineering method for service-based software modeling needs to supply definitive mechanisms for eliciting requirements, constructing precise specifications, selecting appropriate services, and integrating these artifacts coherently into a system model.

S. Liu and Z. Duan (Eds.): SOFL+MSVL 2013, LNCS 8332, pp. 89–103, 2014.
DOI: 10.1007/978-3-319-04915-1_7, © Springer International Publishing Switzerland 2014

Many research efforts have been advanced service-based software modeling from different perspectives, including business process modeling and implementation [1,2,5,18] and service discovery and selection [6,11]. Unfortunately, as summarized by the authors of work [16], almost no approach supports service discovery and selection as part of system modeling. That is, service discovery and selection activities are not coherently integrated into the system modeling phase. Therefore, services may not be effectively and efficiently adopted in the system architecture.

To tackle the above challenge, we have proposed a new approach called *Formal Engineering Framework for Service-based Software Modeling (FEFSSM)* as a solution [12]. FEFSSM integrates service discovery and selection into the entire modeling procedure, aiming to provide a unified engineering approach to constructing precise, comprehensible, and satisfactory specifications of service-based software.

To facilitate the application of FEFSSM in practice, in this paper we describe a supporting tool of the FEFSSM approach. The tool implements the fundamental principle underlying the FEFSSM, offering basic functions that support the involved engineering activities. The practitioner can construct the formal specification gradually through the interaction with the tool.

The rest of this paper is organized as follows. Basic theory of the FEFSSM approach underlying the tool is presented in Sect. 2. Design and implementation of the tool is described in Sect. 3. Section 4 describes an example of modeling a travel agency system to demonstrate the usability of the tool. Section 5 gives the comparison with the related work. Finally, we conclude the paper and point out future research directions in Sect. 6.

2   The FEFSSM Approach

The principle of FEFSSM inherits from the well-established SOFL (Structured Object-oriented Formal Language) formal engineering method [7,9,14,15] but emphasizes the interleaving and interaction of *software modeling* and *service adoption* in building service-based software. The main principle of FEFSSM is illustrated in Fig. 1.

Web service discovery, filtering, and selection activities are carried out sequentially in coupling with the corresponding specification construction activities in a three-step modeling process through the informal, semi-formal and formal stages of specification construction. The rational and technical details of each step are described below.

(1) **Informal specification construction**

The goal of informal specification construction is to acquire requirements as completely as possible at an informal level and discover sufficient candidate services based on the informal requirements. Requirements acquisition is usually achieved through communication between the client and the developer. Since requirements are imprecise at this stage, candidate services are preliminarily explored and filtered using keywords that abstract the corresponding informal

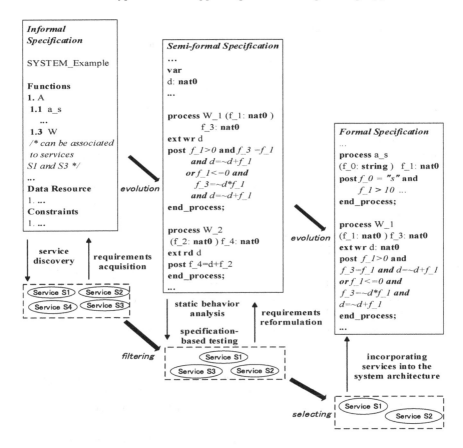

Fig. 1. The FEFSSM approach

requirements. The derived keywords are used to either partially or completely match with the service names or informal descriptions stored in the service repositories. A precise criterion for associating a service as a candidate service to an expected function is defined below.

Criterion 1. *Let $K_r = \{a_1, a_2, ..., a_n\}$ be a set of keywords derived from function F in the informal specification and $K_s = \{b_1, b_2, ..., b_m\}$ be a set of keywords derived from the name and informal descriptions of a service S. Then, S is accepted as a candidate service to be associated with F if and only if the following condition holds:*

$$\exists_{a \in K_r} \exists_{b \in K_s} \cdot is\_substring(a, b)$$

This criterion states that if there exists a keyword derived from a function F in the specification that is a substring (case insensitive) of a keyword derived from the name and informal descriptions of a service S, S is accepted as a candidate service to be associated with F.

In FEFSSM, service searching is in parallel with the functional decomposition. For example, since the developer does not find any candidate service for function A, then A is decomposed into several sub-functions. For each sub-function, the developer tries to explore candidate services. As the result, the sub-function W is associated to two candidate services $S1$ and $S3$. Detailed algorithm that encompasses the procedure of service discovery and functional decomposition is proposed in our previous work [12].

The ultimate informal specification contains three sections: *functions, data resources*, and *constraints*. The *functions* section briefly describes the desired functions of the target system, which are usually organized in a hierarchical structure. The *data resources* section presents the necessary data items for building the system function. The *constraints* section documents the required constraints on either the functions or the data resources.

(2) **Semi-formal specification construction**

The purpose of semi-formal specification construction is to evolve the informal specification into a more precise, complete, and well structured specification that encompasses accurately selecting services as some of its functional components; meanwhile, the services can be used for reformulating the specification. In regard to service selection, services are accurately selected through static behavior analysis and specification-based conformance testing.

– Static behavior analysis

The essential idea of the static behavior analysis is to judge which candidate service is most suitable for implementing each service-associated function. Specifically, the developer extracts potential functions of the services by analyzing their descriptions files (e.g., *WSDL* file) and finally identify the most relevant services for each service-associated function. The relevance of each candidate service to its associated function is represented by a ranking score. The service with the highest ranking score is selected as the most relevant service of its associated function. The ranking procedure can be referred to the corresponding algorithm in our work [12].

As pointed out by Guideline 1 [12], if function F is associated to its most relevant service S, then F is refined into a set of sub-functions $\{f_1, ..., f_n\}$ ($n \geq 1$) where each sub-function f_i is associated to the corresponding operation provided by S. These sub-functions are then transformed into formal *processes* that specify the intended functions precisely. A formal process is written in the SOFL specification language [14], which includes a signature, a pre-condition and a post-condition. The signature includes the input, output, and external variables (or state variables); the pre-condition imposes a constraint on the input variables before executing the process; and the post-condition describes a condition that must be satisfied by the output and external variables after the execution of the process.

After analyzing the descriptions of two candidate services $S1$ and $S3$ of function W, the developer identifies $S1$ as the most relevant service. Then function W is refined into two sub-functions W_1 and W_2. These two sub-functions are further formalized as formal processes W_1 and W_2.

– Specification-based testing
The specification-based conformance testing is aimed at dynamically checking whether a service satisfies the required functions defined by the corresponding formal processes. Test cases are generated from the pre- and post-conditions of the processes and the final decision to accept or reject the service is made by the developer based upon test results analysis and engineering judgements. To facilitate a rigorous testing, each process is converted into an equivalent disjunction of *functional scenarios*, each describing an independent function in terms of the input and output relation [8].

Definition 1. *Let P denote a process and its* post-condition $P_{post} \equiv (C_1 \wedge D_1) \vee (C_2 \wedge D_2) \vee ... \vee (C_n \wedge D_n)$, *where each C_i ($i = 1, ..., n$) is a predicate called a* guard condition *that contains no output variable and D_i a defining condition that contains at least one output variable but no guard condition. Then, each $P_{pre} \wedge C_i \wedge D_i$ is called a* functional scenario.

Functional scenarios are used as the foundation of test data derivation and also the test oracles. One intuitive way to test each service operation is to generate test cases that cover every functional scenario of the associated formal process. To test stateless service operations (i.e. execution results are determined by only the input values), test cases are directly derived from single functional scenarios. To sufficiently test stateful service operations (i.e. executions results are determined by both the input values and internal stateful variables that cannot be directly monitored from the user-end), all pairs of functional scenarios produced by the inter-related processes (i.e. processes that share the same data stores) are adopted for generating test sequences of the corresponding service operations [12].

When services are determined via the conformance testing, the specification can be transformed into a semi-formal specification. All of the related functions, data resources, and constraints in the informal specification are grouped into SOFL *modules*, each containing declarations of *types*, *state variables*, *invariants*, and *processes*. In each module, all of the declarations of types and variables are expressed formally but the logic-related parts such as invariants and processes are expressed informally to represent the expected functions (except service-associated functions, as explained below).

(3) **Formal specification construction**
The final stage of modeling is to transform the semi-formal specification into a formal design specification. The transformation is achieved by formally defining the system architecture into a hierarchical structure and formalizing the pre- and post-conditions of all the processes. The key point is that service-associated processes in the semi-formal specification are used as the foundation for gradually formalizing the entire specification since they have been determined to be part of the target system at the previous modeling stage.

In the formal specification shown in Fig. 1, all the processes including the service-associated process W_1 and process a_s that is not associated to any service, are formally defined.

3   Design and Implementation of the FEFSSM Tool

3.1   Tool Design

The tool is designed and implemented to facilitate the usability of the FEF-SSM. It guides the practitioner to follow the entire engineering process of the FEFSSM approach and support the automation of some specific activities such as the service discovery, service ranking and functional scenario pairs generation. Meanwhile, it also offers appropriate interfaces to handle the interactions between the practitioner and the specification components.

The tool is designed as a three-layered system which provides the major functionalities supporting the application of the FEFSSM. The architecture of this supporting tool is described by Fig. 2.

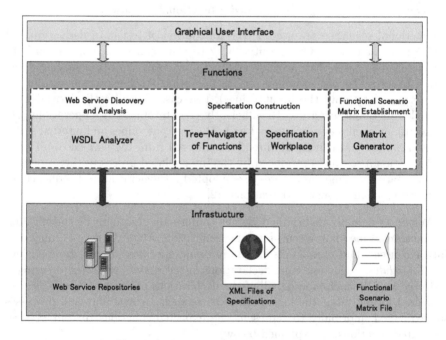

Fig. 2. Architecture of the FEFSSM tool

The infrastructure layer refers to the necessary documents and artifacts that support specification construction and service selection. These artifacts mainly consist of the service repositories information, the specification files and the files of functional scenario matrices. Usually service repositories information documents basic descriptions of the available web services. Specifications are documented in XML files. We use the XML files since the they are machine-readable, platform-independent and can easily represent the hierarchical structures of the processes and other SOFL components. To store the functional scenario pairs for web service testing, functional scenario pairs are organized as functional scenario matrix that is saved as a functional scenario matrix file. Each row of the matrix is a functional scenario pair that can be read by the tool for further test sequence generation.

The function layer consists of three modules: service discovery and analysis module, specification construction module, and functional scenario matrix module. Service discovery and analysis module supports the keyword-based web service discovery and the static behavior analysis, which is performed by a WSDL Analyzer. The analyzer can extract detailed interface information from the WSDL files of the available web services.

The module of specification construction is responsible for documenting the specifications. Specifically, we provide a graphical tree-navigator as a short-cut for function decomposition and documentation. The practitioner can directly manage the hierarchy structures of expected functions rather than manually typing them. Specification workplace performs the basic functions for editing specifications in different modeling phases.

Functional scenario matrix module contains a matrix generator for constructing the functional scenario matrices for test sequence generation.

3.2   Tool Implementation

The tool is implemented in Java language under the Eclipse environment. Figure 3 gives a screenshot of the main interface of the tool.

The text edition area located in the left-side is the workplace for specification construction. The practitioner can shift the three tabs on the top of the text edition area to edit the specifications in different stages. This screenshot shows the interface of informal specification construction. The tree-navigator is in the middle part, which is labelled as *"hierarchical"*. A tree structure of expected functions is described by the navigator in which each node is an expected function. By right-clicking the node, the practitioner can decompose, delete, edit the function or search candidate services. Discovered services are listed in the area labelled as *"Discovered Services of Function"*. The right-side of this interface lists all the available services in the service repositories.

Specification Construction. Specification construction is implemented by the specification workplace and the tree-navigator.

Specification workplace offers the basic functions for constructing specifications, focusing on the writing and reading operations on the XML files of the potential informal, semi-formal and formal specifications. Figure 4 shows an example of the informal specification stored as an XML file.

In this XML file, hierarchical structures of the functions are represented by the hierarchy of the XML elements. For example, function *Lowest_1* is the child node of function *Function_1_Child_1* that is the child node of its higher-level function *Function_1*. Associated services of each function are also documented

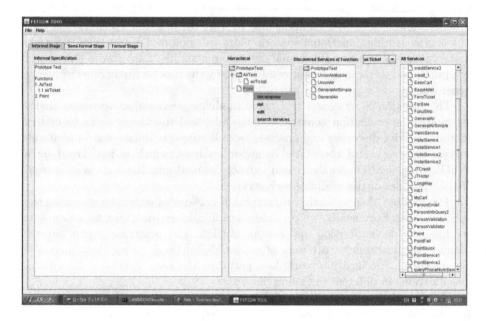

Fig. 3. The screenshot of the main interface of the tool

in the XML file. In this example, after the keyword-based service searching, basic information of a discovered service *JTHotel* is recorded and associated to function *Lowest_1*. As one advantage of the XML format, we can easily locate any element of the specification using *XPath* commands.

The tool provides the practitioner with a tree-navigator to directly decompose, delete or edit the expected functions. Service discovery can also be carried out by this navigator. In the navigator shown in Fig. 3, function *AirTest* and its sub-function *airTicket* and function *Point* are displayed in a consistent hierarchical structure of the textual specification. By right-clicking any function in the navigator, the practitioner can decide to modify the function (i.e. decompose, delete or rename the function) or start the keyword-based service searching for the function.

3.3   Service Discovery and Analysis

Criterion 1 of the keyword-based service discovery is implemented by a matching algorithm. A set of keywords stored in array *key* are splitted into single keywords. Each keyword is then compared with each service name stored in array *allServices*. The discovered services are collected as candidate services that are associated to the specified function in the informal specification. The associations between candidate services and the expected function are added into the XML file of the specification. For example, service *JTHotel* is associated to function *Lowest_1*, which is described in Fig. 4.

```
<?xml version="1.0" encoding="UTF-8"?>
-  <informal_spec lid="0" name="AnExample">
   -  <functionalDescription>
      -  <functions>
         -  <functionItem content="Function_1">
            -  <functionalDescription>
               -  <functions>
                  -  <functionItem content="Function_1_Child_1">
                     -  <functionalDescription>
                        -  <functions>
                           -  <functionItem content="Lowest_1">
                              <service name="JTHotel" score="0" wsdl=
```

Fig. 4. XML file of informal specification

Following the FEFSSM approach, the practitioner needs to analyze the candidate services based on their interface descriptions to extract the potential functional behaviors and then identify the most relevant services for further conformance testing. The analysis is realized by the Service Analyzer through analyzing the WSDL files of the services. Figure 5 describes the kernel operations of this analyzer.

```
public Opr[] getOperations(String wsdl){
...
List oprlist = XPath.selectNodes(doc, "//wsdl:portType//wsdl:operation");
...
}

public parameterModel[] singleTypeAnalysis(String analysisName, String wsdl){
// extract parameter information from WSDL
List list1 = XPath.selectNodes(doc, "//xs:schema/xs:element[@name='"+analysisName+"']/xs:complexType//xs:element");
...
}
```

Fig. 5. Operations for analyzing WSDL file

The interface information, including the available operations and their input/output parameters of each service, is extracted from the WSDL files by two methods *getOperations* and *singleTypeAnalysis*. The tool also offers a graphical interface for dealing with the relevance score ranking, which will be demonstrated in the next section.

3.4   Functional Scenario Matrix Establishment

Functional scenario matrix is constructed by the tool for conformance testing. The code shown in Fig. 6 implements the matrix generation.

For N functional scenarios accepted by method *matrixOperation*, array *result* records the N^2 functional scenario pairs. Each element of this array is a pair of functional scenarios, which is established by the two *for* loop statements.

```
public static String[] matrixOperation(String[] scenarios){
  String[] result = new String[scenarios.length*scenarios.length];
  int index=0;
  for(int i = 0; i < scenarios.length; i++){
   for(int j = 0; j < scenarios.length; j++){
    String temp=(String)scenarios[i]+","+(String)scenarios[j];
      result[index]=temp;
      index++;
      ...
```

Fig. 6. Operation of functional scenario matrix generation

4   An Example

To demonstrate the usability of the tool, we have conducted an example of modeling a *Travel Agency System* (*TAS*) using this prototype tool. Some students in our research group act as the practitioner to model the TAS.

TAS modeling starts from the informal specification construction. The practitioner records the expected functions using the tree-navigator of the tool. In the navigator, the practitioner defines a function *Hotel Operation* and then tries to discover available web services to implement this functions. Meanwhile, corresponding textual informal specification is updated in the specification edition area. A set of keywords is then given by the practitioner to search candidate services. The service discovery procedure is described by Fig. 7.

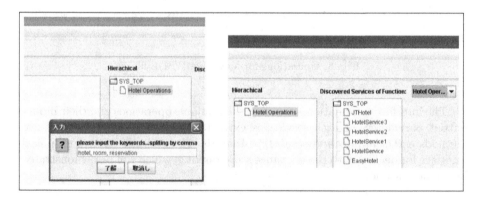

Fig. 7. Keyword-based service discovery

In the left part of Fig. 7, three keywords *"hotel"*, *"rooms"* and *"reservation"* are decided. As the result of service searching, six candidate services, for example, service *JTHotel*, are listed in the interface, which is shown by the right part of this figure. Names of all the discovered services match the keyword *"hotel"*.

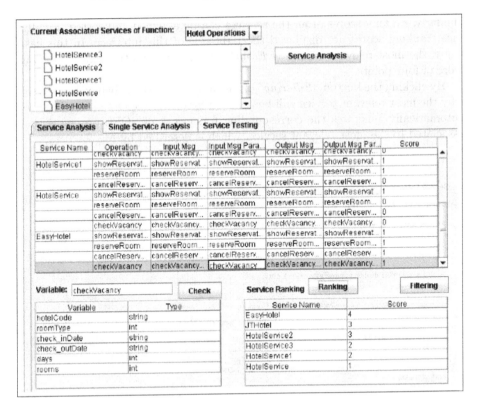

Fig. 8. Static behavior analysis of services

When the informal specification is finished, by shifting the *"semi-formal stage"* tab, the practitioner can start the semi-formal specification construction. The first step of this stage is to carry out the static behavior analysis of the candidate services. Figure 8 shows the interface for static behavior analysis of candidate services.

Static behavior analysis is invoked when the practitioner clicks the button *"Service Analysis"*. The interface information, including the service names, operations, and input/output messages of all the candidate services associated to the corresponding function, are listed in a table. For example, service *EasyHotel* has an operation *checkVacancy*. The input message of this operation is also named as *checkVacancy*. The practitioner can select this message and check its detailed variables by clicking the button *"Check"*. For instance, six variables (e.g., *hotel-Code*, *roomType*, *rooms* and etc.) constitute the message *checkVacancy*. Based on the detailed descriptions of each service operation, the practitioner can judge which operation is necessary for implementing the expected function and then assign the ranking scores for the operations. The practitioner accepts operation *checkVacancy* of service *EasyHotel* after a thorough understanding of its input and output variables, then this operation gets one point as its ranking score.

Similarly, ranking scores of all the services can be assigned and sorted. Finally, these ranking scores are displayed the right-side of this interface. In this case study, the most relevant service is *EasyHotel* since its gets the highest ranking score of four points.

By clicking the button *"Filtering"* on the interface of static behavior analysis, only the most relevant service will be reserved for conformance testing. The tool automatically generates the corresponding framework of SOFL processes that associated to the most relevant service, which is described by Fig. 9.

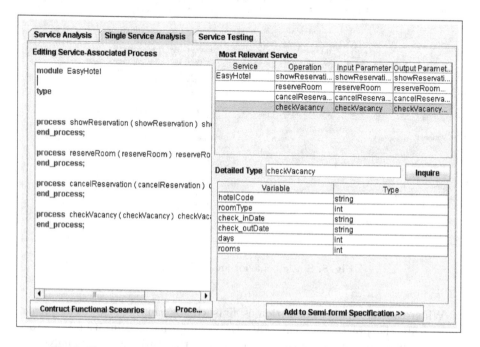

Fig. 9. Formalizing the processes associated to the most relevant service

For the most relevant service *EasyHotel*, the tool automatically generates four processes that correspond to its four operations. The input and output structures are also constructed. For example, process *checkVacancy* which takes variable checkVacancy as its input data is generated. The practitioner can further clarify the data types referring to the corresponding parameters of the service operations. When the data structures of the processes are determined, formal functional scenarios of these processes can be defined. Once all the functional scenarios of the processes are constructed, functional scenario matrix can then be generated. Figure 10 describes the procedure of defining formal functional scenarios of the processes and the generated functional matrix.

Each functional scenario is assigned with an identifier. For instance, functional scenario *f_1* stands for the functional scenario of a successful inquiry of reservation. In our example, for the four processes associated to the candidate

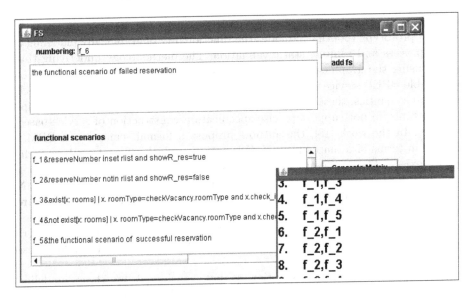

Fig. 10. Interface of functional scenarios construction

service *EasyHotel*, eight functional scenarios are constructed. As the result, a 64*2 functional scenario matrix is generated. For example, the fourth row in the matrix is functional scenario pair (f_1, f_4).

Based on the functional scenario matrix, test sequences are derived for the conformance testing of services. Currently, test data generation cannot be fully supported by the prototype tool. Another testing tool developed by our group can be exploited to finish the testing [10]. As an important task of our future research, we will make efforts to integrate the functionalities of the previous testing tool into the FEFSSM tool so that the conformance testing can be more effective and efficient.

Assume the services are determined, the practitioner can proceed to construct the semi-formal and formal specifications, which are supported by the corresponding specification editing areas.

5   Related Work

Various tools have been developed to support service-based software modeling from different perspectives. One category of them focuses on service-based software modeling based on business process modeling techniques (e.g., BPMN). A CASE tool called WebRatio is extended to support model-driven services integration [4]. The extended tool supports the high-level business process modeling of BPMN notations and detailed services mashup application modeling using WebML language. A service-oriented business process modeling tool is proposed in work [3]. It supports the generation of business process model from BPMN-based business process meta-model with highlighted web service characteristic and automatic translation and deployment features. The authors of work [5] report a prototype tool that provides the functionality of graphically modeling a BPEL process and running static validation. The methodology underlying this tool is using the graphical aspect of BPMN in order to facilitate modeling of executable BPEL service orchestrations. However, since BPMN notation is lack of formal semantics, these BPMN-based modeling methodologies and their supporting tools do not support precise specification construction of service-based software. In the work [18], the authors propose a formal semantics of BPMN defined in terms of a mapping to YAWL nets, for which efficient analysis techniques exists. The proposed mapping has been implemented as a supporting tool. In the work [17], the authors also propose formal semantics of the BPMN notation. These approaches and tools contribute to the service-based software modeling, especially from the perspective of modeling notations while appropriate service-based software modeling methodology is not addressed. Practitioners are demanding engineering methodologies to guide them effectively exploit these techniques.

Moreover, web services selection is not considered by these modeling approaches or techniques. As the authors of work [16] summarize, few approaches support service discovery and selection as part of the design process of service-based systems. Work [16] proposes a method that is relevant to our FEFSSM, in which services discovery and selection are integrated into the entire service-based software modeling process. Specifically, the service discovery in work [16] is carried out through semantics-based matching. Services are not required to be dynamically invoked through the matching process. Service selection in our FEFSSM methodology is realized via formal specification-based conformance testing in which services are dynamically tested after a preliminary keyword-based matching and a static analysis procedures.

6 Conclusion

To facilitate service-based software modeling, we present an interactive tool that supports the FEFSSM approach. We illustrate the theory of FEFSSM underlying the tool and describe its design and implementation. An example of modeling a travel agency system (TAS) is illustrated to demonstrate the usability of the tool.

At present, the tool supports the engineering process and most activities of the FEFSSM while the conformance testing of service selection has not been fully realized. In our future research, we will complete the tool so that the FEFSSM approach can be applied more effectively in practice. We are also interested in the techniques of constructing high-quality service-based software system.

Acknowledgement. This research is supported by SCAT research Foundation. This research is also supported by IDEA4CPS, MT-LAB (VKR Centre of Excellence), Shanghai Knowledge Service Platform for Trustworthy Internet of Things No. ZF1213 and NSFC Project No.91118007.

References

1. http://www.bpmn.org/ (2011) (Online)
2. http://docs.oasis-open.org/wsbpel/2.0/wsbpel-v2.0.pdf (2011) (Online)
3. Bai, L., Wei, J.: A service-oriented business process modeling methodology and implementation. In: International Conference on Interoperability for Enterprise Software and Applications China, 2009, IESA '09, April 2009, pp. 201–205 (2009)
4. Bozzon, A., Brambilla, M., Facca, F., Carughu, G.: A conceptual modeling approach to business service mashup development. In: IEEE International Conference on Web Services (ICWS), July 2009, pp. 751–758 (2009)
5. Decker, G., Kopp, O., Leymann, F., Weske, M.: BPEL4Chor: extending BPEL for modeling choreographies. In: International Conference on Web Services (ICWS), July 2007, pp. 296–303 (2007)
6. Klusch, M., Fries, B., Sycara, K.: Automated semantic web service discovery with OWLS-MX. In: Fifth International Joint Conference on Autonomous Agents and Multiagent Systems (AAMAS), Hakodate, Japan, May 2006, pp. 915–922 (2006)
7. Liu, S., Chen, Y., Nagoya, F., McDermid, J.: Formal specification-based inspection for verification of programs. IEEE Trans. Softw. Eng. **99** (2011, PrePrints)
8. Liu, S.: Integrating specification-based review and testing for detecting errors in programs. In: Butler, M., Hinchey, M.G., Larrondo-Petrie, M.M. (eds.) ICFEM 2007. LNCS, vol. 4789, pp. 136–150. Springer, Heidelberg (2007)
9. Liu, S., McDermid, J., Chen, Y.: A rigorous method for inspection of model-based formal specifications. IEEE Trans. Reliab. **59**(4), 667–684 (2010)
10. Liu, S., Nakajima, S.: A "Vibration" method for automatically generating test cases based on formal specifications. In: 18th Asia-Pacific Software Engineering Conference (APSEC2011), Ho Chi Minh, Vietnam, December 2011, pp. 73–80 (2011)
11. Meditskos, G., Bassiliades, N.: Structural and role-oriented web service discovery with taxonomies in OWL-S. IEEE Trans. Knowl. Data Eng. **22**(2), 278–290 (2010)
12. Miao, W., Liu, S.: A formal engineering framework for service-based software modeling. IEEE Trans. Serv. Comput. **6**(4), 536–550 (2013)
13. Papazoglou, M.P., Traverso, P., Dustdar, S., Leymann, F.: Service-oriented computing: state of the art and research challenges. Computer **40**, 38–45 (2007)
14. Liu, S.: Formal Engineering for Industrial Software Development Using the SOFL Method. Springer, Heidelberg (2004)
15. Liu, S., Offutt, A.J., Ho-Stuart, C., Sun, Y., Ohba, M.: SOFL: a formal engineering methodology for industrial applications. IEEE Trans. Softw. Eng. **1**, 24–45 (1998)
16. Spanoudakis, G., Zisman, A.: Discovering services during service-based system design using UML. IEEE Trans. Softw. Eng. **36**(3), 371–389 (2010)
17. Wong, P.Y.H., Gibbons, J.: A process semantics for BPMN. In: Liu, S., Maibaum, T., Araki, K. (eds.) ICFEM 2008. LNCS, vol. 5256, pp. 355–374. Springer, Heidelberg (2008)
18. Ye, J., Sun, S., Song, W., Wen, L.: Formal semantics of BPMN process models using YAWL. In: Second International Symposium on Intelligent Information Technology Application, December 2008, vol. 2, pp. 70–74 (2008)

A Supporting Tool for Syntactic Analysis of SOFL Formal Specifications and Automatic Generation of Functional Scenarios

Shenghua Zhu[1]([⊠]) and Shaoying Liu[2]

[1] Graduate School of Computer and Information Sciences, Hosei University, Tokyo, Japan
shenghua.zhu.7h@stu.hosei.ac.jp

[2] Faculty of Computer and Information Sciences, Hosei University, Tokyo, Japan
sliu@hosei.ac.jp

Abstract. SOFL formal specifications have been proved to be useful and expressive enough in describing functional requirements for software development. And based on SOFL formal specifications, many techniques have been proposed to provide us with effective solutions for software verification and validation. To support these techniques, a tool support for analysis of specifications is necessary. However, such a tool is still not available. In this paper, we present our work on a supporting tool. This tool supplies two fundamental functions: syntactic analysis of SOFL formal specifications and automatic generation of functional scenarios. By syntactic analysis, we can get syntactic information of SOFL formal specifications. The tool creates an xml file for storing and reusing this syntactic information. Functional scenarios are well-structured predicate expressions, which could be derived from formal specifications. Many formal specification-based techniques require the generation of functional scenarios. Our tool also supports automatic generation of functional scenarios on the basis of the syntactic information.

Keywords: SOFL · Formal specifications · Syntactic analysis · Functional scenarios

1 Introduction

SOFL formal specifications generally consist of two parts: modules and corresponding CDFDs (Control Data Flow Diagram). Modules are responsible for precisely defining the requirements and CDFDs provide a graphic explanation of the cooperation of processes in each module. Because SOFL benefits both the advantages of formal notations and graphic expressions, SOFL has the "talent" to describe both functional requirements and the architecture of software. In additional, based on SOFL formal specification, many techniques have been proposed to provide us with effective solutions for software verification and validation. SOFL could be used practically in real software development.

However, compared with some other formal language, SOFL is restricted by tool supporting, especially for some fundamental functions. In order to make it more practical, we hence implemented a supporting tool for SOFL. This tool supplies two

S. Liu and Z. Duan (Eds.): SOFL+MSVL 2013, LNCS 8332, pp. 104–117, 2014.
DOI: 10.1007/978-3-319-04915-1_8, © Springer International Publishing Switzerland 2014

fundamental functions: syntactic analysis of SOFL formal specifications and automatic generation of functional scenarios. By syntactic analysis, we can get syntactic information of SOFL formal specifications. The tool creates an xml file for storing and reusing this syntax information. Functional scenarios are well-structured predicate expressions, which could be derived from formal specifications. Many formal specification based techniques require the generation of functional scenarios [1, 2]. In our tool, we also realized automatic generation of functional scenarios on the basis of syntax information. Our work is expected to be effective in reducing time and budget by a large margin in applying SOFL to a real software development.

The remainder of this paper is organized as follows. Section 2 talks about the background of our work including features of SOFL, definition of functional scenarios and brief introduction to strategy design. Section 3 describes in details about our tool, which includes two core components: a parser for SOFL and a processor for generating functional scenarios. Section 4 mentions some related work. Section 5 makes a conclusion of our current work and points out how it could support future research.

2 Background

SOFL is short for Structured Object-Oriented Formal Language, which was proposed in Liu's paper [3]. In order to make it more adaptable for practical software development, the designer considered overall the advantages of formal notation, structured methods and object-oriented method, and successfully found out a complementary approach to integrate these three ideas into one formal language. Formal specifications written in SOFL should be encapsulated in a series of modules. Each module represents a high-level system or low-level sub-system and one module also could be decomposed further to lower-level modules. In each module, we should abstract all involved resources, declare them by classifications and define the main processes (operations) to complete the functionality. For each process, it uses pre-condition to describe the assumed initial state and post-condition to clarify the expected final state. Pre- and post-conditions are common predicate expressions, in which sub-predicate clauses could be connected by logic connectors without no regular pattern.

As mentioned before, SOFL formal specifications are synthesis of many kinds of descriptions, including description for resources' definition and declaration, description for operations, while functional scenarios are predicate expressions which have been well classified and partitioned according to information mainly extracted from operations.

In order to generate functional scenarios from formal specifications, firstly we need to clarify the format of an operation specification and the concept of functional scenario. Here for simplicity, we adopt Liu's notation in [4] for operations of SOFL formal specifications.

Definition 1: Let $OP(\text{OP}_{iv}; \text{OP}_{ov})[\text{OP}_{pre}; \text{OP}_{post}]$ denotes an operation of SOFL formal specifications, in which OP_{iv} represents set of input variables whose values should not be changed by this operation, and OP_{ov} represents set of output variables whose values could be newly produced or updated by this operation, and OP$_{pre}$ OP$_{post}$ represent pre- and post-conditions of *OP* respectively.

Then we define functional scenarios based on the criterion 1.

Definition 2: Functional scenarios are predicate expressions matched with specific pattern. Let $\sim OP_{pre} \land C_i \land D_i$ denotes one function scenario, and each function scenario serves as one disjunctive clause of the following disjunction: $(\sim OP_{pre} \land C_1 \land D_1) \lor (\sim OP_{pre} \land C_2 \land D_2) \lor \ldots \lor (\sim OP_{pre} \land C_n \land D_n)$. This disjunction is called a *functional scenario form*. In one functional scenario, C_i is called "guard condition", which contains no output variables and satisfies $C_i \land C_j = false (i \neq j)$; D_i is called "defining condition", which involves at least one output variable, and defines the expected final state of output variables. Guard conditions and defining conditions come from OP$_{post}$; both of them are a collection of sub-predicates of OP$_{post}$.

The algorithm, for generating function scenarios from formal specifications, has been discussed in Liu's paper [5]. In order to describe the algorithm, we also need notations below:

$V_{oe}(OP, E)$: denotes the set of variables from OP_{ov} which occur in the predicate E.

$[1 \ldots n]$: denotes the set of integers $\{1, 2, \ldots, n\}$.

$A \equiv B$: means that A is the same with B both syntactically and semantically.

Algorithm:

Step 1: Convert the post-condition OP$_{post}$ to disjunctive normal form: $P_1 \lor P_2 \lor \ldots \lor P_n$, where each $P_t(t \in [1 \ldots n])$ is a conjunction of atomic predicates or the negation of atomic predicates. An atomic predicate could be a relation (saying $x > y * 5 + z$), a boolean variable, a truth value, or a strict quantified expression. Here if $OP_{post} \equiv true$ or $OP_{post} \equiv false$, go to **step 8**; else go to next.

Step 2: For each $P_t \equiv R_1 \land R_2 \land \ldots \land R_m (m \geq 1)$, construct the partition $\{B_1, B_2\}$ for the set $\{R_1, R_2, \ldots, R_m\}$ that satisfies the conditions:

$$(1) \quad R_i \in B_1 \Rightarrow V_{oe}(OP, R_i) = \varnothing, i \in [1 \ldots m]$$
$$(2) \quad R_i \in B_2 \Rightarrow V_{oe}(OP, R_i) \neq \varnothing, i \in [1 \ldots m]$$

Step 3: For each predicate set B_k where $k \in \{1, 2\}$, if $B_k \neq \varnothing$, then form the conjunction $Q_k^t \equiv \land_{i \in s} R_i$, where $s = \{i \in [1 \ldots m] | R_i \in B_k\}$; otherwise, let $Q_k^t \equiv true$.

Step 4: Express P_t as the conjunction of every such Q_k^t : $P_t \equiv Q_1^t \land Q_2^t$. Here Q_1^t corresponds to the guard condition, which involves no output variables in OP_{ov}. Q_2^t corresponds to the defining condition, which contains at least one output variable.

Step 5: Construct the partition $\{A_1, A_2, \ldots, A_w\}$ for the set $\{P_1, P_2, \ldots, P_n\}$ obtained from No 4 that satisfies the condition: $P_i, P_j \in A_k \Rightarrow Q_1^i = Q_1^j$ assuming $P_i \equiv Q_1^i \land Q_2^i$ and $P_j \equiv Q_1^j \land Q_2^j$, $i, j \in [1 \ldots n], k \in [1 \ldots w]$.

Step 6: For each A_k, form a predicate $P_{A_k} \equiv {}^\sim OP_{pre} \land Q_1 \land (\lor_{l \in [1 \ldots u]} Q_2^l)$, assuming $P_1, P_2, \ldots, P_u$ are members of A_k, $u \neq n$, and each $P_t \equiv Q_1 \land Q_2^l$, where Q_1 is the common guard condition and Q_2^l is a defining condition. The decorated pre-condition

$\sim OP_{pre} = OP_{pre}[\sim x/x]$ denotes the predicate by substituting the initial state $\sim x$ for the final state x in OP_{pre}.

Step 7: Form the disjunction $P_{A_1} \vee P_{A_2} \vee \ldots \vee P_{A_w}$, which is the functional scenarios form (FSF) for OP, where each P_{A_k} denotes a functional scenario. Then go to **Step 9**.

Step 8: Form the conjunction $\sim OP_{pre} \wedge OP_{post}$ as the functional scenarios form (FSF) for OP.

Step 9: The end.

3 Our Work on the Supporting Tool

The tool consists of two core components. One is a parser for SOFL formal specifications, and the other is a processor in charge of automatic transformation. The parser is designed to parse SOFL formal specifications and store syntax tree information in an xml file for reuse. In the xml file, each tag corresponds to one grammar node of SOFL. The processor will take the syntax tree information (xml file) as input, generate functional scenario forms, and store these functional scenario forms back into the xml file. We have defined the format of functional scenario form in the xml file, based on the definition of functional scenarios as we talked in Sect. 2. Figure 1 shows an overview constitution of the tool.

3.1 Parser for SOFL Formal Specification

When we are to develop a parser for a specific language, generally the first task is to know what kind of lexical symbols are legal and how they are arranged in a reasonable way, defined by the grammar. The two questions determine the design of strategy for the most important parts of the parser.

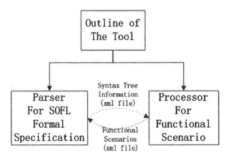

Fig. 1. This figure shows the two core components of the tool. The parser produces the syntax tree information and creates an xml file to store it. After this, the processor will run the algorithm for generating functional scenarios, and store functional scenario forms back into the xml file.

Table 1. The chart shows all legal classifications of symbols in SOFL.

Key value	1	2	3	4
Classification	Enumeration	Character	String	Number
Key value	5	6	7	8
Classification	Identifier	Reserved word	Comment	Separator

We have made a summary about all legal classifications of symbols that could be accepted by SOFL. They are listed as follows in Table 1.

We pick the "identifier" to explain that identifiers in SOFL should maintain what kind of features and how we construct the acceptor to receive an identifier from the texture stream. The "identifier" should start with an English letter and after that could consist of letters and digits (from 0 to 9). This rule can be described in an alternative way, which is more intuitive. We build a finite state machine for accepting "identifier" in SOFL as figured in Fig. 2.

For the grammar of SOFL, also could referred to Liu's publication, we find that it is defined by top-down architecture. In the most top level, the formal specification is abstracted in one grammar node, which is called "specification". The "specification" is decomposed to some grammar nodes in the lower level, which are restricted to list in order. Continuously, all grammar nodes could be decomposed further and at last reach the terminal node, which are symbols that could be accepted directly by lexical analyzer. We pick up one part of the grammar to give a straightforward image.

One part of the grammar defining the module of SOFL:

```
Module ::=
        "module" Identifier [ "/" ( Identifier | "SYSTEM_"Identifier) ] ";"
                Module_body
        "end_module"
Module_body ::=
        ["const" Const_declaration ";" ]
        ["type" Type_declaration ";" ]
        ["var" Var_declaration ";" ]
        ["inv" Inv_definition ";" ]
        ["behav" Behavior ";" ]
        Process_function_specifications
```

Here we use some notations, in which double quotation marks quote a terminal node (a symbol), brackets mean the content is optional, round brackets and vertical

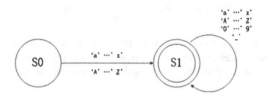

Fig. 2. The figure shows finite state machine for identifier in SOFL.

bars cooperate to imply a multiple selection. We can find that this kind of description is easy to understand for readers, but not suitable for syntactic analysis program. So the first work for us is to rewrite the grammar to make it adaptable for realization. The translation is like the following.

Module -> "module" Identifier S1 ";" Module_body "end_module"

S1 -> epsilon | "/" S2

S2 -> Identifier | "SYSTEM_" Identifier

Module_body -> S3 S4 S5 S6 S7 Process_function_specifications

S3 -> epsilon | "const" Const_declaration ";"

S4 -> epsilon | "type" Type_declaration ";"

S5 -> epsilon | "var" Var_declaration ";"

S6 -> epsilon | "inv" Inv_definition ";"

S7 -> epsilon | "behav" Behavior ";"

Notations used here is almost the same with the ahead. Each line of these sentences is called "grammar deduction formula". In each formula, it contains only nonterminal grammar nodes and terminal nodes. Terminal nodes are symbols which could be accepted by lexical analyzer and nonterminal nodes are able to be coded as methods which are responsible for the syntactic analysis of according units.

So far, we have got an overview about the question domain of the parser. The next step is to design for the implementation. If we view the parser as a software project, We need to decompose the whole task and depict the architecture of the software. Figure 3 shows the architecture of the parser.

The parser includes four components, lexical analyzer, syntactic analyzer, type generator, and xml file constructor. Each component could be decomposed to the third level, of which these are able to be implemented by program units. The core function of a parser is syntactic analysis. As we explained before, the feature of SOFL's grammar determines that top-down analysis strategy is convenient. During the approach of syntactic analysis, we also need to register all symbols and make a symbol table for potential semantic analysis to some extent. Beside of these, we need to design a robust mechanism for exception handling and recovery. We use Fig. 4 to explain the main procedure of top-down syntax analysis.

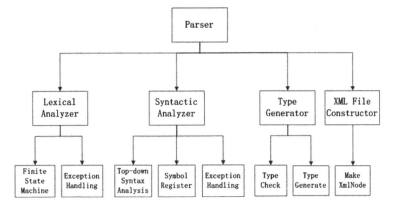

Fig. 3. The figure shows the whole architecture of the parser.

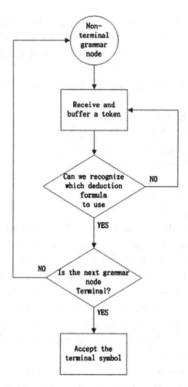

Fig. 4. The figure shows how top-down syntactic analysis works.

Because terminal nodes could be directly provided by lexical analyzer, terminal grammar nodes usually are easy to deal with, and do not need to make methods for them. In Fig. 5, we focus on how to deal with nonterminal grammar nodes. As we mentioned previously, nonterminal grammar nodes should be realize as methods, according to the grammar deduction formulae. So when we are faced with multiple selections about which formula to use and cannot recognize it based on the left-most symbol, we choose to look forward more symbols for help.

After we have figured out the strategy for both lexical and syntactic analysis, we need to consider how to record useful information. The corresponding function is supplied by symbol register. We build a specific data structure named "symbol table" for SOFL. In the symbol table, symbol's information, such as namespace, value, type and so on, will be recorded well. The following table shows this data structure.

Table 2. This chart shows data structure of symbol table.

Field 1	Field 2	Field 3	Field 4	Field 5
Namespace	VariableList	BasicTypeList	SetTypeList	SeqTypeList
Field 6	Field 7	Field 8	Field 9	Field 10
MapTypeList	ComTypeList	ProdTypeList	SignTypeList	UnionTypeList

Table 3. This chart shows data structure of SetType.

Field 1	Field 2
SymbolName	ElementTypeName

All These lists mean array lists of variables and types. We have also defined data structure for them. We take SetType for example.

3.2 Processor for Generating Functional Scenarios

After the work of parser, an xml file is created for the storage of syntax tree information. Each section, in the formal specifications, could be extracted separately from this file. As we have analyzed before, functional scenarios are corresponding directly to the section of process in one module. At this stage, we are able to visit all well-classified information that may help for generating functional scenarios.

The processor will take this kind of xml file as input and generate functional scenarios for each process. At last, we shall organize the functional scenarios into functional scenario forms (FSF), and append FSF to its' appropriate position in the xml file. In this way, we can get access to both information of each process and its correlated FSF.

So far we have been clear about the input and output of this processor. Considering about the algorithm which has been explained in Sect. 2, the first task should be transforming post-condition into disjunctive normal form (DNF). From now on, we are willing to take a predicate $((a \lor b) \land c) \Leftrightarrow (d \Rightarrow e)$ as example to demonstrate how we implement the algorithm. The predicate stands for post-condition of a process,

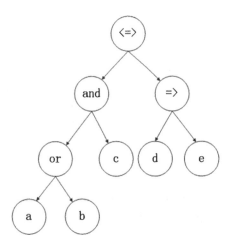

Fig. 5. The figure shows the syntax tree of the example post-condition.

in which a, b, c, d and e are atomic predicates. It may seem simple, but we think it is fine and enough to represents general situations when we face with this matter.

First of all, we shall build a syntax tree from what is stored in xml file. In this case, the syntax tree should look like Fig. 5.

The algorithm for transforming post-condition to DNF is arranged as following:

Step 1: Search nodes of the syntax tree in root-first order, and for each node if the value of currently visited node is "<=>", replace the node with sub-tree like following

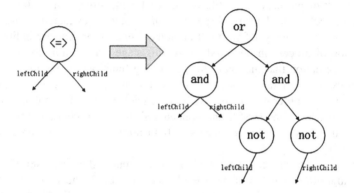

Step 2: Search nodes of the syntax tree in root-first order, and for each node if the value of current node is "=>", replace the node with sub-tree like the following

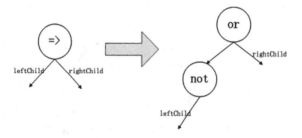

Step 3: Search nodes of the syntax tree in root-first order, and for each node if there exists "not" disorder, that means "not" node's child is not atomic predicate, replace the node with sub-tree like the following

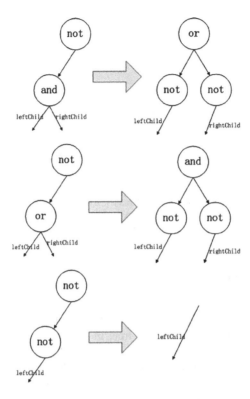

Step 4: Search nodes of the syntax tree in root-first order, and for each node if there exists "and/or" disorder, that means "or" node becomes the child of "and", replace the node with sub-tree like the following

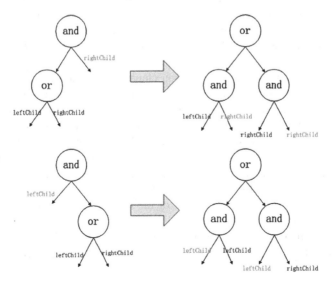

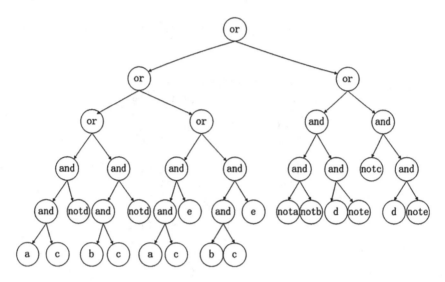

Fig. 6. The figure shows DNF of the example post-condition.

Since the post-condition has been transformed into DNF, considering of the data structure we used, we have got a binary tree, in which "or" nodes are ancestors of "and" nodes and "not" nodes should be connected directly with atomic predicate nodes. In case of the example we mentioned before, the Fig. 6 give a view.

We can easily find out each conjunction clause, which is a sub-tree whose root is the first "and" node. There exist six conjunction clauses in the DNF. They are $a \wedge c \wedge \neg d, b \wedge c \wedge \neg d, a \wedge c \wedge e, b \wedge c \wedge e, \neg a \neg b \wedge d \wedge \neg e$, and $\neg c \wedge d \wedge \neg e$.

According to the algorithm of generating functional scenarios, for each conjunction clause, we need to make a partition for separating atomic predicates by whether they contain output variables. If "a" and "c" contain no output variable, they are called "guard condition". On the other side, "b", "d" and "e" are called "defining condition". The next step we shall do is to rearrange these conjunction clauses. The six conjunction clauses should be rewrite to be $a \wedge c \wedge \neg d, c \wedge b \wedge \neg d, a \wedge c \wedge e, c \wedge b \wedge e, \neg a \wedge \neg b \wedge d \wedge \neg e$, and $\neg c \wedge d \wedge \neg e$.

The last step is to combine conjunction clauses of which the defining conditions are the same. Because guard condition and defining condition of a conjunction clause are stored in an array list, by searching each node in this array list, we can judge whether one defining condition is covering the other and at the same time the other is also covering the original one. If $A \subseteq B \wedge B \subseteq A$, we can make a conclusion two set of defining conditions are same. If there exist any two conjunction clauses whose defining conditions is the same, we shall combine them by merging the guard conditions of them by connector of logic "or". In case of this example, the conjunction clauses should keep themselves, because of the defining conditions of each one are unique among them.

So we can finally generate functional scenarios in this form $\sim OP_{pre} \wedge C_i \wedge D_i$. All guard conditions and defining conditions of the example are listed in Table 4.

Table 4. This chart shows guard condition and defining condition of each functional scenario for the example.

	C (guard condition)	D (defining condition)
Functional scenario 1	$a \wedge c$	$\neg d$
Functional scenario 2	C	$b \wedge \neg d$
Functional scenario 3	$a \wedge c$	E
Functional scenario 4	C	$b \wedge e$
Functional scenario 5	$\neg a$	$\neg b \wedge d \wedge \neg e$
Functional scenario 6	$\neg c$	$d \wedge \neg e$

We have tested this tool by several SOFL formal specifications, one of which defines the requirements of a goods delivery system. We are willing to take that as an example input to show the main interface of our tool in Fig. 7.

The central textural area demonstrates the SOFL formal specification. If there exist some syntactic errors, the tool will collect information for the position where error happens and report them in the below frame. Key words are highlighted in blue and the character where error is located is highlighted in red in Tables 2, 3 and 4.

After parsing, an xml file storing both syntax tree information and functional scenario forms is created. For this test case, corresponding xml file is showed in Fig. 8.

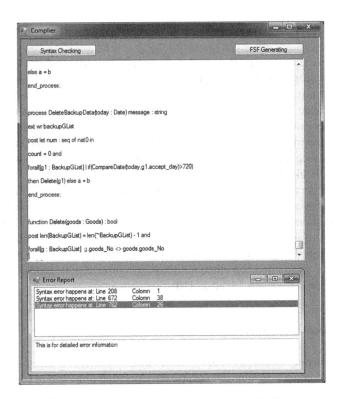

Fig. 7. The figure shows main interface of this tool.

Fig. 8. The figure shows the main output of this tool: xml file storing syntax information and functional scenarios.

4 Related Work

Tool support is significantly important for applying formal methods into practice. There are many formal languages with powerful tool. One famous example is VDM. As introduced in [6], "Overture" is developed to be a common open-source platform integrating a range of tools for constructing and analyzing formal models of systems using VDM. Nowadays, "Overture" has been updated to be a stable and mature platform, but restricted by features of VDM, it could not support effectively on describing the architecture of whole software. There are also other tools supporting formal language like JML and Alloy. They are introduced in [7, 8].

Functional scenario-based techniques also gain more and more attentions in research. Reference [1] proposes an automated functional scenario-based formal specification animation method. Reference [2] talks about their work on an experiment for assessment of a functional scenario-based test case generation method, which is improved from FSBT (functional scenario-based testing) proposed in [9]. For functional scenarios' generation, a method for automatic generation of functional scenarios from SOFL CDFD has been talked in [10].

5 Conclusion and Future Work

In this paper, we implemented a tool for automatically generating functional scenarios from SOFL formal specifications. Based on the algorithm proposed in Liu's paper, we explained the construction of the tool and how it works by a simple but fine example.

We also used several SOFL formal specifications as test cases to test the tool. The test result shows the expected functionalities are well-realized and this tool is able to effectively support functional scenario based research.

In the future, we intend to develop and improve a support environment for constructing system by using SOFL formal specification. This tool is just a prototype tool, but it completes some fundamental requirements. On the basis of this tool, we are looking forward to searching a reasonable way to support "functional scenario- based test case generation" and "functional scenario-based formal specification translation".

Acknowledgments. This work has been conducted as a part of "Research Initiative on Advanced Software Engineering in 2012" supported by Software Reliability Enhancement Center (SEC), Information Technology Promotion Agency Japan (IPA).

References

1. Li, M., Liu, S.: Automated functional scenarios-based formal specification animation. In: 19th Asia-Pacific Software Engineering Conference (APSEC 2012), IEEE CS Press, Hong Kong (2012) (to appear)
2. Li, C., Liu, S., Nakajima, S.: An experiment for assessment of a "functional scenario-based" test case generation method. In: International Conference on Software Engineering and Technology (ICSET 2012), pp. 64–71 (2012)
3. Liu, S., Offutt, A.J., Ho-Stuart, C., Sun, Y., Ohba, M.: SOFL: A formal engineering methodology for industrial applications. IEEE Trans. Softw. Eng. **24**(1), 24–45 (1998)
4. Liu, S ., Nakajima, S.: A decompositional approach to automatic test case generation based on formal specifications. In: 4th IEEE International Conference on Secure Software Integration and Reliability Improvement, Singapore, pp. 147–155, 9–11 June 2010
5. Liu, S., Chen, Y., Nagoya, F., McDermid, J.: Formal specification-based inspection for verification of programs. IEEE Trans. Softw. Eng. **38**(5), 1100–1122 (2012)
6. Larsen, P.G., Battle, N., Ferreira, M., Fitzgerald, J., Lausdahl, K., Verhoef, M.: The overture initiative integrating tools for VDM. ACM Softw. Eng. Notes **35**(1), 1–6 (2010)
7. Leavens, G.T., Cheon, Y.: Design by contract with JML. http://jmlspecs.org (2005)
8. Jackson, D.: Alloy: a lightweight object modeling notation. ACM Trans. Softw. Eng. Methodol. **11**(2), 256–290 (2002)
9. Liu, S., Nakajima,S.: A decompositional approach to automatic test case generation based on formal specifications. In: 4th IEEE International Conference on Secure Software Integration and Reliability Improvement, Singapore, pp. 147–155, 9–11 June 2010
10. Li, M., Liu, S.: Automatically generating functional scenarios from SOFL CDFD for specification inspection. In: 10th IASTED International Conference on Software Engineering, Innsbruck, Austria, pp. 18–25, 15–17 Feb 2011

SOFL Specification Animation with Tool Support

Mo Li[1]($\boxtimes$) and Shaoying Liu[2]

[1] Graduate School of Computer and Information Sciences,
Hosei University, Tokyo, Japan
mo.li.3e@stu.hosei.ac.jp
[2] Department of Computer and Information Sciences,
Hosei University, Tokyo, Japan
sliu@hosei.ac.jp

Abstract. Formal specification animation is a very useful technique for verification and validation. It provides the end users and field experts with an intuitive way to observe the operational behaviour of software system described by the formal specification. Several tools have already been built to support animations of specifications written in different formal languages. In this paper, we describe the design of a tool that can support the animation of specification written in Structure Object-oriented Formal Language (SOFL). The animation strategy underlying the tool uses system functional scenario as a unit and data as connection among independent operations involved in one system functional scenario. A system functional scenario defines a behaviour that transforms input data into the output data through a sequential execution of operations. It is the target of animation. In the animation, data is used to connect each operation in a specific scenario. The data can be provided by the user or generated automatically. It will help the user and the developer to understand the system. We explain the whole animation process step by step and present a prototype at the end of the paper.

Keywords: Formal method · Specification · Animation · Tool

1 Introduction

Formal specification animation is an effective technique for specifications verification and validation. The purpose of animation is to provide an intuitive way for the end user and domain expert to monitor the states of a behaviour so that they do not need to read the formal specification which is fulfilled with mathematical or logical formulas. Usually, a tool is required to support the animation

This work has been conducted as a part of "Research Initiative on Advanced Software Engineering in 2012" supported by Software Reliability Enhancement Center (SEC), Information Technology Promotion Agency Japan (IPA).

S. Liu and Z. Duan (Eds.): SOFL+MSVL 2013, LNCS 8332, pp. 118–131, 2014.
DOI: 10.1007/978-3-319-04915-1_9, © Springer International Publishing Switzerland 2014

process since it faces a lot of challenges in practice and one of the challenge is that formal specification is complex and difficult to understand. A tool is needed to hide the complexity and derive the intuitive information for the user. Several tools have been built to support animation of specification written in different formal languages, such as ANGOR [1], B-Model animator [2], and ZAL animation system [3]. Most of them require a translation from a formal specification language to an executable programming language, so that the animation can be done automatically. But the translation may imposes many restrictions to the style of the specifications written in a formal notation and this would bring inconvenience to the developer.

In this paper, we describe the design of a tool for SOFL [4] specification animation. There is no further restrictions to the language or style of specification. In the tool, the end user or field expert can animate the specification on the Conditional Data Flow Diagram (CDFD, a part of SOFL specification) directly, and we think it is a very good way to connect user, developer and formal specification. The animation strategy underlying the tool uses system functional scenario as a unit and data as connection among independent operations involved in one system functional scenario. System functional scenario is used as unit of an animation since it presents a specific behaviour of the system, and the behaviour is the target or object of animation. In order to animate the entire specification, all of the potential behaviours, or system functional scenarios, should be animated. Usually, a system functional scenario is defined as a sequence of operations that process a group of input data to a group of output data. Each operation in scenario is connected by intermediate data, and it is the reason why we use data as connection in animation.

One of the advantages of using data for animation is that the end user can observe each behaviour by monitoring the states of it. The states of behaviours are presented as the input and output data of each operation involved. The tool allows users to select providing the data themselves or letting the data generated automatically. If users select to provide the data for animation, they usually provide the most typical data of the system. Meanwhile, the users need to guarantee that the data they provide satisfies the pre- and post-conditions. If users want to let the data generated automatically, the data generation method would generate the data that satisfies the pre- and post-conditions. But the generated data may not present the specific circumstance users want to animate. We will introduce how to animate a scenario step by step in Sects. 2 and 3.

The prototype is implemented on the bases of a framework that is built to help developers specifying SOFL specification. The framework includes the editors of informal specification, formal specification, and CDFD, etc. All the specifications are well organized and stored in the well formatted files under this framework. It provides a fundamental to further utilization of the formal specifications. The prototype is now a part of the framework, and it contains functions of deriving system functional scenario and animating a specific scenario. Section 4 describes the framework and prototype in details.

The remainder of this paper is organized as fellows. Section 2 describes the animation strategy and the animation process. Section 3 briefly introduces the specific methods of system functional scenarios derivation and data generation used in the tool. The framework for specifying SOFL specifications and the prototype is described in Sect. 4. Section 5 gives a brief overview of related work. Finally, in Sect. 6 we conclude the paper and point out future research directions.

2   Animation Strategy and Process

As mentioned previously, we use the system functional scenario as the basic unit in animation. Each system scenario presents a specific function of the system. Since the goal of a formal specification animation is to validate the potential behaviours of the specification, we suggest that every possible system functional scenario defined in the specification should be animated. A system scenario defines a specific kind of operational behaviour of the system through a sequential executions of operations. And a specific operational behaviour is usually presented to end users as a pair of input and output, that is, given an input, the result of a behaviour of the system results in a certain output. The definition of a system functional scenario is detailed in Definition 1.

Definition 1. *A **system functional scenario**, or **system scenario** for short, of a specification is a sequence of operations* $d_i[OP_1, OP_2, ..., OP_n]d_o$, *where* d_i *is the set of input variables of the behaviour,* d_o *is the set of output variables, and each* $OP_i(i \in \{1, 2, ..., n\})$ *is an operation.*

The system scenario $d_i[OP_1, OP_2, ..., OP_n]d_o$ defines a behaviour that transforms input data item d_i into the output data item d_o through a sequential execution of operations $OP_1, OP_2, ..., OP_n$. Actually, other data items are used or produced within the process of executing the entire system scenario but not being presented. For example, the first operation OP_1 in the system scenario receives the input data item d_i and produces a data item, which is the input data item of operation OP_2. Operation OP_2 cannot be executed without the output data item of OP_1. We call these data items *implicit data items*. In order to show the behaviour of system step by step in an animation, the implicit data items in system scenario should be presented explicitly. When presenting implicit data items explicitly is necessary, we use $[d_i, OP_1, d_1, OP_2, d_2, ..., d_{n-1}, OP_n, d_o]$ to present a system scenario, where d_1 indicates the output data item of OP_1 or input data item of OP_2.

For example, Fig. 1 shows the CDFD of a simplified ATM. There are only to functions included in this simple specification: *withdraw* and *show balance*. Based on the definition of system functional scenario, five scenarios defined in the specification is listed as follows:

- {*withdraw_com*}[*Receive_Command, Check_Password, Withdraw*]{*cash*}
- {*withdraw_com*}[*Receive_Command, Check_Password, Withdraw*]{*err2*}
- {*withdraw_com*}[*Receive_Command, Check_Password*]{*err1*}

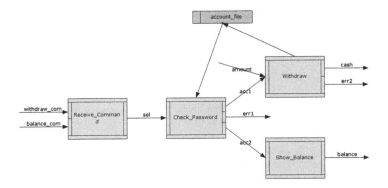

Fig. 1. CDFD of a simple ATM

– {*balance_com*}[*Receive_Command, Check_Password*]{*err1*}
– {*balance_com*}[*Receive_Command, Check_Password, Show_Balance*]{*balance*}

Such a system functional scenario clearly describes how the final output data is produced by a sequence of processes based on the input data. Note that the input data and output data indicate the sets of variables when talking about the concept of system scenario or a specific system scenario of an behaviour. Under the context of animation, the input and output data are instances rather than concepts. They indicate sets of values of the input and output variables.

To animate a specific system scenario, the data is used to connect each operation involved in the scenario. Since the data is restricted by the pre- and post-conditions of process, the data present a real environment of the behaviour. The user and experts can observe the behaviour by monitoring the data. There are two ways to collect the data for animation. The first way is to let the user providing the data. The advantage of this way is that the data provided by user is usually the most typical data. The provided data presents the circumstance that the user cares about. Meanwhile, the user have to guarantee that the data satisfies the pre- and post-condition, otherwise the data would be meaningless. The alternative way of collecting data is to generate data automatically. The generation method does not require translating the formal specification to any executable program. One of the obvious disadvantage of the method is that the generated data may not present the specific circumstance users want to animate. No matter which way the user use, the data provide a concrete point of views of the behaviour.

When collecting input and output data for a single process, the operation functional scenarios of the process have to be extracted first. By operation functional scenario, we mean an predicate expression derived from the pre- and post-condition of a process, which precisely defines the relation of a set of input and output data. Liu first gives a formal definition of operation functional scenario [5] and we repeat it here to help the reader understand the rest of this paper.

process **Check_Password**(id: nat0, sel: bool, pass: nat0)

　　　　　acc1: Account | err1: string | acc2: Account

ext　　rd Account_file

pre　　true

post　　(exists![x: Account_file] | ((x.id = id and

　　　　　　　　　　　　　　x.password = pass) and

　　　　(sel = true and acc1 = x or

　　　　sel = false and acc2 = x)))

　　　　or

　　　　not(exists![x: Account_file] | (x.id = id and

　　　　　　　　x.password = pass)) and

　　　　　　　err1 = "Reenter your password or insert

　　　　　　　　　　the correct card"

end_process

Fig. 2. Specification of process "Check_Password"

Definition 2. *Let $OP(OP_{iv}, OP_{ov})[OP_{pre}, OP_{post}]$ denote the formal specification of an operation OP, where OP_{iv} is the set of all input variables whose values are not changed by the operation, OP_{ov} is the set of all output variables whose values are produced or updated by the operation, and OP_{pre} and OP_{post} are the pre and post-condition of operation OP, respectively.*

Definition 3. *Let $OP_{post} \equiv (C_1 \wedge D_1) \vee (C_2 \wedge D_2) \vee ... \vee (C_n \wedge D_n)$, where each $C_i(i \in \{1, ..., n\})$ is a predicate called a "**guard condition**" that contains no output variable in OP_{ov} and $\forall_{i,j \in \{1,...,n\}} \cdot i \neq j \Rightarrow C_i \wedge C_j = false$; D_i a "**defining condition**" that contains at least one output variable in OP_{ov} but no guard condition. Then, a formal specification of an operation can be expressed as a disjunction $(\sim OP_{pre} \wedge C_1 \wedge D_1) \vee (\sim OP_{pre} \wedge C_2 \wedge D_2) \vee ... \vee (\sim OP_{pre} \wedge C_n \wedge D_n)$. A conjunction $\sim OP_{pre} \wedge C_i \wedge D_i$ is called an **operation functional scenario**, or **operation scenario** for short.*

Note that we use $\sim x$ and x to represent the initial value before the operation and the final value after the operation of external variable x, respectively. The decorated pre-condition $\sim OP_{pre} = OP_{pre}[\sim x/x]$ denotes the predicate resulting from substituting the initial state $\sim x$ for the final state x in pre-condition OP_{pre}. We treat a conjunction $\sim OP_{pre} \wedge C_i \wedge D_i$ as an operation functional scenario because it defines an independent behaviour: when $\sim OP_{pre} \wedge C_i$ is satisfied by the initial state (or intuitively by the input data), the final state (or the output data) is defined by the defining condition D_i.

The reason why we need the operation functional scenario is that the definition of SOFL allows the process to receive more than one exclusive input or output data. In a specific system functional scenario, only one pair of input and output data of each process is involved. For instance, the process "Check_Passwork" of the simple ATM system in Fig. 1 is formally defined in the specification shown in Fig. 2. There are three operation functional scenario contained in this specification.

1. $(\exists x \in Account\_file \cdot x.id = id \wedge x.password = pass) \wedge sel = true \wedge acc1 = x$
2. $(\exists x \in Account\_file \cdot x.id = id \wedge x.password = pass) \wedge sel = false \wedge acc2 = x$
3. $\neg(\exists x \in Account\_file \cdot x.id = id \wedge x.password = pass) \wedge err1 =$ "Reenter your password or insert the correct card"

If the system functional scenario {balance_com}[Receive_Command, Check_Password, Show_Balance]{balance} is under animation, there is no doubt that the second operation functional scenario should be selected to collect input and output data for the process "Check_Passwork".

After the introduction of our animation strategy, we would describe how to apply the strategy in practice. For a given formal specification, the following stages supply a procedure for systematically performing the animation.

Stage 1. *Derive all possible* ***system scenarios*** *from the formal specification.*

Different methods are used to derived system functional scenario from formal specification written in different formal languages. For example, for a formal specification language containing graphic specification, the system scenarios can be derived based on the topology of the graph. On the other hand, for a formal specification language that does not contain graphic specification, the system scenarios can be derived based on the data dependency among operations. For SOFL specification, we derive system functional scenarios from the topology of the CDFD. We will introduce the specific automatic approach for deriving all possible system scenarios in next section.

Stage 2. *Let $d_i[P_1, P_2, ..., P_n]d_o$ be a selected* ***system scenario***. *Derive related* ***operation scenarios*** *of each $P_i(i \in \{1, 2, ..., n\})$ from its specification and get a set of* ***operation scenarios*** $\{OS_1, OS_2, ..., OS_n\}$, *where OS_i is the related* ***operation scenario*** *of P_i.*

According to our animation strategy, only one system scenario should be selected to animate each time. For any selected system scenario, the related operation scenario of each operation involved should be derived from the formal specification. Since an operation scenario of an operation defines an independent relation between its input and output under a certain condition, only one operation scenario of an operation can be involved in the selected system scenario. Therefore, the second stage of entire animation process should be deriving related operation scenarios.

As the start point of a system functional scenario, the input data of the first process in the system scenario should be collected first. Actually, the input data of the first process is the only input that need to be collected from the user or generated by data generation method. The input data of the following processes is the output data of the previous processes.

Stage 3. *Let $\sim S_{pre}^1 \wedge C_i^1 \wedge D_i^1$ be the related operation scenario of the first operation P_1 in the selected system scenario. The input data should be collected and satisfy the predicate expression $\sim S_{pre}^1 \wedge C_i^1$.*

The input data generated in Stage 3 is actually the input of the selected system scenario. It can be used as bases to collect output data of P_1. The output data collected should satisfy the predicate expression $\sim S_{pre}^{1*} \wedge C_i^{1*} \wedge D_i^1$, which can be created by applying the input data to predicate expression $\sim S_{pre}^1 \wedge C_i^1 \wedge D_i^1$. The output data of P_1 then be used as input data of P_2 to collect output data of P_2. Repeating this procedures, the output data of entire system scenario can be generated eventually. This idea is reflected in Stage 4.

Stage 4. *Use the input data generated in Stage 3 and the operation scenarios derived in Stage 2 to generate the output data for each operation and entire system scenario.*

So far, all of the data involved in a selected system scenario has been generated. And the behaviour can be simulated by using the data involved in it. The end users and field experts can monitor the states of the behaviour during its execution, and analyse whether the specification meets their requirement.

Stage 5. *Repeat Stage 2 to Stage 4 until all the* **system scenarios** *derived in Stage 1 are animated.*

Animating all possible behaviours of the system is required by our animation strategy. The process of animating a specific behaviour should be repeated until all of the potential behaviours have been animated.

3   Design of the Tool

According to our animation strategy, there are two steps in the animation process. The first step is to derive all possible system functional scenario, and the second step is to collect input and output data for all involved processes of a specific system functional scenario. In this section, we first introduce the method of deriving system functional scenario briefly, and then describe how to collect input and output data under the two ways mentioned above.

3.1   Deriving System Scenario

We choose deriving functional scenarios from a CDFD because it is extremely difficult to automatically generate scenarios from a process specification directly. Form the introduction of SOFL, we know that process specification uses mathematical notation to define processes in a module, and it is not designed to present the architecture or logic between different processes. If deriving functional scenarios from process specifications, it requires parsing the entire specification to determine which two processes are connected. It is obviously not a cost-effective approach. On the contrary, deriving scenarios from the CDFD will be more cost-effective, because the CDFD is specifically designed to describe the relations among the processes, and we can derive functional scenarios based on the topology of CDFD.

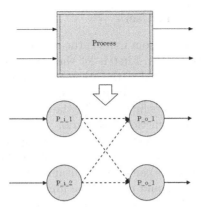

Fig. 3. The decomposition of a process

In order to generate all possible scenarios, the first step is to decompose the CDFD. This can be realized by decomposing every process in the CDFD. Each process can be decomposed into a corresponding graph. Figure 3 illustrates the decomposition of a process. In the original CDFD, the port list on the left side of a process is input port list, in which each input port is ordered from top to bottom, we use a number to label each port. The output ports of a process are labelled in the same way. In the corresponding graph, each node represents one port of the process, one input port or output port.

Each node in the corresponding graph has a name, consisting of three parts: the first character of the process's name, the identification of input or output port, and the port number. Different nodes are connected by two kinds of edges, solid edges and dotted edges. The solid edge represents the data flow in original CDFD and the dotted edge represents the mapping relationship inside the process. Like the data flows connecting two different processes in CDFD, the solid edges connect one input port node and one output port node that belong to different processes. Contrasts to the solid edges, the dotted edges represent the implicit relation in process. We use dotted edges to explicitly present this kind of relation because the ports that belong to the same port list are exclusive. If a process has more than one input port and output port, we need to find all possible combinations between its input ports and output ports. So that we can find all possible functional scenarios. The dotted edges represent such possible combinations or relations. In practice, just one dotted edge in each process can be valid each time. It means at each time process receiving and sending data from the input port and output port which are concerned by the valid dotted edge.

By using the decomposition method, one CDFD can be decomposed to a graph that contains only input port nodes and output port nodes. The nodes in the decomposed graph is linked by solid and dotted edges. The process of deriving all possible system functional scenarios can be realized as finding all possible paths in the decomposed graph. For the space sake, we will not explain this method further. The details of this method is included in [8].

3.2   Collecting Data from Users

The process of collecting data from users is the easiest way of collecting data. It can be separated into two steps. First is let the user provide data, and second is to check whether the provided data satisfy the related operation functional scenarios. The two steps are usually mixed in practice. For example, in the beginning of an animation, users first provides the input data for the first process, P_1, in the selected system functional scenario. Then, the users should check whether the input data they provide satisfy the predicate expression $\sim S^1_{pre} \wedge C^1_i$, a part of the related operation functional scenario of process P_1. If the input data satisfy the expression, the users can provide output data of P_1 based on the input data. Otherwise, the users should provide the input data again. Once the users provide the output data of P_1 successfully, the output data of P_1 will be used as the input data of the second process, P_2. This procedure will continue until the output of the entire system functional scenario are successfully provided.

To facilitate the users to check whether the data they provide satisfy a specific predicate expression, we use fault tree in our tool to help the users to do the judgement. We first apply the provided data to the predicate expression, and than decompose the expression using a tree structure, Each node in this tree presents an atomic expression. Since the fault tree technique is well known, we do not do any further explanation here.

3.3   Generating Data Automatically

The automatic data generation method underlying our tool is first introduced in [6]. The advantage of this method is that there is no need to translate the formal specification to any executable program. Here we give a brief introduction of the principle of the method.

As described previously, an *operation scenario* is expressed as a conjunction $\sim OP_{pre} \wedge C_i \wedge D_i$. To derive input data based on the *operation scenario*, it must be decomposed first. The decomposing process is divided into following two steps:

- **Step 1: Eliminate Defining condition.** The defining condition D_i is eliminated first since the execution of program only requires input values. The input data generation depends on the pre-condition and guard condition, and defining condition usually do not provide the main information for input data generation. The conjunction after eliminating defining condition is $\sim OP_{pre} \wedge C_i$, called "*testing condition*".
- **Step 2: Convert to disjunctive normal form.** The remainder of the *operation scenario* is translated into an equivalent disjunctive normal form (DNF) with form $P_1 \vee P_2 \vee ... \vee P_n$. A P_i is a conjunction of atomic predicate expressions, say $Q^1_i \wedge Q^2_i \wedge ... \wedge Q^m_i$.

Let $Q(x_1, x_2, ..., x_w)$ be one of the atomic predicate expressions $Q^1_i, Q^2_i, ..., Q^m_i$ mentioned previously. The variables $x_1, x_2, ..., x_w$ is a subset of all the input variables. The values for the input variables involved in each atomic predicate expression Q can be generated using a set of algorithms that deals with the following three situations, respectively. Here we are using variables of numerical types as examples for convenience.

Table 1. Input data generation algorithm

No. of Algorithms	$\ominus$	Algorithms of test case generation for x_1
1	$=$	$x_1 = E$
2	$>$	$x_1 = E + \Delta x$
3	$<$	$x_1 = E - \Delta x$
4	$\leq, \geq, \neq$	Similar to above

- **Situation 1:** If only one input variable is involved and $Q(x_1)$ has the format $x_1 \ominus E$, where $\ominus \in \{=, <, >, \leq, \geq, \neq\}$ is a relational operator and E is a constant expression, using the algorithms listed in Table 1 to generate test cases for variable x_1.
- **Situation 2:** If only one input variable is involved and $Q(x_1)$ has the format $E_1 \ominus E_2$, where E_1 and E_2 are both arithmetic expressions which may involve variable x_1, it is first transformed to the format $x_1 \ominus E$, and then apply Situation 1.
- **Situation 3:** If more than one input variables are involved and $Q(x_1, x_2, ..., x_w)$ has the format $E_1 \ominus E_2$, where E_1 and E_2 are both arithmetic expressions possibly involving all the variables $x_1, x_2, ..., x_w$, first randomly assigning values from appropriate types to the input variables $x_2, x_3, ..., x_w$ to transform the format into the format $E_1 \ominus E_2$, and then apply Situation 2.

Note that if one input variable x appears in more than one atomic predicate expression, it needs to satisfy all the expressions in which it is involved.

To define the generated input data precisely, we use a set of states of input variables, called *input case*, to present the one-to-one correspondence between each input variable and its value. The *input case* is denoted as I_c and defined as follows.

Definition 4. *Let $OP_{iv} = \{x_1, x_2, ..., x_r\}$ be the set of all input variables of operation OP and $Type(x_i)$ denotes the type of $x_i (i \in \{1, 2, ..., r\})$. Then $I_c = \{(x_i, v_i) | x_i \in OP_{iv} \land v_i \in Type(x_i)\}$. If $(x_i, v_i) \in I_c$, we write $I_c(x_i) = v_i$.*

After automatically collecting the input data, the next step is to generate output data. The same algorithm can be used. The similar process is described as follows.

- **Step 1: Verify the given input data.** For any given input case I_c, evaluate the predicate $(\sim OP_{pre} \land C_i)[I_c(x_i)/x_i]$, which is the result of substituting the variable x_i with the value of variable x_i in the *testing condition* $\sim OP_{pre} \land C_i$. The result of true means that the given input data can be processed by the operation, and the output data can be produced based on the input data.

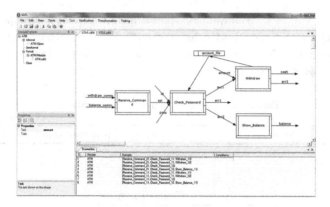

Fig. 4. Scenario explorer

- **Step 2: Substitute input variables.** Substitute the input variables in *operation scenario* with the corresponding values in I_c, and get a new predicate $\sim OP^*_{pre} \wedge C_i^* \wedge D_i^* = (\sim OP_{pre} \wedge C_i \wedge D_i)[I_c(x_i)/x_i]$, which merely contains output variables.
- **Step 3: Convert to disjunctive normal form.** Translate the conjunction $\sim OP^*_{pre} \wedge C_i^* \wedge D_i^*$ into an equivalent disjunctive normal form (DNF) with form $P_1^* \vee P_2^* \vee ... \vee P_n^*$. A P_i^* is a conjunction of atomic predicate expressions, say $Q_i^{*1} \wedge Q_i^{*2} \wedge ... \wedge Q_i^{*m}$.
- **Step 4: Generate values for output.** For each $Q_i^{*j}(j \in \{1, 2, ..., m\})$, use the algorithms explained in previous subsection to generate values for output variables.

Similar to the definition of *input case*, we define *output case* to present output variables and their generated values formally.

Definition 5. *Let* $OP_{ov} = \{y_1, y_2, ..., y_k\}$ *be the set of all input variables of operation OP and* $Type(y_i)$ *denotes the type of* $y_i (i \in \{1, 2, ..., k\})$. *Then* $O_c = \{(y_i, v_i) | y_i \in OP_{ov} \wedge v_i \in Type(y_i)\}$. *If* $(y_i, v_i) \in O_c$, *we write* $O_c(y_i) = v_i$.

4   Framework and Prototype

The prototype is implemented on the bases of a framework that is built to help developers specifying SOFL specification. The framework includes the editors of informal specification, formal specification, and CDFD, etc. All the specifications are well organized and stored in the well formatted files under this framework. It provides a fundamental to further utilization of the formal specifications. Now, the prototype has been a component of the framework. In this section, we introduce some functions that related to the animation.

The implementation prototype is corresponding to the two steps. The first step is to derive system functional scenario. Figure 4 shows the snapshot of

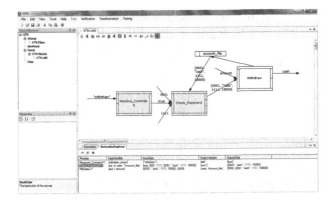

Fig. 5. Animation board

Table 2. Opération scenarios involved in the selected system scenario

Process	Operation scenario
Received_Command$_{11}$	$withdraw = $ "$withdraw$" $\land sel = true$
Check_Password$_{11}$	$x.id = id \land x.password = pass) \land sel = true \land acc1 = x$
Withdraw$_{11}$	$amount \leq \sim x.balance \land x.balance$
	$= \sim x.balance - amount \land cash = amount$

derivation. The CDFD is the system shown in Fig. 1. Here we chose the first scenario {withdraw_com}[Receive_Command, Check_Password, Withdraw]{cash} to animate. The corresponding operation functional scenario is listed in Table 2.

Figure 5 shows the snapshot of animation. The data collected is listed at the lower part of the window. Each row shows the input and output data for a single process. For example, the first row list the input and output of process "$Receive_Command_{11}$". The CDFD in the center of the window shows the mid-step of animation, and the process "$Check_Password_{11}$" is under animated.

5   Related Work

Formal specification animation is an effective technique for the communication between users and developers. Tool support animation can make such communication easier. In this section, we introduce some existing work on specification animation.

Liu and Wang introduced an animation tool called SOFL Animator for SOFL specification animation [7]. It provides syntactic level analysis and semantic level analysis of a specification. When performing animation, the tool will automatically translate the SOFL specification into Java program segments, and then use some test case to execute the program. In order to provide reviewers a graphic presentation of the animation, SOFL Animator uses Message Sequence Chart (MSC) to present the simulation of the operational behaviours.

MSC is also adopted in other animation approach as a framework to provide a graphical user interface to represent animation. Stepien and Logrippo built a toolset to translate LOTOS traces to MSC and provide a graphic animator [9]. The translation is based on the mappings between the elements of LOTOS and MSC. Combes and his colleagues described an open animation tool for telecommunication systems in [1]. The tool is named as ANGOR, and it offers an environment based on a flexible architecture. It allows animating different animation sources, such as formal and executable language like SDL and scenario languages like MSC.

6   Conclusions and Future Work

In this paper, we describe a tool to support SOFL specification animation. The animation strategy is introduced first and then the prototype is presented. Comparing to other existing tool, the advantage of our work is that there is no requirement to translate formal specification to executable program. This means there is no further request for the developers about the style of specification. We provide two ways for users to collect data for animation. Each way shows different aspects of the system to users. We think the data can give the users a concrete point of view, and help them to understand the behaviours of the system. But only the animation is not enough to validate the formal specification, in the future, we hope to combine the inspection technique with animation. The inspection contains a list of question and require the users to think rather than observation only. We hope the combination of these two techniques can make validation more effective and efficiency.

References

1. Combes, P., Dubois, F., Renard, B.: An open animation tool: application to telecommunication systems. Int. J. Comput. Telecommun. Netw. **40**(5), 599–620 (2002)
2. Waeselynck, H., Behnia, S.: B model animation for external verification. In: Proceedings of the Second IEEE International Conference on Formal Engineering Methods, pp. 36–45 (1998)
3. Morrey, I., Siddiqi, J., Hibberd, R., Buckberry, G.: A toolset to support the construction and animation of formal specifications. J. Syst. Softw. **41**(3), 147–160 (1998)
4. Liu, S.: Formal Engineering for Industrial Software Development Using the SOFL Method. Springer, Heidelberg (2004). ISBN 3-540-20602-7
5. Liu, S., Nakajima, S.: A Decompositional approach to automatic test case generation based on formal specification. In: Fourth IEEE International Conference on Secure Software Integration and Reliability Improvement, pp. 147–155 (2010)
6. Li, M., Liu, S.: Automated functional scenarios-based formal specification animation. In: Proceedings of the 19th Asia-Pacific Software Engineering Conference (APSEC 2012), pp. 107–115. IEEE CS Press, Hong Kong (2012)
7. Liu, S., Wang, H.: An automated approach to specification animation for validation. J. Syst. Softw. **80**, 1271–1285 (2007)

8. Li, M., Liu, S.: Automatically generating functional scenarios from SOFL CDFD for specification inspection. In: 10th IASTED International Conference on Software Engineering, Innsbruck, Austria, pp. 18–25 (2011)
9. Stepien, B., Logrippo, L.: Graphic visualization and animation of LOTOS execution traces. Comput. Netw.: Int. J. Comput. Telecommun. Netw. **40**(5), 665–681 (2002)
10. Liu, S., Chen, Y., Nagoya, F., McDermid, J.A.: Formal specification-based inspection for verification of programs. IEEE Trans. Softw. Eng. **21**(2), 259–288 (2011). IEEE Computer Society Digital Library, IEEE Computer Society
11. Liu, S.: Integrating specification-based review and testing for detecting errors in programs. In: Butler, M., Hinchey, M.G., Larrondo-Petrie, M.M. (eds.) ICFEM 2007. LNCS, vol. 4789, pp. 136–150. Springer, Heidelberg (2007)
12. Miller, T., Strooper, P.: Model-based specification animation using testgraphs. In: George, C.W., Miao, H. (eds.) ICFEM 2002. LNCS, vol. 2495, pp. 192–203. Springer, Heidelberg (2002)

Formal Specification
and Application

An Approach to Declaring Data Types for Formal Specifications

Xi Wang[✉] and Shaoying Liu

Department of Computer Science, Hosei University, Tokyo, Japan
xi.wang.y2@stu.hosei.ac.jp, sliu@hosei.ac.jp

Abstract. Data type declaration is an important activity in formal specification construction, which results in a collection of custom types for defining variables to be used in writing formal expressions such as pre- and post-conditions. As the complexity of software products rises, such a task will become more and more difficult to be handled by practitioners. This paper proposes an approach to facilitate the declaration of data types based on a set of *function patterns*, each designed for guiding the description of one kind of function in formal expressions. During the application of these patterns, necessary data types will be automatically recognized and their definitions will be gradually refined. Meanwhile, formal expressions will be modified to keep their consistency with the type definitions. A case study on a banking system is presented to show the validity of the approach in practice.

1 Introduction

Formal specification serves as the foundation of many software verification techniques, such as formal specification-based testing and inspection. It documents software behaviors in formal expressions, such as pre- and post-conditions, with a set of state variables of the envisioned system. These state variables needs to be formally defined with custom data types. Therefore, declaring appropriate data types is the first and important step for formal specification construction.

As the complexity of software rises, data type declaration becomes more difficult to manage and more likely to result in defected data types. Type checking technique and model transformation have been introduced to facilitate such an activity [1–3]. The former detects static type errors to prevent erroneous formal descriptions while the latter allows data to be described in certain intermediate language easier to use and provides a method for transforming the data model into formal data types. Unfortunately, they fall short of meeting practitioners' demand. First, relations between types and functions to be described is not considered, i.e., type definitions incapable of or unsuitable for describing the intended functions are not able to be identified. Secondly, no guidance or automated assistant is provided during the declaration process. Lastly, the consistency between formal expressions and type definitions cannot be guaranteed. In a formal specification f, if a type definition t is changed into t', all the formal

S. Liu and Z. Duan (Eds.): SOFL+MSVL 2013, LNCS 8332, pp. 135–153, 2014.
DOI: 10.1007/978-3-319-04915-1_10, © Springer International Publishing Switzerland 2014

expressions involving state variables defined with t need to be manually modified to be consistent with the new definition t'.

To deal with the above problems, this paper puts forward an approach to supporting data type declarations for formal specifications. Its underlying principle is that types should be defined to meet the need of correctly and concisely describing related functions. Type definitions will evolve as function description proceeds until all the expected functions are properly represented in formal expressions.

In this approach, *function pattern* is adopted to assist the writing of formal expressions [4]. Each *function pattern* provides a framework for formalizing one kind of function through interactions. Describing functions in formal expressions is to select appropriate patterns and apply them. During the application process, necessary data types can be automatically recognized and their definitions will be refined. Specifically, when applying each selected pattern, we use *function-related declaration* to guide the refinement of the related data types. It consists of two steps for different stages of the application process: *property-guided declaration* and *priority-guided declaration*.

We also give a method for updating formal expressions as their involved data types are refined to keep the consistency. When a type definition is modified after the application of a pattern, the formal expressions affected by such modification will be fully explored. For each formal expression, the method first retrieves the pattern applied for writing it and the application process of the pattern. Based on the retrieved information and the modified type definition., the formal expression is automatically updated.

Since we believe that object identification is an intelligent activity that cannot be manipulated by machines, the approach is not expected to be total automatic and requires human effort when creative decisions need to be made.

It should be noted that the proposed approach is language-independent. We choose SOFL as an example formal notation to illustrate the approach because of our expertise. A formal specification in SOFL comprises a set of modules in a hierarchical structure where lower level modules describe the detailed behavior of their upper level modules. Each module is an encapsulation of processes, which describe functions in terms of pre- and post-conditions, within the specific specification context of the module. Relation between these processes are reflected by a CDFD (Condition Data Flow Diagrams) which specifies interactions between them via data flows and stores. The independency of each module allows us to discuss the production approach on the module level and a complete set of data types will be achieved after applying the approach to all the modules included in the specification. For more details in SOFL, one can refer to [5,6].

The remainder of this article is organized as follows. Section 2 summarizes the related work. To facilitate the understanding of the proposed approach, some fundamental concepts are first introduced in Sect. 3, including data context and function pattern. Based on these concepts, the declaration approach is explained in detail in Sect. 4 and a case study is presented in Sect. 5 to illustrate the approach. Finally, Sect. 6 concludes the paper and points out the future works.

2   Related Work

We know of no existing approach that provides assistance throughout the whole data type declaration process, although some researches have been concerned with certain aspects of the problem.

To ensure type compliance and absence of erroneous descriptions, typecheckers are designed and implemented for various formal specification languages with different type systems. Jian Chen et al. [2] develop a simple but useful set of rules for type checking the object-oriented formal specification language Object-Z and an earlier version of the type checker for Z is given in [7]. For the Vienna Development Method (VDM), the most feature-rich analytic tool available is VDMTools which includes syntax- and type-checking facilities [1,8]. Syntax checking results in positional error reporting supported by an indication of error points. Type-checking can be divided into static type-checking and dynamic type-checking. The former checks for static semantics errors of specifications including incorrect values applied to function calls, badly typed assignments, use of undefined variables and module imports/exports, while the latter aims at avoiding semantic inconsistency and potential sources of run-time errors. As one of the major components in the Rodin tool for Event-B, static checker analyses Event-B contexts and Event-B machines and generates feedback to the user about syntactical and typing errors in them [9,10]. Prototype Verification System (PVS) extends higher order logic with dependent types and structural and predicate subtypes. In addition to conventional type-checking, it returns a set of proof obligations TCCs (Type Correctness Conditions) as potent detectors of erroneous specifications and provides a powerful interactive theorem prover that implements several decision procedures and proof automation tools [11,12]. Tan et al.[13] presents a type checker for formal specifications of software systems described in Real-Time Process Algebra, which is able to handle three tasks: identifier type compliancy, expression type compliancy and process constraint consistency. Xavier et al.[14] defines the type system of formal language Circus which combines Z, CSP and additional constructors of Morgan's refinement calculus, and describes the design and implementation of a corresponding type checker based on the typing rules that formalize the type system of Circus.

The quality of the declared data types can be significantly improved by the supporting tools listed above, unfortunately practitioners are still complaining about the difficulties in identifying real objects by formal data type definitions, the lack of effective guidelines throughout the declaration process and everlasting appearance of errors implicitly explained. Despite the use of "semantic analysis" in some of these tools' underlying theories, it refers to the semantics of the embedded type system that is part of the built-in mechanism, rather than the semantics of ideas in users' mind. By contrast, our approach tries to connect the semantics of specifications with the corresponding system behaviors through data types and evaluate the appropriateness of the declared types on the real semantic level. Moreover, the given systematic guidance in the overall declaration process specifies how to reach the appropriate data types step by step while checking the correctness of the result of each step, which alleviates burdens of manual design.

There are also some researches done for transforming models in intermediate languages to formal data type definitions. These intermediate languages provide accessible visualization of object relation models and therefore simplify the object identification process. In [3], entity relationship models are treated as the basis for producing VDM data types in specifications. Colin Snook et al. [15] propose a formal modeling technique that emerge UML and B to benefit from both languages where the semantics of UML entities is defined via a translation into B. Anastasakis et al.[16] presents an automated transformation method from UML class diagrams with OCL constraints to Alloy which is a formal language supported by a tool for automated specification analysis. The problem, however, lies in the fact that identifying and defining objects are separated from functions to be described in these methods and totally depending on the developer's initial understanding of the real system. Hence our approach would be more reliable in declaring data types for function description and practitioners can utilize models in graphical representations as supplementary materials.

3   Preliminaries

3.1   Data Context

Constants and variables compose a data context under which formal expressions in formal specifications can be written and become analyzable. The formal definition of *data context* is given as follows.

Definition 1. *A data context is a 4-tuple (C, T, V, vt) where C is the set of constants, T is the set of custom data types, V is the set of variables and $vt : V \rightarrow T$ is the type function that determines the data type of each variable in V.*

To facilitate automated analysis and improve specification readability, each variable in the data context is required to be defined as a custom type in our approach, i.e., for each $v \in V$, there exists a type t in T that satisfies $vt(v) = t$. For example, when describing an ATM system, a password should be defined as a variable of a custom type declared as *string*. Although the built-in type *string* itself is capable of representing the nature of password and one can define the required password as a variable of *string* type, it fails to distinguish the object from others that are also defined as *string*, such as error messages. In addition, modification on the definitions of all the password entities in the specification can be easily manipulated by modifying the definition of the corresponding custom type.

3.2   Function Pattern

A function pattern provides a framework for formalizing one kind of function. Different from traditional ones, function pattern is designed to be applied in a full automated way. For each unit function intended to be described, the developer will be first guided to select a proper function pattern and then a formal expression will be generated by automatic application of the pattern. The definition of function pattern is given as follows.

Definition 2. *A function pattern p is a 6-tuple $(id, E, PR, \Delta, \Phi, \Psi)$ where*

- *id is a unique identify of p written in natural language*
- *E is a set of elements that needs to be specified to apply p, which can be assigned with 3 kinds of values: choice value (CV) generated by choosing from several candidate items, variable value (VV) composed of constants and system variables, and property value (PV) that specifies properties of certain objects*
- *PR is a property set including properties of the pattern p or properties of the elements in E*
- *$\Delta : PR \to \mathcal{P}(E \cup \{p\})$ indicates the objects involved in each property $pr \in PR$ which may include p and elements in E.*
- *$\Phi : SN \times (E \cup \mathcal{P}(PR)) \to E \cup \mathcal{P}(PR)$ indicates a set of rules including element rules and property rules where*
  - *each $sn : SN$ denotes the sequence number of the rule it associated with*
  - *$\exists_1 x : E \cup \mathcal{P}(PR) \cdot \Phi(1, null) \to x$*
  - *$\forall i : SN, e : E \cdot e' = \Phi(i, e) \Rightarrow e' \in E \wedge e' \neq e(e' = \Phi(i, e)$ denotes an element rule where e' should be specified after e)*
  - *$\forall i : SN, PR_i : \mathcal{P}(PR) \cdot PR_j = \Phi(i, PR_i) \Rightarrow PR_j \in \mathcal{P}(PR) \wedge (\forall pr : PR_i \cdot pr \notin PR_j)(PR_j = \Phi(i, PR_i)$ denotes a property rule where properties in PR_j will be hold if each property in PR_i is satisfied)*
  - *$\forall PR_i, PR_j : \mathcal{P}(PR) \cdot (\exists i : SN \cdot (i, PR_i) \in dom(\Phi) \wedge (i, PR_j) \in dom(\Phi)) \Rightarrow ((\forall pr_i : PR_i \cdot pr_i = true) \Rightarrow (\exists pr_j : PR_j \cdot pr_j = false))$*
- *$\Psi : \mathcal{P}(PR) \to exp$ produces a formal result exp when certain properties in PR are satisfied iff*
  $\forall PR_i, PR_j : dom(\Psi) \cdot (\forall pr_i : PR_i \cdot pr_i = true) \Rightarrow (\exists pr_j : PR_j \cdot pr_j = false)$

Since patterns are categorized and each pattern holds a distinguishable *id* that reflects, on an abstract level, the function it is able to describe, developers can easily select the most suitable pattern. After the selection decision of certain pattern p is made, elements in E_p will be required to be specified under the guidance produced by the rules in Φ_p. The obtained element information is then analyzed within the context of Ψ_p to determine its corresponding formal result.

But such a formal result may still contain informal statements composed of pattern *id* and element information, which indicates that further formalization needs to be conducted by applying the reused patterns with the attached element information. For example, suppose a formal result involving informal statement "$p'(v_1, v_2)$" is achieved where $E_{p'} = \{e_1, e_2, e_3\}$ and $\exists_{i,j \in SN_{p'}} \cdot (i, e_1) \to e_2 \wedge (j, e_2) \to e_3$, it should be further formalized by replacing the informal statement with the formal result generated by applying p' with e_1 and e_2 set as v_1 and v_2 respectively. This procedure will not be terminated until reaching a formal expression.

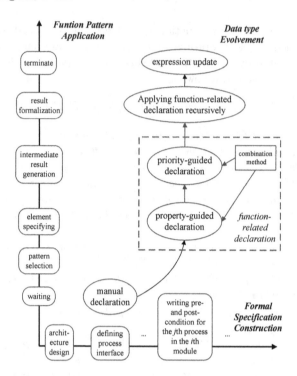

Fig. 1. The outline of the data type declaration approach

4   The Approach to Declaring Data Types

4.1   Approach Outline

The proposed approach regards data type declaration as an evolution process along with the writing of formal expressions based on function patterns. This evolution process starts with a modulized formal specification and terminates when the detailed behavior of each module is precisely given. Figure 1 shows the outline of the approach where x-axis and y-axis indicate the pattern application process and the formal specification construction process respectively.

On the assumption that specification architecture is already established where modules are organized in a hierarchical structure and processes of each module are connected by their interfaces, developers will first be required to manually declare data types for defining these interfaces. Since process behaviors is not considered in this stage, the declared data types only reflects the initial idea of the intended functions and will be refined as the function details are clarified.

Then the description of individual processes is started where each process should be attached with a pair of pre- and post-condition. For each pre-/post-condition, a pattern suitable for describing the expected function will first be selected. The selected pattern is then applied. Step 1 is to guide the specifying of its elements and step 2 is to generate an intermediate formal result based on the specified elements. During these two steps, *function-related declaration* is carried out to declare new types and refine the existing type definitions where *property-guided declaration* is carried out on step 1 and *priority-guided declaration* is carried out on step 2. The former guides the refinement of type definitions under the principle that all the properties inferred from the specified elements should be satisfied while the latter provides suggested definition of certain types according to the priority attribute associated to Ψ of the selected pattern. These two techniques share a type combination method that refines the existing type definitions by combining different definitions of the same type. For example, suppose pattern p is selected to write a formal expression and type t is initially declared as definition def_1 for specifying element e_1 of p. When specifying element e_2, *property-guided declaration* leads to a suggestion that t should be defined as definition def_2 to enable the correct representation of the value assigned to e_2. If def_1 is not equal to def_2, the combination method will be applied to refine def_1 with def_2 by combining them into a new definition for declaring t.

If the generated intermediate result contains informal expressions, formalization of the result is needed. Since it is performed by applying the patterns indicated by the informal expressions, *function-related declaration* can be repeatedly manipulated to further refine the data types of the specification. When the formalization process terminates with a formal expression, a refined data context is obtained. Finally, *expression update* is carried out where all the formal expressions that are inconsistent with the refined data context are updated.

Serving as the critical techniques in the described declaration approach, *function-related declaration* and *expression update* will be presented in details respectively.

4.2   Function-Related Declaration

Function-related declaration guides the refinement of data types to enable the application of the selected function patterns. It adopts *property-guided declaration* and *priority-guided declaration* in declaring data types for specifying element and generation intermediate result, respectively. Before presenting the detailed techniques in *function-related declaration*, some necessary concepts are introduced first.

Definition 3. *Given a data context dc and a pattern p, $es_p^{dc} : E_p \rightarrow \mathcal{P}(Choices) \cup Exp_{dc} \cup \mathcal{P}(Props_{dc})$ is an element state of p under dc revealing the value of each element $e \in E_p$ where*

- *Choices denotes the universal set of choice values*
- *Exp_{dc} is the universal set of formal expressions within context dc and each $exp_{dc} \in Exp_{dc}$ is a sequence: $N^+ \rightarrow C_{dc} \cup V_{fsc} \cup Operator$ where Operator is the set of operators in formal notations*
- *$Props_{dc}$ denotes the universal set of property values within context dc and for each prop $\in Props_{dc}$, $inVar(prop)$ is adopted to denote the variables involved in prop.*

It should be noted that es_p denotes all the possible element states of p, i.e., set $\{es_p^{dc_1}, ..., es_p^{dc_i}, ...\}$ where $\{dc_1, ..., dc_i, ...\}$ is the universal set of data contexts.

Definition 4. *Given a data context dc and a pattern p, function $satisfy_p^{dc}$: $PR_p \times ES_p^{dc} \rightarrow boolean$ denotes satisfaction relations between properties and element states where each $es_p^{dc} \in ES_p^{dc}$ is a possible element state of p under dc and $satisfy_p^{dc}(pr, es_p^{dc})$ indicates $\forall_{e \in \Delta(pr)} \cdot es_p^{dc}(e) \neq \varnothing \wedge pr$ is satisfied by es_p^{dc}.*

Definition 5. *Given a data context dc and a pattern p, $condSatisfy_p^{dc} : es_p \rightarrow \mathcal{P}(\ominus_p)$ is a conditional satisfaction function iff*

$-$ $es_0 \in es_p \wedge \forall_{e \in dom(es_0)} \cdot es_0(e) = \varnothing \Rightarrow$
  $condSatisfy_p^{dc}(es_0) = \ominus_p$
$-$ $condSatisfy_p^{dc}(es_p^{dc}) = R \Rightarrow$
  $\forall_{PR_i \in dom(R)} \cdot \forall_{pr \in PR_i} \cdot (satisfy_p^{dc}(pr, es_p^{dc}) \vee$
  $((\exists_{e \in \Delta(pr)} \cdot es_p^{dc}(e) = \varnothing) \wedge$
  $(pr, es') \notin dom(satisfy_p^{dc})))$
  where $es' \subset es_p^{dc} \wedge \forall_{e \in dom(es_p^{dc} - es')} \cdot$
  $es_p^{dc}(e) = \varnothing \wedge (\forall_{e' \in dom(es')} \cdot es(e') \neq \varnothing)$

Due to the fact that the type combination method is employed in both *property-guided declaration* and *priority-guided declaration*, it is first introduced.

Type Combination. Type combination is an operation that combines two different definitions of the same type into an appropriate new definition for declaring that type. The result of the operation is determined by certain properties held by the definition pair. Considering that it is impossible to combine all kinds of definition pairs automatically, the strategy of the operation is to deal with syntactic issues by machines and ask the developer to handle the semantic problems.

In order to precisely describe various properties of definition pairs, the concept of *subtype* is introduced and formally defined as follows.

Definition 6. *Given a custom type ct, $subType(ct)$ denotes the subtype of ct where*

$-$ *ct is basic type $\Rightarrow subType(ct) = \varnothing$*
$-$ *ct is composite type with each field f_i defined as type $t_i \Rightarrow subType(ct) = \{(f_1, t_1), ..., (f_n, t_n)\}$*
$-$ *ct is product type with the ith field defined as type $t_i \Rightarrow subType(ct) = \{1 \rightarrow t_i, ..., n \rightarrow t_n\}$*
$-$ *ct is set or sequence type with each element defined as type $t \Rightarrow subType(ct) = t$*
$-$ *ct is mapping type with domain defined as type t_i and range defined as t_j $\Rightarrow subType(ct) = (t_i, t_j)$*

Table 1. Solution table for type combination

Property of definition pair			Combination solution
	basic		human effort
	set/sequence		$sol(subType(d), subType(d'))$
	composite	$subType(d) \subset subType(d')$	$def = d'$
		$\overline{dom(subType(d)) = dom(subType(d'))}$ $\wedge \exists_{(f,t)\in subType(d),(f',t')\in subType(d')} \cdot$ $f = f' \wedge t \neq t'$	$\forall_{(f,t)\in subType(d)} \cdot$ $\exists_{(f,t')\in subType(d')} \cdot t \neq t'$ $\Rightarrow sol(t,t')$
$buildIn(d)$ $= buildIn(d')$		......	......
	product	$rng(subType(d)) \subset rng(subType(d'))$	$def = d'$
		......	......
	map	$\overline{dom(d) = dom(d') \wedge rng(d) \neq rng(d')}$	$sol(rng(d), rng(d'))$
		$dom(d) = rng(d') \wedge rng(d) = dom(d')$	human effort
		......	......
	$buildIn(d)$ and $buildIn(d')$ are basic types		human effort
$buildIn(d)$ $\neq buildIn(d')$	$buildIn(d) = composite\wedge$ $buildIn(d') = set$	$\exists_{(f,t)\in subType(d)} \cdot t = d'$	$def = d$
		......	......
	$buildIn(d) = composite\wedge$ $buildIn(d') = mapping$	$d = dom(d') \vee d = rng(d')$	$def = d'$
		......	......
	......	......	......

Based on the definition, we try to summarize possible properties of definition pairs and figure out the corresponding combination solutions. Table 1 (with formal notations in SOFL) shows part of the work where $buildIn(t)$ denotes the built-in type that type t belongs to and def indicates the result definition of the combination operation. For each pair of type definition d and d' where $d \neq d'$, a combination solution $sol(d, d')$ can be found by matching the definition pair against the properties listed in the table.

It can be seen from the table, properties of definition pair are classified into two categories: properties where d and d' belong to the same built-in type and properties where d and d' belong to different build-in types. The first category is further divided into five sub-categories that cover all the built-in types (in SOFL) and a solution is provided for each specific property within each built-in type. For example, the first "basic" denotes the property that d and d' belongs to the same basic type and its corresponding solution "human effort" indicates the combination of such kind of definition pair needs intelligent decision and the developer will be asked to give the operation result based on d and d'. More specific properties are provided with combination solutions if both d and d' are composite types. The second property within "composite" category and its corresponding solution mean that if d and d' owns the same fields and some of them are declared as different types, the combination method should be conducted on each pair of different types to achieve $sol(d, d')$. Within the second category, all combinations of different built-in types are considered and only parts of them are listed in the table for the sake of space. For instance, if d and d' are declared as different basic types, only human effort is able to figure out the proper definition. In case d is a composite type and d' is a set type, the combination result should be d if one of the fields in d is defined as d'.

Property-Guided Declaration. Figure 2 shows the main procedure of *property-guided declaration* for each selected pattern p within data context dc where cE

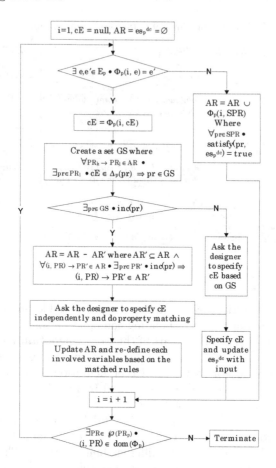

Fig. 2. The main procedure of the property-guided declaration

denotes the element currently being specified, AR denotes the set of activated rules and $inc(pr)$ denotes that the developer identifies the property pr as being inconsistent with the expected function.

Rules in Φ_p are applied sequentially according to their attached sequence numbers and when dealing with those who own the same number, the one with its required conditions satisfied will be activated. For each $i(0 < i \leq maximum$ $sequence\ number)$, if i corresponds to a set of property rules $R \subset \Phi_p$, the rule $(i, SPR) \to SPR' \in R$ will be identified where all the properties in SPR can be satisfied. Meanwhile, a set of new properties SPR' will be obtained and added to AR. If i corresponds to an element rule, cE will be set as $\Phi_p(i, cE)$ which is the next element waiting to be specified. To assist the value assignment to cE, activated rules that lead to properties of cE will be extracted from set AR and these properties form a property set GS. After confirming that all the properties in GS are consistent with the desired function, the developer needs to assign a value to cE based on GS. In case that certain properties in GS violate the expected function, the activated rules that lead to these properties form a set AR' and will be deleted from AR. Then the developer will be required to specify cE manually and property matching will be carried out to obtain the rules that match the given value.

In addition to the value v assigned to cE by the developer, set $CR : \mathcal{P}(\mathcal{P}(\Phi_p))$ serves as another critical participant in property matching which satisfies:

$$\forall_{R \in CR} \cdot (\forall_{(m,x),(n,y) \in dom(R)} \cdot m = n \wedge$$
$$\forall_{R' \in CS - \{R\}} \cdot \forall_{(k,x') \in R, (l,y' \in R')} \cdot k \neq l)$$
$$\wedge \forall_{(no,Pr) \in dom(AR')} \cdot \exists_{R \in CR} \cdot \forall_{(no',Pr') \in dom(\Phi_p)} \cdot$$
$$(no = no' \wedge \exists_{pr \in \Phi_p(no',Pr')} \cdot cE \in \Delta(pr))$$

Each set $R \in CR$ comprises all the candidate rules for substituting one of the rules that lead to properties violating the expected function. With the given v, dc will be updated accordingly and property matching can be by the following algorithm where RS denotes the set of rules that match the given v:

$$RS = temp = \{\};$$
$$for\ each\ R \in CR\{$$
$$\quad for\ each\ Pr \to Pr' \in R$$
$$\quad\quad if\ (satisfy_p^{dc}(Pr', es_p^{dc}) = true)$$
$$\quad\quad\quad temp = temp \cup \{Pr \to Pr'\};$$
$$\quad if\ (\mid temp \mid = 1)$$
$$\quad\quad for\ the\ only\ element\ sr\ \ RS = RS \cup \{sr\};$$
$$\quad else\{$$
$$\quad\quad tempP = \{\};$$
$$\quad\quad for\ each\ Spr \to Spr' \in temp$$
$$\quad\quad\quad tempP = tempP \cup \{Spr\};$$
$$\quad\quad display\ all\ the\ items\ in\ tempP\ and$$
$$\quad\quad ask\ the\ developer\ to\ choose$$
$$\quad\quad\quad the\ most\ appropriate\ one\ ``item;"$$
$$\quad\quad RS = RS \cup \{r\}\ where$$
$$\quad\quad\quad r \in temp \wedge \exists_{y \in \mathcal{P}(\Phi_p)} \cdot r = item \to y; \}\}$$
$$return\ RS;$$

This algorithm helps explore a set RS containing all the rules in $\mathcal{P}(\Phi_p)$ consistent with the function intended to be described which is reflected by the values assigned to elements. These rules will then be added into set AR and for each rule $Spr \to Spr'$, data context dc will be updated according to Spr.

Priority-Guided Declaration. The main idea of priority-guided declaration is to provide suggested definition of concerned types based on Ψ after assigning values to pattern elements. Rules in each Ψ are attached with priority attributes which help select a most appropriate one when elements are incompletely specified or no rule can be applied according to the specified elements.

Definition 7. *Given a pattern p, $PS_p : \mathcal{P}(\mathcal{P}(\ominus_p))$ is the priority set of p iff*

- $\forall_{ps_i \in PS_p} \cdot \exists_{es_p^{dc} \in es_p} \cdot condSatisfy_p^{dc}(es_p^{dc}) = ps_i$
- $\forall_{R \in \mathcal{P}(\ominus_p)} \cdot \exists_{es_p^{dc} \in es_p} \cdot condSatisfy_p^{dc}(es_p^{dc}) = R \Rightarrow$
  $R \in PS_p$

Definition 8. *Given a pattern p, $\tau_p : \ominus_p \times PS_p \to N^+$ determines the priority of each rule in $\ominus_p$ where $\tau_p(r, ps_i) = n$ means that $r \in \ominus_p$ is ranked as the nth rule in set ps_i.*

Based on the definition, priority-guided declaration is conducted as the following steps for each selected pattern p within formal specification context fsc.

1. Ask the developer to provide element information, and define types and variables when necessary, which results in an element state es_p^{fsc}.
2. Analyze priority set PS_p and extract the item $ps \in PS_p$ that satisfies $condSatisfy_p^{fsc}(es_p^{fsc}) = ps$.
3. Sort set ps into a sequence $psSeq$ where
   $\forall i, j : int \cdot 0 < i < j \leq | psSeq | \Rightarrow$
   $\quad \tau_p(psSeq(i), ps) > \tau_p(psSeq(j), ps)$
4. Set $rule = psSeq(k)$ where k is initialized as 1. Provide the properties involved in $rule$ for the developer to assist the declaration of relative types and variables.
5. If the suggestion is not accepted and $k \leq | psSeq |$, set $k = k + 1$ and repeat step 4-5. Otherwise terminate.

4.3   Expression Update

In contrast to the traditional formal specification construction method that requires formal expressions to be written manually, function patterns enables automatic generation of formal expressions based on the given values of necessary elements. Therefore, instead of grammar checking, the essential idea of expression update in our approach is to record the element values specified during the pattern application process and reuse that information to update the original formal expression. For an expression exp generated through the application process ap of the pattern p, if exp becomes erroneous under the refined data context, it will be replaced by a new expression generated by applying p again based on ap.

Definition 9. *Given a pattern p_0, sequence $(p_0, es_{dc_0}^{p_0}, exp_0, p_1, es_{dc_1}^{p_1}, exp_1, ...,$ $p_n, es_{dc_n}^{p_n}, exp_n)$ is the application process of p_0 where*

- $p_1, ..., p_n$ *are the reused patterns*
- *each $es_{dc_i}^{p_i}$ denotes the element state after all the elements in E_{p_i} are specified*
- *exp_0 denotes the intermediate formal result produced by applying p_0 with specified elements in $es_{dc_0}^{p_0}$, which can be represented as $exp_0 = p_0(es_{dc_0}^{p_0})$*

– each $exp_i(0 < i \leq n)$ denotes the intermediate formal result generated by replacing certain informal part in exp_{i-1} with $p_i(es^{p_i}_{fsc_i})$, which can be represented as $exp_i = exp_{i-1} \oplus p_i(es^{p_i}_{dc_i})$ where $exp_i = p_i(es^{p_i}_{dc_i})$ if $exp_{i-1} = \varnothing$
– exp_n is the resultant formal expression

Definition 10. *Given a data context dc, $vdept_{dc} : T_{dc} \rightarrow V_{dc}$ reveals dependent relations between types and variables where $vdept_{dc}(t) = V$ indicates that for each variable $v \in V$, the definition of $vt_{dc}(v)$ involves type t.*

Definition 11. *Given a data context dc and a pattern p, $sdept^p_{dc} : T_{fsc} \rightarrow \mathcal{P}(es^{dc}_p)$ reveals dependent relations between types and element values where*

$$sdept^p_{dc}(t) = Es^{dc}_p \Rightarrow$$

$$\forall_{e \rightarrow vl \in Es^{fsc}_p} \cdot (vl \in Exp^{dc}_p \wedge$$
$$\exists_{i \in N^+, v \in V_{dc}} \cdot (i, v) \in vl \wedge v \in vdept_{dc}(t)$$
$$\vee(vl \in Props_{dc} \wedge \exists_{v \in inVar(vl)} \cdot v \in vdept_{dc}(t))$$

Assume that the data context dc has been modified into dc', the update of each formal expressions exp previously written through application process $ap = (p_0, es^{p_0}_{dc_0}, exp_0, p_1, es^{p_1}_{dc_1}, exp_1, ..., p_n, es^{p_n}_{dc_n}, exp_n)$ is conducted as the following algorithm where $def_{dc}(t)$ denotes the definition of type t under dc.

$$if(\exists_{(i,v) \in exp} \cdot (vt_{dc}(v) \neq vt_{dc'}(v)) \vee$$
$$(\exists_{t \in T_{dc}} \cdot t \in T_{dc'} \wedge v \in vdept_{dc}(t) \wedge$$
$$v \in vdept_{dc'}(t) \wedge def_{dc}(t) \neq def_{dc'}(t))\{$$
$$exp_{-1} = \varnothing;$$
$$\text{for each } p_i \text{ in } ap\{$$
$$if(\exists_{t \in T_{dc}, e \rightarrow vl \in es^{p_i}_{dc}} \cdot t \in T_{dc'} \wedge$$
$$def_{dc}(t) \neq def_{dc'}(t) \wedge e \rightarrow vl \in vdept_{dc}(t))$$
$$exp'_i = exp'_{i-1} \oplus p_i(es^{p_i}_{dc'});$$
$$else$$
$$exp'_i = exp'_{i-1} \oplus temp \text{ where } exp_i = exp_{i-1} \oplus temp\}$$
$$exp = exp'_n;\}$$

The algorithm first checks whether there exist variables or types used in exp with definitions being modified. If so, the application of pattern p_0 will be restarted with element information $es^{p_0}_{dc}$ and further formalization will be conducted by applying the rest of the reused patterns in ap with their element information sequentially. Before generating formal expression for each pattern p_i, the value of each element indicated by $es^{p_i}_{dc}$ will be analyzed to determine its change caused by the update of the data context. Expression exp_i can be directly used to formalize the current formal result exp'_{i-1} if no difference is found between $es^{p_i}_{dc}$ and $es^{p_i}_{dc'}$. Otherwise, $p_i(es^{p_i}_{dc'})$ will be produced to replace the corresponding informal part of exp'_{i-1}.

5   Case Study

A case study on a banking system is presented to show the feasibility and effectiveness of the proposed approach in practice. The system allows for the management of various currency types and mainly provides four services for authorized customers: *deposit, withdraw, account information display* and *currency exchange*. Since architecture design is not discussed in this paper, we assume that it has already been done and the result is a CDFD shown in Fig. 3 where rectangles drawn with input and output ports are processes and other three are datastores. It can be seen from the figure, neither type definitions nor relation between the input and output of each process is provided in the CDFD, and it only specifies the interfaces of the included processes and demonstrates their relation with data flows represented as solid lines and control flows represented as dotted lines. For example, process *Id_confirm* owns one input port and two output ports, and when receiving data flow *inputInf*, it will be activated and generate data flow *inf* or *warning* when terminated. If *inf* is generated, it will reach process *Selection* which produces one of the four possible outputs according to the available control flow.

Based on the CDFD, necessary data types can be declared to meet the need of accurately describing the behavior of each enclosed process sequentially. Due to space limitation, we take process *Id_confirm* and *Withdraw* as examples. For the process *Id_confirm*, manual declaration is first required for defining its inputs and outputs. According to the expected behavior of the process, one can easily response with the following definitions:

$Num = string, Psd = string, Msg = string,$
$Inf = composed\ of$
$\quad\quad inf\_num : Num$
$\quad\quad inf\_psd : Psd$
$\quad\quad end$
$inputInf : Inf, warning : Msg, inf : Inf$

No pre-condition is needed in the process and the informal idea of the post-condition is that if the provided ID information can be found in the datastore *account_store*, data flow *inf* will be produced. Otherwise, error message *warning* will be displayed to the customer. Such idea leads us to the selection

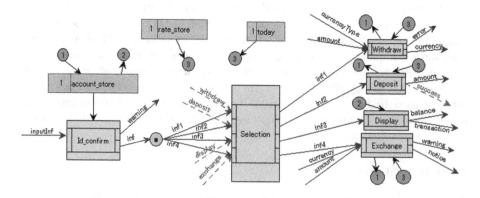

Fig. 3. The CDFD of the example banking system

Table 2. Pattern "belongTo"

id	belongTo
expl	A relation between 2 objects where one is part of another
E	$\{element, container : VV, specifier : null \mid PV\}$
PR	$\{dt(element) = T, dt(container) = set\ of\ T,$ $specifier = f_i, specifier = null, ...\}$
Ψ	$\{\{dt(element) = T, dt(container) = set\ of\ T\}$ $\xrightarrow{a}\ element\ inset\ container,$ $\{dt(element) = T, dt(container) = seq\ of\ T\}$ $\xrightarrow{b}\ element\ inset\ elems(container),$ $\{dt(element) = set\ of\ T, dt(container) = T \rightarrow T'\}$ $\xrightarrow{c}\ belongTo(elemetn, dom(container)),$ $\{dt(element) = set\ of\ T, dt(container) = composite$ $specifier = f_i\}\ \xrightarrow{d}\ element\ inset\ container.f_i,$ $\{dt(element) = T \rightarrow T', dt(container) = T \rightarrow T',$ $specifier = null\}\ \xrightarrow{e}\ element\ subset\ container,$ $\{dt(element) = seq\ of\ T, dt(container) = set\ of\ product,$ $specifier = null\}\ \xrightarrow{f}\ exists[e : container] \mid$ $forall[i : N^+] \mid element(i) = e(i), ...\}$

of pattern *belongTo* as shown in Table 2 where $dt(v)$ indicates the data type of the element e in E. It is used to describe a relation where one object is part of another. There are three elements in the pattern: *element* denoting the member object, *container* denoting object that *element* belongs to and *specifier* denoting constraints on their relations which can be assigned with either *null* or a property value. The application of pattern *belongTo* starts from the requirement of specifying these three elements. Apparently, *element* is *inputInf* and container is *account_store* which has not been defined. In case that *specifier* is not decided yet, the generation of an intermediate result begins and *priority-guided declaration* will be carried out according to the priority knowledge given in Table 3. Suppose the developer uses "*AccountFile*" to represent its type, priority set $ps_1(\cup)$ is then selected and rule a is first suggested which indicates that the type *AccountFile* should be defined as *set of Inf*. Assume that the suggestion is accepted, the formal expression for describing the "belongTo" relation is automatically generated and the post-condition of process *Id_confirm* will be written as:

$if\ (inputInf\ inset\ account\_store)$
$then\ inf = inputInf$
$else\ warning = \text{"Invalid user."}$

Table 3. Priority in pattern "belongTo"

Rule	Priority set				
	$ps_1(\cup)$	$ps_2(a,b,c,d)$	$ps_3(a,b,e)$	$ps_4(a,b,f)$	...
a	1	3	2	2	
b	2	4	3	3	
c	3	1	-	-	
d	4	2	-	-	
e	5	-	1	-	
f	6	-	-	1	
...					

Table 4. Pattern "alter"

id	alter
expl	To describe the altering of certain system variable
E	$\{obj : VV, decompose : Boolean,$ $specifier, onlyOne : Boolean, new\}$
PR	$\{the\ pattern\ is\ reused, dt(obj) = basic,$ $dt(obj) = set\ of\ composite(with\ each\ field\ as\ f_i),$ $dt(obj) = T \to T', decompose = false, ...\}$
Φ	$\{(1, null) \xrightarrow{a} obj, (2, \{dt(obj) = basic\}) \xrightarrow{b}$ $\{decompose = false\}, ..., (3, obj) \xrightarrow{c} decompose,$ $(4, \{dt(obj) = basic\}) \xrightarrow{d} \{specifier = null\},$ $(4, \{dt(obj) = set\ of\ composite(with\ each\ field\ as\ f_i)$ $, decompose = true\}) \xrightarrow{e} \{specifier : \mathcal{P}(\{f_i\})\},$ $(4, \{dt(obj) = T \to T', decompose = true\}) \xrightarrow{f}$ $\{specifier : (\{constraints(dom), constraints(rng),$ $constraints((dom, rng))\}, dom \mid rng),$ $..., (5, decompose) \to specifier, ...\}$
Ψ	$\{\{the\ pattern\ is\ not\ reused, dt(obj) = T \to T'$ $decompose = true, specifier = (dom = x, rng),$ $new = alter\} \to alter(obj(x)), ...\}$

Notice that no formal expression was written before the application of pattern *belongTo*, expression update is therefore not needed.

Since the data types and functions involved in the process *Selection* are simple enough to be manually written and the data context will not be affected after the description, data type declaration during the construction of process *Withdraw* is presented based on the type definitions declared for the process *Id_confirm*. Process *Withdraw* takes the intended currency type and amount as inputs and currency or error messages as outputs, which can be manually defined as:

$CurrencyType = string, Amount = real,$
$currencyType : CurrencyType, amount : Amount$
$currency : Amount, error : Msg$

The pre-condition is also true and the post-condition should clarify how the account information in *account_store* is altered when the withdraw operation is successfully done. Therefore, pattern *alter* will be selected to describe such function, which is shown in Table 4 where $constraints(x)$ denotes certain constraints on object x. It contains four elements for depicting the altering of system variables: *obj* denoting the object to be altered, decompose meaning to replace the whole given *obj* by a new value if it is designated as true and to modify parts of the given *obj* if it is designated as false, *specifier* denoting the description of the parts to be altered within *obj*, *onlyOne* meaning there exists only one part consistent with the description in *specifier* if it is designated as true and new indicates the new values for replacing the corresponding parts to be altered. Figure 4 reveals the property-guided declaration process during the application of the pattern.

The above application process results in an definition "$Inf \rightarrow AccountInf$" for type $AccountFile$ that is more appropriate for describing process $Withdraw$.

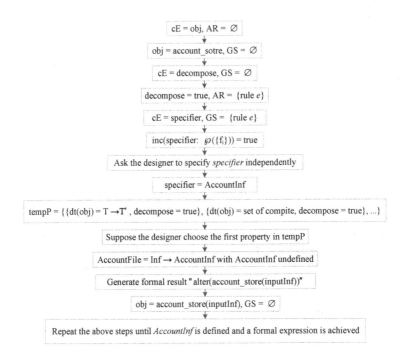

Fig. 4. The priority-guided declaration process during the application of the pattern "alter"

Thus, the original definition *set of Inf* needs to be refined by applying the combination method. According to the solution table for type combination, the definition of type *AccountFile* should be refined as: $Inf \rightarrow AccountInf$.

Due to the refinement of the definition of type *AccountFile* and the use of the type in the post-condition of process *Id_confirm*, formal expression previously generated by applying the pattern *belongTo* needs to be updated accordingly. The application process of the pattern *belongTo* for the post-condition of process *Id_confirm* can be described as:

$$(belongTo, \{element \rightarrow inputInf,$$
$$container \rightarrow account\_store,$$
$$specifier = null\},$$
$$\text{``}inputInf\ inset\ account\_store\text{''})$$

According to the algorithm for expression update, formal expression "*inputInf inset account_store*" will be transformed into:

$$belongTo(\{element \rightarrow inputInf,$$
$$container \rightarrow account\_store,$$
$$specifier = dom\}, newExp)$$

where *account_store* is defined as a map type and element *specifier* is modified into "*dom*" in the refined data context. By analyzing the above expression in the context of the Ψ of the pattern *belongTo*, formal expression "*inputInf inset dom(account_store)*" will be generated as the value of *newExp* to replace the original one.

Following the similar procedures for describing process *Withdraw*, the data context can be gradually refined while the pre- and post-conditions of the rest processes *Deposit*, *Display* and *Exchange* are specified. After completing the description of the last process *Exchange*, a set of appropriate data types for the example banking system is established.

6   Conclusion

This paper proposes an approach to assist the declaration of data types for formal specifications along with the function description in formal expressions. After the architecture of the formal specification is determined, the approach helps adjust the type definitions to fit the expected functions captured and formally described by applying function patterns. Besides, as the data types are refined, their consistency with the written formal expressions will be maintained by applying the involved patterns again based on their history application information.

In order to investigate the performance of the approach when being applied to more complicated systems, an empirical case study is intended to be held in the future. For example, as complexity rises, the update of expressions in accordance with specification context will be more difficult and less likely to be automatically done.

Furthermore, only tool implementation could bring the proposed approach into practice and allow practitioners to benefit from the assistance expected to be provided, which is also part of our future work.

Acknowledgement. This work has been conducted as a part of "Research Initiative on Advanced Software Engineering in 2012" supported by Software Reliability Enhancement Center (SEC), Information Technology Promotion Agency Japan (IPA).

References

1. Gorm, L.P., Nick, B., Miguel, F., John, F., Kenneth, L., Marcel, V.: The overture initiative integrating tools for vdm. SIGSOFT Softw. Eng. Notes **35**(1), 1–6 (2010)
2. Chen, J., Durnota, B.: Type checking classes in object-z to promote quality of specifications (1994)
3. Vadera, S., Meziane, F.: From English to formal specifications. Comput. J. **37**(9), 753–763 (1994)
4. Wang, X., Liu, S., Miao, H.: A pattern system to support refining informal ideas into formal expressions. In: Dong, J.S., Zhu, H. (eds.) ICFEM 2010. LNCS, vol. 6447, pp. 662–677. Springer, Heidelberg (2010)
5. Liu, S.: Formal Engineering for Industrial Software Development. Springer, Heidelberg (2004)
6. Liu, S., Offutt, A., Ho-Stuart, C., Sun, Y., Ohba, M.: Sofl: a formal engineering methodology for industrial applications. IEEE Trans. Softw. Eng. **24**(1), 24–45 (1998)
7. http://spivey.oriel.ox.ac.uk/mike/fuzz/
8. John, F., Gorm, L.P., Shin, S.: Vdmtools: advances in support for formal modeling in vdm. SIGPLAN Not. **43**(2), 3–11 (2008)
9. Abrial, J.R.: Modelling in Event-B: System and Software Design. Cambridge University Press, Cambridge (2010)
10. Abrial, J.R., Butler, M., Hallerstede, S., Hoang, T., Mehta, F., Voisin, L.: Rodin: an open toolset for modelling and reasoning in event-b. Int. J. Softw. Tools Technol. Transf. (STTT) **12**, 447–466 (2010). doi:10.1007/s10009-010-0145-y. http://dx.doi.org/10.1007/s10009-010-0145-y (Online)
11. Owre, S., Shankar, N.: A brief overview of PVS. In: Ait Mohamed, O., Muñoz, C., Tahar, S. (eds.) TPHOLs 2008. LNCS, vol. 5170, pp. 22–27. Springer, Heidelberg (2008)
12. Rushby, J., Owre, S., Shankar, N.: Subtypes for specifications: predicate subtyping in pvs. IEEE Trans. Softw. Eng. **24**(9), 709–720 (1998)
13. Tan, X., Wang, Y., Ngolah, C.: A novel type checker for software system specifications in rtpa. In: Canadian Conference on Electrical and Computer Engineering, vol. 3, May 2004, pp. 1549–1552 (2004)
14. Xavier, M., Cavalcanti, A., Sampaio, A.: Type checking circus specifications. Electr. Notes Theor. Comput. Sci. **195**, 75–93 (2008). http://dx.doi.org/10.1016/j.entcs.2007.08.027 (Online)
15. Snook, C., Butler, M.: Uml-b: Formal modeling and design aided by uml. ACM Trans. Softw. Eng. Methodol. **15**(1), 92–122 (2006). http://doi.acm.org/10.1145/1125808.1125811 (Online)
16. Anastasakis, K., Bordbar, B., Georg, G., Ray, I.: UML2Alloy: a challenging model transformation. In: Engels, G., Opdyke, B., Schmidt, D.C., Weil, F. (eds.) MODELS 2007. LNCS, vol. 4735, pp. 436–450. Springer, Heidelberg (2007)

Detection Method of the Second-Order SQL Injection in Web Applications

Lu Yan, Xiaohong Li, Ruitao Feng, Zhiyong Feng, and Jing Hu$^{(\boxtimes)}$

Tianjin Key Laboratory of Cognitive Computer and Application,
School of Computer Science and Technology, Tianjin University, Tianjin, China
{luyan,xiaohongli,rtfeng,zyfeng,mavis_huhu}@tju.edu.cn

Abstract. Web applications are threatened seriously by SQL injection attacks. Even though a number of methods and tools have been put forward to detect or prevent SQL injections, there is a lack of effective method for detecting second-order SQL injection which stores user inputs into the back-end database. This paper proposes a detecting solution that combines both static and dynamic methods for second-order SQL injection. This solution first analyzes source code to find out the vulnerable data item pair which probably has second-order SQL injection vulnerability and then transforms it into an effective test sequence. After that, test sequence and malicious inputs are combined together for testing. Assessment of this solution in four applications and practical use show its effectiveness in the detection of second-order SQL injection.

Keywords: Second-order SQL injection · Static analysis · Dynamic testing · Web application

1 Introduction

Nowadays, a large number of data-driven web applications have been developed to provide a variety of services, and thereupon SQL injection vulnerability has become a serious security threat to such web applications [1, 2]. As one kind of SQL injections, the second-order SQL injection is just as harmful as the first-order equivalent, which allows the attacker to access to the back-end database and steal confidential data. However, it is subtler and more difficult to be detected [4] since the malicious input, as injected into a web application, is stored in the back-end database rather than executed immediately [3]. When another request is under processing, the malicious input is introduced to build SQL statement dynamically, which will change the semantics of the original SQL statement and achieve attacks.

Currently, there are generally three types of methods to detect SQL injection vulnerabilities which are static analysis, dynamic testing and run-time monitoring. However, these methods mainly focus on the first-order SQL injection attack and only few of them support the second-order SQL injection detection.

In the static analysis, literatures [5, 6] utilize static taint analysis method and detect vulnerabilities by tracking the flow of untrusted values through a program and checking whether these values flow into sensitive sinks. They regard user inputs as untrusted but ignore the credibility of data extracted from the database, so they have

S. Liu and Z. Duan (Eds.): SOFL+MSVL 2013, LNCS 8332, pp. 154–165, 2014.
DOI: 10.1007/978-3-319-04915-1_11, © Springer International Publishing Switzerland 2014

trouble achieving the second-order SQL injection detection. Pietraszek and Berghe [7] discover vulnerabilities by adding metadata to user inputs so as to distinguish between the user input and application's source code and finally perform checks on the parts of user inputs. However, there is still some uncertainty and mistakes caused by considering all data retrieving from database as untrusted which expands the scope of untrusted data. Literatures [8, 14] have the same problem as well. Besides these problems, misinformation may be introduced because static analysis methods do not create an actual attack instance to determine vulnerabilities.

For the dynamic testing methods, Halfond et al. [9] define the testing for vulnerabilities into three phases: information gathering, attack generation and response analysis. Testers identify the possible points by using web crawling or social engineering, and then according to the attack pattern library, test cases are generated on these points. Finally testers analyze the application's responses to determine whether the attacks succeed. Most vulnerability scanning tools using the above method are able to discover the first-order SQL injection, but fail to identify the second-order SQL injection [10–12]. To discover the second-order SQL injection, currently, it depends on testers' experience about the possible points where the malicious input is possibly stored and then used to build SQL statement [4]. However, with the increase of the code size and the functionality, manual testing depending on testers' experience to generate test cases cannot guarantee results.

As to the runtime monitoring approach, Halfond and Orso [13] model the SQL queries contained in the application's code as legitimate queries and then at runtime check dynamically-generated queries which add user inputs against legitimate queries. Queries that violate the legitimate one exist SQL vulnerabilities and are prevented. This method can detect a second-order SQL injection attack, but the accuracy of modeling the SQL query determines the accuracy of the method. Moreover, runtime overhead is inevitable. In literature [14], a monitor embedding framework DESERVE is proposed which identifies exploitable statements from source code based on static slicing technique and embeds monitor code for those statements. Then the enhanced programs execute the exploitable statements in a separate test environment. However, this method suffers from some uncertainty caused by taking the change in the numbers of fetched, changed rows and objects in database as a sign of judging attacks, which may not change in an attack. DESERVE also assumes that all data from database are dangerous which will be improved in their future work [14]. In addition, DESERVE introduces delay for each exploitable statement and needs to increase 2.1 %–8.5 % code.

Second-order SQL injections are prevalent (and will continue to be) and existing methods and tools do not perform well [10]. To the author's knowledge, it still lacks effective detection method for the second-order SQL injection. Therefore, in this paper we put forward a systematic method to achieve the detection of the second-order SQL injection vulnerability. In the static analysis phase, the source code is analyzed and the storing process and triggering process which may brings in the second-order SQL injection vulnerability can be found out. Storing process stores the user input into database, while triggering process means retrieving input value from the database and building a SQL statement. In the dynamic testing phase, malicious input is submitted in the storing process and the existence of vulnerability can be determined by observing the system response after calling the triggering process.

Paper arrangement is as follows. Section 2 illustrates the principle of the second-order SQL injection. Section 3 gives the formal definition of data item, the recognition criterion and test sequence in the detection method. Section 4 presents the second-order SQL injection detection method. Section 5 shows the experiment results and analysis. At last is the conclusion.

2   Second-Order SQL Injection Principle

Figure 1 shows a classic example [15] which illustrates the process of the second-order SQL injection. In a website where an "admin" account exists, the attacker registers another account "admin'--". Here is the code:

```
String name = escape(request.getParameter(''Name''));
String pwd = escape(request.getParameter(''Pwd1''));
String sql1 = ''insert into user(username, password)
values('''+name+''','''+pwd+''')'';
result = stm.executeUpdate(sql1);
```

The application properly escapes the single quote in the input before storing, which causes the single quote to be treated as string literal rather than string termi-nator. By using escaping, it will be stored as "admin'--" in the database but not cause string termination issues when building the statement. When the attacker wants to update the password of account "admin'--", the system will first confirm the validity of the origin password. The code might look like this:

```
String name = escape(request.getParameter(''Name''));
String oldpwd = escape(request.getParameter(''oldpwd''));
String newpwd = escape(request.getParameter(''newpwd''));
String sql2 = ''select * from user where
username ='''+name+''' and password ='''+oldpwd+''''';
result = stm.executeQuery(sql2);
```

After the validity confirmation, the stored username "admin'--" is retrieved from database and a new SQL statement is built up by following code:

```
String sql3 = ''update user set password = '''+newpwd+'''
where username = '''+result.getString(''username'')+''''';
result = stm.executeQuery(sql3);
```

The statement executed by database is as follows:

```
update user set password = '1' where username = 'admin'--'
```

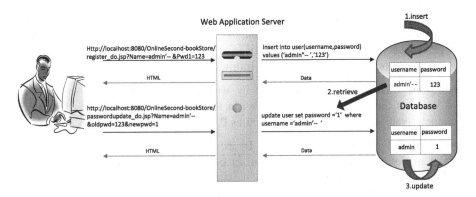

Fig. 1. An instance of the second-order SQL injection

As double-dash is the standard form of the SQL single-line comment, which means that we never even execute code after "--", the actual query is *update user set password = '1' where username = 'admin'*. The password of "admin" rather than "admin'--" is changed and thus attack is achieved.

3   Formal Definitions in Detection Method

The implementation of the second-order SQL injection attack contains two processes, storing process and triggering process. Storing process is to store user input into a field in database table and triggering process is to retrieve the stored field and concatenate it into a dynamic SQL statement. Therefore, the two processes can be linked through the retrieved field. In order to find the interrelated two processes in which the second-order SQL injection vulnerability may exist, we define the data item and recognition criterion in the detection method as follows:

Definition 1. Categorical Attribute θ is a 2-tuple $<p, q>$. The symbol p represents the source of value provided to column in the SQL statement and $p \in \{$input, db$\}$. "Input" represents that the value derives from user input and "db" means that the value is retrieved from the database. The symbol q denotes whether that column is in the "where" clause of SQL statement and $q \in \{$true, false$\}$.

Definition 2. Data Item d is a 3-tuple $<Y, y, \theta>$ where Y represents the name of the SQL statement operating field, namely column name, y denotes the original parameter that provides value concatenated to Y and θ is the categorical attribute in Definition 1. Mark the set of data item d as $\mathbf{D}$. If $d.\theta = <$input, false$>$, d is called the input data item and the set is marked as $\mathbf{D_i}$. If $d.\theta = <$db, false$>$ or $<$db, true$>$, d is called the database data item and the set is marked as $\mathbf{D_b}$. If $d.\theta = <$input, true$>$, d is called other data item and the set is marked as $\mathbf{D_o}$. It can be derived that $\mathbf{D} = \mathbf{D_i} \cup \mathbf{D_b} \cup \mathbf{D_o}$ and $\mathbf{D_i} \cap \mathbf{D_b} = \Phi$, $\mathbf{D_b} \cap \mathbf{D_o} = \Phi$, $\mathbf{D_o} \cap \mathbf{D_i} = \Phi$.

Recognition Criterion. We refer to the data item pair $<d_1, d_2>$ as a vulnerable one only if $d_1 \in \mathbf{D_i}$, $d_2 \in \mathbf{D_b}$ and $d_1.Y = d_2.y$. The vulnerable data item pairs denote those that probably have the second-order SQL injection vulnerabilities.

In addition, in order that dynamic testing can be carried out automatically by sending the HTTP requests, the vulnerable data item pair needs to be transformed into HTTP requests which trigger the execution of SQL statements. So we define HTTP request, functions and test sequence as follows:

Definition 3. The HTTP request sent by web application $\eta = \{<m, n> \mid m \in \mathbf{P},$ $n \in \mathbf{V}\}$. $\mathbf{P}$ is the set of parameter names in the HTTP request and $\mathbf{V}$ is the set of parameter values. The set of η is marked as $\mathbf{\Gamma}$.

Definition 4. Function $f_1 : \mathbf{D} \rightarrow \mathbf{S}$, $\forall d \in \mathbf{D}$, $\exists s = f_1(d) \in \mathbf{S}$. $\mathbf{D}$ is the set of data items shown in Definition 2, $\mathbf{S}$ represents the set of SQL statements in the source code, $f_1(d)$ means that data item d builds SQL statement s. Function f_2: $\mathbf{S} \rightarrow \mathbf{\Gamma}$, $\forall s \in \mathbf{S}$, $\exists r = f_2(s) \in \mathbf{\Gamma}$, $f_2(s)$ means that the statement s is triggered by HTTP request r. Therefore, function $f = f_1 f_2$ denotes the mapping of data item to the HTTP request.

Definition 5. Test sequence $<r_1, r_2>$, where $r_1 = f(d_1)$, $r_2 = f(d_2)$. It is an ordered pair of HTTP requests sent to test the second-order injection.

4 Detection Method of the Second-Order SQL Injection

The second-order SQL injection detecting method combines both static and dynamic methods. In the static analysis phase, the source code is analyzed and the vulnerable data item pair can be found out. In the dynamic testing phase, the test sequence and the test input are generated and incorporated together and then tests are carried out. The flow chart of the method is shown in Fig. 2.

4.1 Determine the Vulnerable Data Item Pair

With the aim of finding out the vulnerable data item pair, firstly the source code of application is scanned and SQL statements (including select, insert, update, delete) along with the operated fields (the column name in the SQL statement) are extracted using regular expressions to match.

Secondly, the data item for each field extracted before is built. According to Definition 2, Y is the extracted column name. Then the static backward slicing technology [16] is introduced to track the value concatenated to field Y in the SQL statement. The method computes the slice of the execution of the extracted SQL statement, C(s, V) where s is the line of code executing SQL statement and V initially is the string variable containing the SQL statement. If a function related to user input is contained in the slice and it affects the value of the variable concatenated to a specific column in the computed SQL statement, the value of data item can be determined from user input ($\theta.p = $ input) and the parameter name in the function is assigned to y. On the other hand, if the functions are related to database processing and execute "select" SQL statement instead of processing user input, the value of data item can be determined from the database ($\theta.p = $ db) and the retrieved field name is assigned to y. Table 1 lists the functions related to user input and database. Afterwards, the method fills $\theta.q$ with true or false according to whether Y exits in "where" clause in SQL statement and then classifies the data item as $\mathbf{D}_i$, $\mathbf{D}_b$ or $\mathbf{D}_o$ based on θ in Definition 2.

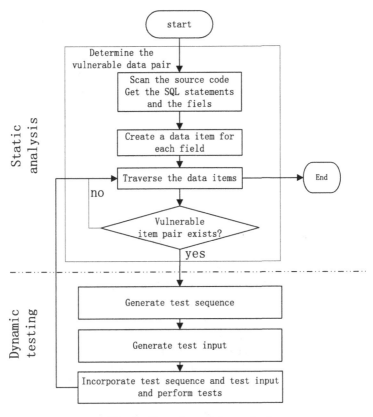

Fig. 2. Flow chart of the method

Table 1. Related functions to determine the source of the value

Programming language	Functions related to user input	Functions related to database
Java	getParameter ()	executeQuery()
	getParameterValues ()	executeUpdate()
	getQueryString ()	execute()
		executeBatch()
PHP	$_GET	mysql_query()
	$HTTP_GET_VARS	mysql_db_query()
	$_POST	mysql_unbuffered_query
	$HTTP_POST_VARS	odbc_execute()
	$_REQUEST	odbc_exec()

Thirdly, the data items in set $\mathbf{D_b}$ are traversed. For a specific database data item d_2, if there is an input data item d_1, which meets the recognition criterion $d_1.Y = d_2.y$, the ordered pair $<d_1, d_2>$ can be regarded as a vulnerable data item pair which probably has the second-order SQL injection vulnerability.

The instance shown in Sect. 2 is analyzed and the vulnerable data item pair is demonstrated in Fig. 3 to clarify these definitions and the detection method. Table 2

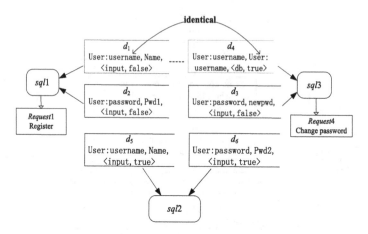

Fig. 3. The vulnerable data item pair in the instance

Table 2. Meaning of symbols in Fig. 3

symbol	meaning
request	HTTP request
sql	SQL statement
d	Data item in SQL statement
sql ← d	Data item constitutes SQL statement
d_1 ----- d_2	Vulnerable data item pair $<d_1,d_2>$, red means input data item, green means database data item
request ← sql	SQL statement is triggered by HTTP request

shows the meaning of symbols in Fig. 3. Through scanning the source code of the application, three SQL statements and their fields are got. In the SQL statement $sql1$ there are two data items d_1 and d_2. The first operating field is "username" column in the "user" table, which means $d_1.Y$ = user:username. Since the slice $C(stm.excu$-$teUpdate(sql1), sql1)$ contains function processing user input $getParameter$ ("Name") and the function affects the value of variable "name" concatenated to $d_1.Y$, the value of data item d_1 is from user input and the parameter "Name" in the function is recorded as $d_1.y$ = Name. As the value is from user input and the field is not in the "where" clause, $d_1.\theta$ = <input, false> and thus d_1 is an input data item.

As to the statement $sql3$ which contains data items d_3 and d_4, the operating field $d_4.Y$ = user:username. Since the function $executeQuery(sql2)$ in the slice is related to database, executes "select" statement and affects the value concatenated to $d_4.Y$, the value of data item d_4 is from database and the retrieved column name of the table is record, namely $d_4.y$ = user:username. As the value is from database, d_4 is a database data item. The other data items d_2, d_3, d_5, d_6 can be obtained in the same way.

Since $d_1.Y = d_4.y$ and $d_1 \in \mathbf{D}_i$, $d_4 \in \mathbf{D}_b$ which meet the recognition criterion, $<d_1, d_4>$ is a vulnerable data item pair.

4.2   Generation of Test Sequence

In order to get the mapping relationship between the SQL statements and the HTTP requests, namely function f_2 in Definition 4, we employ HTTP proxy and SQL proxy to catch the HTTP request and the triggered SQL statement separately in the normal use of the web application. As a result, each HTTP request and the SQL statement that is triggered by it can be got and also the function f_2. And according to scanned result in the start of Sect. 4.1, we can know which SQL statement the data item belongs to and thus get function f_1 in Definition 4. Then according to the Definition 5, the vulnerable data item pair $<d_1, d_2>$ is transformed into the corresponding test sequence $<r_1, r_2>$.

4.3   Generation of Test Input

The principle of triggering the second-order injection is that parts of the malicious input is interpreted into the code and changes the semantics of the original SQL statement. Since it is the same as the first-order injection, the malicious inputs of first-order SQL injection also apply to the second-order. So we refer to the classification and formal description of the first-order SQL injection in literatures [17] and [18] to constitute malicious data set. The test input data is constituted by legitimate data set which contains the data in HTTP requests recorded by HTTP proxy and malicious data set which contains some instances of the formal description.

4.4   Perform Tests

When incorporating malicious input with the test sequence, the first request in test sequence is searched to find the parameter which has the same name as $d1.y$ The value of this parameter is replaced with the data from the malicious data set. The other parameters use the data from the legitimate data set, which are not changed.

The test cases are executed through sending HTTP requests in the order of the test sequence. If the storing process fails when sending the first request, the second one will not be sent and the next test sequence is put into testing. If the malicious input is successfully stored in the database, the second request is sent and the existence of vulnerability can be determined through the second response.

5   Test Results and Analysis

5.1   Test Subjects

In order to verify the feasibility and effectiveness of the second-order SQL injection detection methods proposed in this paper, we evaluated the method on four web application that reflect in functions and structures the typical characteristics of the current web applications. Two of them, SchoolMate-1.5.4 and WebChess-1.0.0, downloaded from http://sourceforge.net use PHP as the programming language and

Table 3. Test result

Program	The method in this paper			Pixy	Appscan
	Number of vulnerable data item pairs	Number of pairs that finally find vulnerabilities	Number of second-order SQL injection vulnerabilities	Number of second-order SQL injection vulnerabilities	Number of second-order SQL injection vulnerabilities
SchoolMate	5	1	1	0	0
WebChess	7	0	0	0	0
SecondhandBookstore	3	1	1	0	0
HotelManageSystem	5	2	2	0	0

MySQL as the back-end database. SchoolMate is a web application for managing school's classes and information and WebChess is an online game for playing chess with other users. The others, SecondhandBookstore and HotelManageSystem, developed by different teams of students as a project of class, use Java as the programming language and MySQL as the back-end database. SecondhandBookstore is an online second-hand bookstore where users can sell and buy second-hand books and HotelManageSystem is a web application for booking rooms online.

5.2 Results and Analysis

The test result is shown in Table 3. Through static analysis, 20 vulnerable data item pairs are found and then through dynamic testing, 4 of them are confirmed having second-order SQL injection. Static analysis tool Pixy [6] and dynamic testing tool Appscan8.0 [19] are also used to scan these web applications, but no problems about the second-order SQL injection are found.

The vulnerabilities found in the applications are shown in Table 4. In SchoolMate, the method found the second-order injection vulnerability in header.php. The code of it is shown below and some unimportant code is omitted for brevity.

```
$query = mysql_query(''select schoolname from schoolinfo'');
$schoolname = mysql_result($query,0);
...
$query = mysql_query(''UPDATE schoolinfo SET schoolname =
\''''.htmlspecialchars($_POST[''schoolname'']).''\'',...where
schoolname = '$schoolname' LIMIT 1 '');
```

The application updates the value of *schoolname* in table *schoolinfo* with user input and also uses the retrieved value of *schoolname* to build SQL statement dynamically. So through static analysis, the vulnerable data item pair is $<d_1, d_{12}>$ where d_1 is <schoolinfo:schoolname, schoolname, <input, false>> and d_{12} is <schoolinfo: schoolname, schoolinfo:schoolname, <db, true>>.

Table 4. Vulnerabilities found in applications

Program	Pair number	Vulnerable data item pair	Test sequence	Parameter assigned by malicious input	Number of test cases	Number of test cases that exposed vulnerabilities
SchoolMate	1	$<d_1, d_{12}>$	$<r_1, r_1>$	schoolname	10	4
SecondhandBookstore	2	$<p_7, p_8>$	$<q_5, q_6>$	author	10	2
HotelManageSystem	3	$<m_1, m_5>$	$<n_1, n_4>$	Name	10	5
	4	$<m_3, m_5>$	$<n_2, n_4>$	Name	10	5

Since $r_1 = f(d_1)$, $r_1 = f(d_{12})$, $<d_1, d_{12}>$ is transformed into test sequence $<r_1, r_1>$. The storing process and the triggering process use the same request r_1, but r_1 is sent twice with different inputs. We take one pair of generated malicious inputs for analysis. The value of parameter *schoolname* in the first r_1 is replaced with "tju' or $1 = 1$--" and sent. After that, the second r_1 that retains the original input "nku" in the legitimate set is sent. We got the second response that *schoolname* is updated successfully to "nuk". In order to compare the response, we repeat the process with another malicious input "tju' or $1 = 2$--" and the response is that *schoolname* is not updated to "nuk". Due to the difference between two responses of the second r_1, we determine the existence of the vulnerability. The vulnerable pair 2 in Secondhand-Bookstore is similar to SchoolMate.

For the HotelManageSystem, although most of the SQL statements use parameterized statements to avoid injections, the second-order SQL injection still exists. Because the application only use parameterized statements for SQL statements that obviously accept user input and use concatenated string for ones not. Consequently, the malicious input is successfully stored into the database by using parameterized statements and then the malicious input is retrieved to dynamically build a SQL statement which causes injection.

Test results verify that the proposed method which combines static analysis and dynamic testing is an effective method for detecting second-order SQL injection vulnerabilities in the web applications.

Compared with the previous static method, this method analyzes not only the user input but also the data out of the database. Moreover, by using recognition criterion, this paper can find the vulnerable data item pair, which tracks the flow of user input through the database. At the same time, this method generates concrete attack instances to determine the existence, which is more convincing.

Compared with the previous dynamic method in which vulnerability scanners fail to detect any second-order SQL injection, the proposed method takes advantages of system's internal information and can associate the storing and triggering processes, thus identifying existing vulnerabilities. Compared to manual testing, this method does not rely on the experience of test personnel and is able to recognize the functionality of the program that needs to check, which effectively improves the efficiency of testing.

Besides, our method does not produce additional load and does not need to modify the source code in contrast to the run-time monitoring method.

6   Conclusion

Based on the deep analysis of the second-order injection principle, a detection method to discover second-order SQL injection vulnerability is proposed and experimentally demonstrated in this paper. The method combines the advantages of static analysis and dynamic testing which reduces the false warnings and makes up the lack of inter information respectively. The static part analyzes not only the user input stored into database but also the data out of the database. More importantly, by using recognition criteria to interrelate two parts above, the method successfully tracks the data through the database and identifies the vulnerable pair. The dynamic part sends HTTP requests transformed from the vulnerable pair to further verify the existence of the vulnerabilities. Further work will focus on developing automated tools for our method and applying the tools to more open source web applications to analyze the accuracy.

Acknowledgement. This work is funded by the National Natural Science Foundation of China (No. 91118003, 61272106, 61003080) and 985 funds of Tianjin University.

References

1. 2011 CWE/SANS Top 25 Most Dangerous Software Errors. http://cwe.mitre.org/top25/index.html
2. OWASP TOP 10 – 2013: The ten most critical web application security risks. https://www.owasp.org/index.php/Top_10#OWASP_Top_10_for_2013
3. Ollmann, G.: Second-order code injection attacks. Technical report. NGSSoftware Insight Security Research (2004)
4. Justin, C.: SQL Injection Attacks and Defense. Syngress Publishing Inc., Boston (2009)
5. Livshits, V.B., Lam M.S.: Finding security vulnerabilities in Java applications with static analysis. In: Proceedings of the 14th USENIX Security Symposium, pp. 271–286 (2005)
6. Jovanovic, N., Kruegel, C., Kirda, E.: Pixy: a static analysis tool for detecting web application vulnerabilities. In: 2006 IEEE Symposium on Security and Privacy, pp. 258–263 (2006)
7. Pietraszek, T., Berghe, C.V.: Defending against injection attacks through context-sensitive string evaluation. In: Valdes, A., Zamboni, D. (eds.) RAID 2005. LNCS, vol. 3858, pp. 124–145. Springer, Heidelberg (2006)
8. Wassermann, G., Su, Z.: Sound and precise analysis of web application for injection vulnerabilities. ACM SIGPLAN Not. **42**(6), 32–41 (2007)
9. Halfond, W.G.J., Choudhary, S.R., Orso, A.: Improving penetration testing through static and dynamic analysis. Softw. Test. Verif. Reliab. **21**(3), 195–241 (2011)
10. Bau, J., Bursztein, E., Gupta, D., Mitchell, J.: State of the art: automated black-box web application vulnerability testing, In: 2010 IEEE Symposium on Security and Privacy, pp. 332–345 (2010)
11. Doupé, A., Cova, M., Vigna, G.: Why Johnny can't pentest: an analysis of black-box web vulnerability scanners. In: Detection of Intrusions and Malware, and Vulnerability Assessment - 7th International Conference, pp. 111–131 (2010)
12. Khoury, N., Zavarsky, P., Lindskog, D., Ruhl, R.: Testing and assessing web vulnerability scanners for persistent SQL injection attacks. In: Proceedings of the 1st International Workshop on Security and Privacy in e-Societies, pp. 12–18 (2011)

13. Halfond, W.G.J., Orso, A.: AMNESIA: analysis and monitoring for NEutralizing SQL-injection attacks. In: 20th IEEE/ACM International Conference on Automated Software Engineering, pp. 174–183 (2005)

14. Mohosina, A., Zulkernine, M.: DESERVE: a framework for detecting program security vulnerability exploitations. In: Proceedings of the 2012 IEEE Sixth International Conference on Software Security and Reliability, pp. 98–107 (2012)

15. Anley, C.: Advanced SQL injection in SQL server applications. An NGSSoftware Insight Security Research (2002)

16. Horwitz, S., Reps, T., Binkley, D.: Interprocedural slicing using dependence graphs. ACM Trans. Program. Lang. Syst. **12**(1), 26–60 (1990)

17. Tian, W., Yang, J.F., Xu J., Si G.N.: Attack model based penetration test for SQL injection vulnerability. In: Proceedings of the 2012 IEEE 36th IEEE Annual Computer Software and Applications Conference Workshops, pp. 589–594 (2012)

18. Wang, J., Phan, R.C.W., Whitley, J.N., Parish, D.J.: Augmented attack tree modeling of SQL injection attacks. In: ICIME 2010 - 2010 2nd IEEE International Conference on Information Management and Engineering, pp. 182–186 (2010)

19. IBM Rational AppScan. http://www-01.ibm.com/software/awdtools/appscan

Applying SOFL to Constructing a Smart Traffic Light Specification

Wahyu Eko Sulistiono[1]([⊠]) and Shaoying Liu[2]

[1] Graduate School of Computer and Information Sciences,
Hosei University, Tokyo, Japan
sulistiono.eko.wahyu.7x@stu.hosei.ac.jp
[2] Department of Computer and Information Sciences,
Hosei University, Tokyo, Japan
sliu@hosei.ac.jp

Abstract. Smart Traffic Light (STL) is a system for controlling traffic lights based on patterns of traffic loads in related intersection. Since this is a safety-critical system, we need to construct an accurate specification to build a firm foundation for implementation of the system. In this paper, we describe how the SOFL formal engineering method is applied to construct a Smart Traffic Light specification through the three-step modeling approach of SOFL that helps us manage the complexity and difficulty of constructing a formal specification.

Keywords: Formal specifications · SOFL · Smart traffic light

1 Introduction

Traffic lights have been used widely to control the traffic in junctions in order to avoid collision and congestion. Collision could be avoided by applying safe signal timing to traffic lights, such as minimum yellow signal duration, while congestion could be managed by determining signal timing that corresponds to traffic loads of the junctions.

Currently, many traffic lights are based on fixed signal timing, which works well if the number of vehicles flowing at each direction does not vary significantly throughout the day. However, in many junctions, such as ones near business district or school, the traffic loads at some directions may change significantly at certain hours. To achieve smooth-flowing traffic, these junctions require traffic lights that could change their signal timing. In this paper, we specify a system called Smart Traffic Light (STL) that uses patterns of traffic loads for determining optimal signal timing.

Since STL is safety-critical system and formal methods are considered capable of delivering accurate specification of such system, we use SOFL, one of the formal methods, to construct this system specification. Compared to other formal methods, SOFL offers benefit: SOFL employs an evolutionary approach in constructing a specification, which helps developers deal with difficulty in creating formal specification. It combines waterfall method and transformations to allow developers start from informal specification and progress in steps into formal specification [1–4].

S. Liu and Z. Duan (Eds.): SOFL+MSVL 2013, LNCS 8332, pp. 166–174, 2014.
DOI: 10.1007/978-3-319-04915-1_12, © Springer International Publishing Switzerland 2014

In this paper we describe how SOFL are employed to construct formal specification of STL. In particular, we describe the development through SOFL three-step modeling. First, we define the system using natural language in informal specification. Second, we define formally all but pre and post condition using SOFL language in semi-formal specification. And finally, we formalize all parts of the system in formal specification.

The remainder of this paper is organized as follows. Section 2 briefly describes SOFL formal engineering method. Section 2 describes the smart traffic light system we devise for this paper. Section 3 discusses how we construct a specification for smart traffic light using SOFL. Section 4 describes our experience and lesson learned from this project. Section 5 discusses related works. Finally, in Sect. 6 we conclude the paper and provide several suggestions for future research.

2 Smart Traffic Light

Current traffic lights generally set to fixed signal timing. This setting, however, could lead to less optimal traffic control when traffic load varies significantly. In order to achieve smooth-flowing traffic, a traffic light needs to adjust its signal timing responding to traffic condition of its junction. In many places, this traffic condition varies forming a pattern. For example, at certain hour and day, the traffic load at direction toward business district increases significantly while at other directions it remains the same. This pattern could be used as consideration when determining signal timing for traffic lights as a way for improving traffic flow.

Smart traffic light (STL) in this paper is a system designed to process historical traffic data to reduce waiting time for vehicles through the traffic roads. In other words, STL uses feedback mechanism to improve its control function. The change in traffic condition will result changes in its control behavior. For example, if one side of the road is getting longer in waiting then the traffic light for that side of the road will have longer green signal.

This system relies on the ability of the elements of the system to communicate to each other in order to coordinate in optimal traffic light control [5]. The system itself comprises of a traffic management center, vehicles, and traffic light controllers, as can be seen in Fig. 1. A traffic management center will function to manage data gathered from others. For example, it will compute green signal duration for each junction. Vehicles are having capability of sending information regarding traffic condition they experience. Last, traffic light controllers are going to use information from traffic management center in controlling their lights.

2.1 Vehicle

In this system, vehicles must transmit traffic data they experience to Traffic Management Center (TMC). To support this, every vehicle is equipped with sensors and wireless communication. The sensor will detect when the vehicle is in queue behind a red light. The vehicle also receives information regarding identity of traffic light where the vehicle in queue for. When the vehicle runs pass through the traffic light,

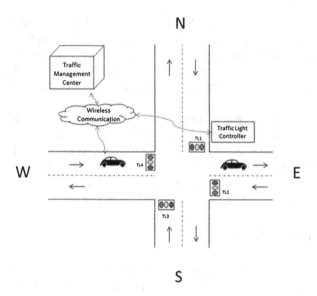

Fig. 1. Smart traffic light

also the sensor will detect it. The process inside vehicle will compute the time taken for queuing and send this information to TMC by wireless communication.

2.2 Traffic Management Center (TMC)

TMC will collect data concerning waiting time to pass a traffic light from all vehicles. This is done by storing data sent by vehicles. Every week, TMC will calculate the average waiting time for every traffic light in same hour for weekday and weekend. For example, TMC will calculate average waiting time for a traffic light in 10.00 in the morning for weekday by averaging all waiting time happened from 10.00 to 11.00 from Monday to Friday. Similarly, TMC will calculate this for weekend, by averaging data happened in Saturday and Sunday. The differentiation happened because the traffic pattern between weekday and weekend is usually different.

By knowing the average waiting time, we can further compute green light timing for every traffic light. We will determine the green time of a traffic light to be proportional to the average waiting time for that traffic light. At the end, TMC will provide this green light timing for all traffic light controllers.

2.3 Traffic Light Controller (TLC)

In each intersection, there are four traffic lights, which are divided to two pairs of traffic lights with the same operation. In Fig. 1 TL1 operation will be the same as TL3 operation, while TL2 operation will be the same as TL4 operation. The operation of the traffic lights will depend on the information about green light timing from TMC. The operation of these traffic lights will be directed by a traffic light controller. One controller is for each junction.

The TLC will fetch information regarding green timing for each pair of traffic lights. Then, this controller will calculate yellow and red light timing. After that, it will turn on traffic lights based on that timing continuously. The same timing will be used for one hour only. After one hour, new timing can be computed and used to run the traffic lights for the next one hour.

The traffic lights in one junction are controlled under one controller to make sure that timing can be run precisely. For example, at the time one pair of traffic lights gets green, the other pair of traffic lights should already be red. If traffic light is controlled independently, then it would need timing synchronization that may be difficult to implement.

In this case study, the system only considers one junction at a time without considering the effect of traffic in other junctions. Furthermore, it is assumed in the current case study, to simplify our system, the junctions do not have traffic light control for pedestrian. Moreover, there is no dedicated turn-right signal.

3   SOFL Specification of Smart Traffic Light

Following SOFL three-step modeling approach, constructing a specification consists of three steps, namely informal specification, semi-formal specification, and finally formal specification. In this section we describes each of these steps for the development of STL specification. In this development we use SOFL Tool, which provides text editor and CDFD diagram editor to support the creation of complete specifications using SOFL language.

3.1   Informal Specification

In informal specification step, we describe requirement of the system using natural language and we structure the requirement of STL into three sections: functions, data resources, and constraints, as shown in the Fig. 2. In this specification, function section describes functionality of STL. We express functionality of vehicle, TMC, and TLC in function 1.1, 1.2, and 1.3 respectively. In each of these functions, we further describe detailed functionality of related element of STL. In data resources section we list two data items: we assume there are 100 junctions for this system and each junction consists of four traffic lights. In constraints section, we describe three constraints. At the end of each constraint, there is a notation (F.1.3), which means this constraint is applied to function 1.3. Note that this reference notation is optional.

3.2   Semi-formal Specification

In the semi-formal specification, we have three tasks. First, we group related functions, data resources, and constraints in modules. Second, we declare any data type needed in this module. Finally, we write pre and post condition for every process in the module using natural language. As an example, Fig. 3 shows semi-formal specification of module Control_Traffic_Light_decom, which represents Traffic Light Controller element of STL.

1 Functions

1.1 For every vehicle, count and send waiting time information each time it passes a traffic light

1.1.1 Start time counter when arriving at the queue behind a red light

1.1.2 Send waiting time information to TMC (Traffic Management Center) after passing the traffic light

1.2 For TMC (Traffic Management Center), compute green signal duration for every traffic light

1.2.1 Calculate the average waiting time at every traffic light for each hour every day from data collected in a week

1.2.2 Calculate the average waiting time at every traffic light for each hour from the data above

1.2.3 Calculate the maximum waiting time for a road at every junction based on traffic light waiting time on that road

1.2.4 Calculate the green signal duration for every road for every hour based on road's waiting time in a junction

1.3 For TLC (Traffic Light Controller), control traffic lights according signal timing from TMC

1.3.1 Set signal timing

1.3.2 Set signal

2 Data Resources

2.1 There are 100 junction.

2.2 Each junction controls 4 traffic lights

3 Constraints

3.1 Traffic signal for one direction is the same as it for the opposite direction. (F1.3)

3.2 Traffic lights display signals following this sequence: green, yellow, red (F1.3)

3.3 Yellow and green signal in one road must be accompanied by red signal at the other road of the same junction (F1.3)

Fig. 2. Informal specification of smart traffic light

```
module Control_Traffic_Light_decom/SYSTEM_TMS

type
GreenDuration = SYSTEM_TMS.GreenDuration;
SignalTiming = composed of
                roadNS_green : nat0
                roadNS_yellow : nat0
                roadNS_red : nat0
                roadWE_red : nat0
                roadWE_green : nat0
                roadWE_yellow : nat0
        end;

var
ext #green_duration_set : set of GreenDuration;
ext #signal_timing : SignalTiming;
ext #junction_no : nat0;

inv
- Traffic signal for one direction is the same as traffic signal for the opposite
  direction
- Traffic lights display signals following this sequence: green, yellow, red
- Yellow and green signal in one road must be accompanied by red signal at the other
  road of the same junction

process Set_Signal_Timing (hourly_trigger : sign, hour: nat0)
        ext rd green_duration_set
               rd junction_no
               wr signal_timing
        pre green_duration_set must contain exactly one tuple for each junction in
           one hour
        post calculate duration of every signal in road A and road B in this junction
end_process;

...

end_module
```

Fig. 3. Semi-formal specification of module Control_Traffic_Light

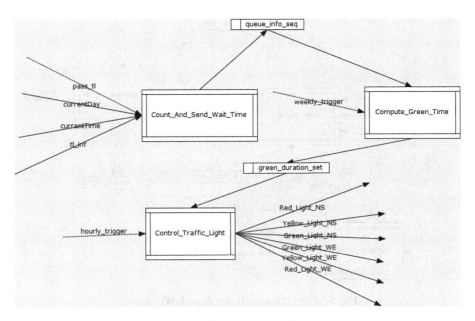

Fig. 4. CDFD of top module

3.3   Formal Specification

In formal specification, from semi-formal specification we develop CDFD diagrams and their module specifications. CDFD will reveal the architecture of the system. It shows the relation between processes. Figure 4 shows CDFD of the top module of STL.

In formal specification, all processes are specified in SOFL language. If a process cannot be specified using pre and post condition, then it may be too complex and therefore need to be decomposed into other modules. In our top module, all processes have to be decomposed into other modules. This decomposition continues until simple processes are achieved. As an example, module Set_Signal_WE does not need decomposition and it can be specified entirely using SOFL language. The CDFD of this module can be seen in Fig. 5 and its module specification can be seen in Fig. 6.

As we complete this formal specification, it can serve as a foundation for implementation of the system.

4   Experience and Lesson

Compared to other formal methods, SOFL has some features that help us reduce the difficulty of creating formal specifications. One of them is CDFD that help us visualize the design architecture. This increases the readability of the specification, which is crucial especially in large specification. Using CDFD we can trace more easily the

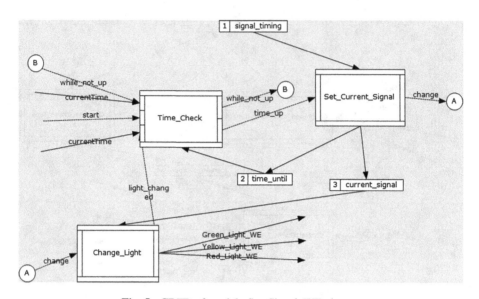

Fig. 5. CDFD of module Set_Signal_WE_decom

```
module Set_Signal_WE_decom/Control_Traffic_Light_decom

type
SignalTiming = Control_Traffic_Light_decom.SignalTiming;
Time = SYSTEM_TMS.Time;
Signal = SYSTEM_TMS.Signal;

var
ext #signal_timing : SignalTiming;
ext time_until : Time;
ext current_signal : Signal;


process Change_Light(change: sign)Green_Light_WE: boolean, Yellow_Light_WE: boolean,
                Red_Light_WE: boolean, light_changed: sign
ext rd current_signal : Signal
pre true
post
    current_signal = <Green> and Green_Light_WE = true and Yellow_Light_WE = false and
    Red_Light_WE = false and bound(light_changed)
or
    current_signal = <Yellow> and Green_Light_WE = false and Yellow_Light_WE = true and
    Red_Light_WE = false and bound(light_changed)
or
    current_signal = <Red> and Green_Light_WE = false and Yellow_Light_WE = false and
    Red_Light_WE = true and bound(light_changed)
end_process

...

end_module
```

Fig. 6. Specification of module Set_Signal_WE_decom

relationships among processes and also the decomposition from top level module to the lowest ones and trace the transformation flow.

In general, constructing a formal specification faces high barrier. The culprit is the difficulties in writing and reading mathematical expression both for developer and user. SOFL method has ameliorated this matter using three-step modeling approach.

It helps developer and user construct the specification in gradual formality. As a result, developer and user can proceed more smoothly in developing the specification. From informal specification which is easily constructed because of the use of natural language and in turn facilitating communication between developer and user, the process proceeds to next steps that introduce formality in part where they have deeper understanding of the system to be built. Finally, they arrived at formal specification. There all are defined formally when they have understood all very well.

In traditional method, natural language is used for writing specification. With that, developers will find it difficult to ensure that there is no inconsistency between parts in the specification. Not only because of the possible ambiguity of natural language, but also lack of tool to think more thoroughly. One important point of using SOFL is that it forces developers to clarify thinking. It helps them think in precise what is going to be built. For example, when the developer defines data type in semiformal specification, they clarify what kind of data will flow between processes or stored in data store. Furthermore, when they writes pre and post condition of processes, they think in precise what kind of input expected and the effect of the transformation to the output of the processes. The consistency among items on the specification is checked. As a result, it is less likely there is wrong data type, because it has already been thought against all related processes.

5   Related Work

SOFL has been used successfully in various case studies. In [3] SOFL is applied to construct a specification for railway crossing controller, a safety-critical and real-time system that produce signal of coming trains and control crossing gates. In [6] insulin pump system, a safety-critical embedded system for controlling insulin injection, also has been constructed using SOFL. In [7] SOFL is also used to carry out case study of auto-cruise control for the purpose of hazard analysis. In [8] SOFL has been tried on non-safety critical system, i.e. university information system. In [9] the specification of automatic automobile driving simulation system is also constructed using SOFL. Finally, [2] employs ATM (Automated Teller Machine) as a case study for evaluating effectiveness of the framework for developing dependable software systems using the SOFL formal engineering method.

Although SOFL has been applied in various case studies, none has constructed a specification for traffic light system. Thus, this paper is the first SOFL case study on traffic light system. Compared to those case studies, this system shares some same characteristic, such as real-time and safety-critical, which are good reasons to employ formal methods like SOFL. Moreover, with more potential features, this system becomes a complex system, which needs such method even more.

6   Conclusion and Future Work

In this paper, we have presented the development of a smart traffic light specification using SOFL formal engineering method. This method helps us deal with the complexity of the system while maintaining preciseness of the specifications. In this case study, the system can be specified through combination of CDFD and module specification.

In the future, we will add more features to STL. We will consider more collaborative work among elements of the system. For example, we are going to coordinate multiple junctions to provide better traffic control. Furthermore, we will develop inspection methods to verify the specification.

Acknowledgement. This work has been conducted as a part of "Research Initiative on Advanced Software Engineering in 2012" supported by Software Reliability Enhancement Center (SEC), Information Technology Promotion Agency Japan (IPA).

References

1. Liu, S.: Formal engineering for industrial software development – an introduction to the SOFL specification language and method. In: Davies, J., Schulte, W., Barnett, M. (eds.) ICFEM 2004. LNCS, vol. 3308, pp. 7–8. Springer, Heidelberg (2004)
2. Liu, S.: A framework for developing dependable software systems using the SOFL formal engineering method. In: 2010 International Conference on Intelligent Computing and Integrated Systems (ICISS), pp. 561–567 (2010)
3. Liu, S., Asuka, M., Komaya, K., Nakamura, Y.: Applying SOFL to specify a railway crossing controller for industry. In: Proceedings of the 2nd IEEE Workshop on Industrial Strength Formal Specification Techniques 1998, pp. 16–27 (1998)
4. Liu, S.: Formal Engineering for Industrial Software Development. Springer, Heidelberg (2004)
5. Wang, Q., Hu, J., Wang, Y., Zhang, Y.: A simulation study for the communication subsystem of wireless traffic information service system. In: 7th International Conference on Information, Communications and Signal Processing 2009, ICICS 2009, pp. 1–6 (2009)
6. Wang, J., Liu, S., Qi, Y., Hou, D.: Developing an insulin pump system using the SOFL method. In: 14th Asia-Pacific Software Engineering Conference 2007, APSEC 2007, pp. 334–341 (2007)
7. Abdullah, A.B., Liu, S.: Hazard analysis for safety-critical systems using SOFL. In: 2013 IEEE Symposium on Computational Intelligence for Engineering Solutions, Singapore (2013)
8. Liu, S., Shibata, M., Sato, R.: Applying SOFL to develop a university information system. In: Proceedings of Sixth Asia Pacific Software Engineering Conference 1999, APSEC 1999, pp. 404–411 (1999)
9. Mat, A., Liu, S.: Applying SOFL to construct the formal specification of an automatic automobile driving simulation system. In: International Conference on Software Technology and Engineering, vol. 3308, pp. 42–48. World Scientific Publishing, Chennai (2009)

Checking Internal Consistency of SOFL Specification: A Hybrid Approach

Yuting Chen[1,2]([envelope])

[1] School of Software, Shanghai Jiao Tong University, Shanghai 200240, China
[2] Shanghai Key Laboratory of Computer Software Testing and Evaluating,
Shanghai, China
chenyt@cs.sjtu.edu.cn

Abstract. A SOFL specification can be written with errors inside, leading to an untrustable situation for implementation. Some techniques, such as specification review and testing, have been proposed to detect and remove the errors from the specification as early as possible. Meanwhile these techniques face strong challenges when applied to practice in that they strongly rely on human intelligence to either cautiously design a review task tree for directing the whole review process, or design some test inputs to "run" the specification. The completeness of the review or testing tasks also remains a problem. In this paper we propose a hybrid approach to checking the internal consistency of a SOFL specification. The internal consistency is an important property indicating that the entire specification can work properly. The essential idea of the hybrid approach is to adopt the different strategies to check the different aspects of the specification: concrete or abstract values are used to check the satisfiability of a process, and the symbolic execution and the deduction techniques can be used to check the internal consistency of the specification at the integration level. We also use a Sort-Search example to illustrate the use of the hybrid approach.

Keywords: Internal consistency · Satisfiability · Symbolic execution · Loop invariant

1 Introduction

A SOFL specification can be written with errors inside, leading to an untrustable situation for implementation. Some techniques, such as specification review [1,2] and testing [3,4], have been proposed to effectively detect and remove the errors from the specification as early as possible. Specification review means to read over the specification, and in each time slot only one manageable component is focused on and one property be selected to be an objective property for review. Specification testing means to generate test cases and then check whether the specification can run as expected. Meanwhile the review and testing techniques face two strong challenges when applied to practice.

S. Liu and Z. Duan (Eds.): SOFL+MSVL 2013, LNCS 8332, pp. 175–191, 2014.
DOI: 10.1007/978-3-319-04915-1_13, © Springer International Publishing Switzerland 2014

Firstly, these techniques strongly rely on human intelligence to either cautiously design a review task tree for directing the review process, or select some test cases for executing the specification. Since human intelligence can definitely cause some occasionality, the review or testing tasks can be various from person to person, leading to the conclusion not convincing. The completeness also remains a problem, because a completion of all the review or testing tasks arbitrarily generated may not be sufficient to conclude that the objective specification is absolutely correct.

Secondly, a specification meeting a complicated property usually require one or more components participate in. Since human engineers (reviewers or testers) are shortage of their abilities in managing all aspects of a complex system, it becomes difficult, if not impossible, for them to take an integration review or testing of the specification and determine whether some complicated properties can be met because all of the components including processes, datastores, dataflows, invariants may contribute to the evaluation of these properties.

In this paper we propose a hybrid approach to checking the internal consistency of a SOFL specification. The internal consistency, as defined in [2], is an important property of a SOFL specification indicating that the entire specification can work properly.

Definition 1. *The internal consistency of a SOFL specification is a property that the outputs can be generated based on its inputs under the condition that the pre- and postconditions of all the processes involved in the execution of the specification evaluated to true.*

The internal consistency of a SOFL specification is obviously necessary for the correctness of the specification. Otherwise the efforts in the implementation may be wasted because there can be no inputs to run the program, or some valid inputs cannot run it. However, a specification against the property is not easy to either review or test because the property needs to be evaluated by all of the processes, invariants, dataflows in the specification. Additionally, a process may not have the unique semantics until the explicit specification is defined. Thereby it may generate nondeterministic outputs, some of which can drive the successors to execute, while the others may not. The latter destroys the internal consistency of the specification, but when and how such outputs are produced is less than clear. A systematic and rigorous method is needed to help the engineers check the internal consistency of a SOFL specification.

The approach proposed is used to verify a specification both at a unit level and at an integration level. As Fig. 1 shows, the approach starts from verifying the satisfiability of each process, to verifying the internal consistency of the entire specification. Different strategies are adopted, depending on the objective sub-properties and the existence of the explicit specifications, to perform the verification: concrete or abstract values are used to check the satisfiability of a process, and the symbolic execution and the deduction techniques can be used to check the internal consistency of the entire specification at the integration level.

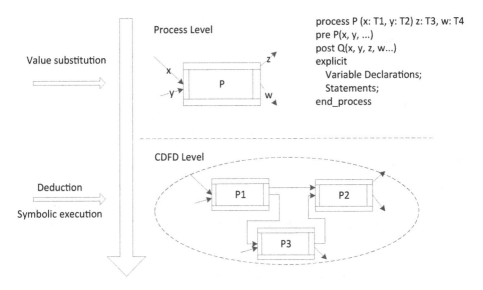

Fig. 1. A framework of checking of the internal consistency of a SOFL specification

The paper is organized as follows. Sections 2 and 3 describe the strategies for verification of a SOFL specification at the unit level and at the integration level, respectively. Section 4 introduces the related work and finally in Sect. 5 we conclude this paper and point out the future research directions.

2   Checking of Satisfiability of Process

A SOFL specification is internally consistent only if all its processes are satisfiable. By saying a process P is "satisfiable" we mean that for any input (along with the external variables of any state), if the precondition evaluates to true, there must exist some output (along with the external variables updated) based on which the postcondition of P evaluates to true. Formally, let $\overrightarrow{in}$, $\overrightarrow{out}$, $\overrightarrow{rd}$, $\overrightarrow{wr}$ be the vectors of the input and output variables, the **rd** and **wr** external variables, respectively.

Definition 2. *The satisfiability of a SOFL process $P(pre, post)$ is defined as*

$$\forall \overrightarrow{in}, \overrightarrow{rd}, \tilde{\overrightarrow{wr}} \cdot pre(\overrightarrow{in}, \overrightarrow{rd}, \tilde{\overrightarrow{wr}}) \wedge inv \Rightarrow \exists \overrightarrow{out}, \overrightarrow{wr} \cdot post(\overrightarrow{in}, \overrightarrow{out}, \overrightarrow{rd}, \tilde{\overrightarrow{wr}}, \overrightarrow{wr}) \wedge inv.$$

For example, let a process $Sort_1$ be defined. $Sort_1$ attempts to, for any array of length greater than 0, sort it in either an ascending or descending order. More specifically, the process overwrites the external variable _array with a sorted sequence, and produces its length as the output.

```
wr _array: seq of int
inv len(_array) > 0
```

```
process Sort₁ (ascending: bool) length: int
ext wr _array
pre true
post length = len(_array) and
    if ~ascending = true
    then forall[i: inds(_array), j: inds(_array)]|
            i < j => _array(i) <= _array(j)
    else forall[i: inds(_array), j: inds(_array)]|
            i < j => _array(i) >= _array(j)
end_process
```

The satisfiability of $Sort_1$ says that for _array and *ascending* of any values, if the invariant (i.e., $len(\_array) > 0$) and the precondition (i.e., *true*) are met before the execution, the values of _array and *length* after execution meet the postcondition (and the invariant).

2.1 Using Value Substitution to Verify Process

The satisfiability of a process $P(pre, post)$ can be evaluated through gradually checking three sub-properties.

Property 1.1. whether the domain of the process defined by $pre \wedge inv$ is non-empty. Otherwise no inputs can drive the process to execute. For example, it requires that there exists at least an input and an _array making $pre \wedge inv$ of $Sort_1$ evaluate to true;

Property 1.2. whether the range of the process defined by $post \wedge inv$ is non-empty. Otherwise the process cannot produce any valid outputs. For example, it requires that there exists at least an output and an _array making $post \wedge inv$ of $Sort_1$ evaluate to true;

Property 1.3. whether P is satisfiable, i.e., for any input in the domain, some values in the range correspond to the input. It means that the process provides with appropriate effects.

A SOFL process can be verified to approve/disapprove the three sub-properties by taking a strategy called *"value substitution"*. In principle, value substitution, like the testing or symbolic execution, is to substitute the process variables either by using either some concrete values or some abstract ones.

Obviously, the Properties 1.1 and 1.2 can get supported once some concrete values are selected from the domain and the range, respectively. Let a snapshot be a state of all external variables assigned with some values. We prefer to select (1) a snapshot S and an input from the domain, and (2) a snapshot S' and an output from the range. We call S and S' the pre- and post-snapshots, respectively.

The concrete values can be intuitively selected or constructed: let all of the external variables related to the process and all of the input variables be assigned with some values, as long as they satisfy the precondition and invariants. For example, S_1 and $Input_1$ are values satisfying the Property 1.1.

$S_1 = (\_array = [2, 4, 8, 10, 7, 5, 3, 1])$
$Input_1 = \{ascending = true\}$

The same thing holds for the post-snapshot and the output. A post-snapshot S_2 and $Output_1$ shown next can be selected from the range of $Sort_1$.

$S_2 = (\_array = [1])$
$Output_1 = \{length = 1\}$

Note that in this example, the Property 1.3 is certainly met by the process when the Property 1.2 is met. It denotes that whatever the pre-snapshot and the input are, S_2 and $Output_1$ can always meet the postcondition. One main reason is that the postcondition of $Sort_1$ is of few relation to the pre-states of the input and the external variables (i.e., the states of these variables before execution).

Thus it is concluded that $Sort_1$ is satisfiable because (1) the pre- and post-condition can be true, and (2) for any input and pre-snapshot satisfying the precondition, we can obtain some output and post-snapshot satisfying the postcondition.

Challenges exist when the postcondition is strongly related to the inputs/external variables. For example, let the process $Sort_2$ be defined as follows. It differs from $Sort_1$ in that it requires $len(\tilde{}\_array) = len(\_array)$ in its postcondition.

```
wr _array: seq of int
inv len(_array) > 0
process Sort₂ (ascending: bool) length: int
ext wr _array
pre true
post len(_array) = len(~_array) and
     length = len(_array) and
     if ~ascending = true
     then forall[i: inds(_array), j: inds(_array)]|
             i < j => _array(i) <= _array(j)
     else forall[i: inds(_array), j: inds(_array)]|
             i < j => _array(i) >= _array(j)
end_process
```

Similarly, the Property 1.1 can be met by $Sort_2$ in that the pre-snapshot S_1 and the input $Input_1$ can satisfy the precondition. The Property 1.2 can be met by the post-snapshot S_2 and the output $Output_1$ if the input and the external variables are not considered. However, since the length of $\tilde{}\_array$ needs to be same as that of $\_array$, $Sort_2$ meets the Property 1.3 only if all the values of $\tilde{}\_array$ are enumerated, while it is not possible for a infinite domain.

A rational solution is to look for a counterexample with respect to the Property 1.3. A counterexample is an instance satisfying

$$(\exists \overrightarrow{in}, \overrightarrow{rd}, \tilde{}\overrightarrow{wr} \cdot pre(\overrightarrow{in}, \overrightarrow{rd}, \overrightarrow{wr}) \wedge inv) \wedge (\nexists \overrightarrow{out}, \overrightarrow{wr} \cdot post(\overrightarrow{in}, \overrightarrow{out}, \overrightarrow{rd}, \tilde{}\overrightarrow{wr}, \overrightarrow{wr}) \wedge inv).$$

Hence given a process, human engineers can creatively find a counterexample, or determine subjectively that no counterexample does exist. In order to verify a process in a more rigorous way, we can use abstract values to analyze the process. Like symbolic execution [5,6], we execute the process as in a normal execution except that input values are either abstract or concrete. An applying of the execution technique helps reason about all the values of the input and the external variables, which is effective when the domain and the range space are large.

For example, let the pre-snapshot $S_3 = (\tilde{}\_array = ARRAY_1)$ and $Input_1 = (ascending = true)$ and $Input_2 = (ascending = false)$, where $ARRAY_1$ be an abstract sequence whose length is $n_{>0}$. A value substitution can produce two constraints on the basis of the pre- and postconditions.

Constraint 1. $let(\tilde{}\_array = ARRAY_1, \tilde{}ascending = true)$ in
   $(len(\_array) = len(\tilde{}\_array)$ and
   $length = len(\_array)$ and
   if $\tilde{}ascending = true$
   then $forall[i: inds(\_array), j: inds(\_array)]|i < j => \_array(i) <= \_array(j)$
   else $forall[i: inds(\_array), j: inds(\_array)]|i < j => \_array(i) >= \_array(j))$

Constraint 2. $let(\tilde{}\_array = ARRAY_1, \tilde{}ascending = false)$ in
   $(len(\_array)=len(\tilde{}\_array)$ and
   $length = len(\_array)$ and
   if $\tilde{}ascending = true$
   then $forall[i: inds(\_array), j: inds(\_array)]|i < j => \_array(i) <= \_array(j)$
   else $forall[i: inds(\_array), j: inds(\_array)]|i < j => \_array(i) >= \_array(j))$

The two constraints can be simplified to

1. $len(\_array)=n$ and $forall[i: inds(\_array), j: inds(\_array)] |i < j => \_array(i) <= \_array(j)$ and $length = n$
2. $len(\_array)=n$ and $forall[i: inds(\_array), j: inds(\_array)] |i < j => \_array(i) >= \_array(j)$ and $length = n$

Let $ARRAY_2 = [1, 2, ...n]$ and $ARRAY_3 = [n, n - 1, ..., 1]$. It is obvious that a post-snapshot $S_4 = (\_array = ARRAY_2)$ and an output $Output_2 = (length = n)$ meet Constraint 1 when $ascending$ is true, and $S_5 = (\_array = ARRAY_3)$ and $Output_2 = (length = n)$ meet Constraint 2 when ascending is false. Since the pre-snapshot S_3 is given using an abstract value, the Property 1.3 gets approved after S_4, S_5, and $Output_2$ are obtained.

2.2   Handling Explicit Specification

An explicit specification can make a process not satisfiable. The explicit specification provides the process with a detailed but abstractly described design, mainly from an algorithmic point of view. Let a process be defined as $P = \{pre\}explicit\_specificaiton\{post\}$. P is of satisfiability if it can consume any input satisfying the precondition and then reach a state satisfying the postcondition through executing the algorithm given in the explicit specification. The process may not be satisfiable due to the wrong algorithm or errors hidden in the explicit specification or postcondition leading to the output not appropriately produced.

For example, let $Sort_2$ be equipped with an explicit specification as next shows. The explicit specification is a SOFL version of an insertion sort algorithm. Insertion sort iterates, consuming one sequence element each repetition and growing a sorted sequence. Note that *swap* is a function to swap two elements in a sequence, whose definition is omitted for the sake of space. A checking of $Sort_2$ with the explicit specification is then conducted to determine wether $Sort_2$ can employ the explicit specification to produce the appropriate results. Since the explicit specification provides with a detailed algorithm, it is of no doubt that the best choice to check $Sort_2$ is to execute the explicit specification like a program.

```
explicit
k: int = 0;
while (k < len(_array)) do
begin
  t: int = k;
  while (t>0 and (ascending = true and _array(t-1) > _array(t) or
    ascending=false and _array(t-1) < _array(t) )) do
  begin
      swap(_array(t-1), _array(t));
    t = t - 1;
  end;
  k = k + 1;
end;
length = len(_array);
```

Although the concrete values can be used to "test" the process, we prefer to adopt the abstract values in the execution due to the completeness. In this way, we reason about all the inputs that take the same path through the process. However, the explicit specification cannot be fully executed using abstract values. The main reason is that a dual loop exists, and the number of iterations is not estimable in that it relates to the length of $\tilde{\ }\_array$ and its values.

An ancillary aid is to use loop invariants. A loop invariant is a statement of the conditions that should be true on entry into a loop and that are guaranteed to remain true on every iteration of the loop. We add two loop invariants into the explicit specification in order to simplify the checking of $Sort_2$. Note that $j : [0, k)$ means $0 \leq j < k$.

```
explicit
k: int = 0;
while (k < len(_array)) do
loop inv (1) 0 <= k and k <= len(_array) and (
        ascending=true and
```

```
       forall[j: [0, k), i: [0, k)]| i<j => _array(i) <= _array(j)
       or
        ascending=false and
       forall[j: [0, k), i: [0, k)]| i<j =>_array(i) >= _array(j))
  begin
   t: int = k;
   while (t>0 && (ascending = true and _array(t-1) > _array(t) or
     ascending=false and _array(t-1) < _array(t) )) do
   loop inv (2) 0 <=t and t <=k and
          (ascending=true and
           forall[j: [1, t), i: [0, j)] |a(i) <= a(j) and
             forall[j: [t, k+1), i: [t, j)] | a(i) <= a(j) and
             forall[j: [t+1, k+1), i: [0, t)] | a(i) <= a(j) or
           ascending=false and
           forall[j: [1, t), i: [0, j)] |a(i) >= a(j) and
             forall[j: [t, k+1), i: [t, j)] | a(i) >= a(j) and
             forall[j: [t+1, k+1), i: [0, t)] | a(i) >= a(j))
   begin
       swap(_array(t-1), _array(t));
     t = t - 1;
   end;
   k = k + 1;
  end;
  length = len(_array);
```

Loop inv (1) ensures that at each time a partial sorted sequence $(\_array[0], ..., \_array[k-1])$ exists and waits for the insertion operation. Loop inv (2) ensures that at each insertion step, let t be the position at which the element to be inserted, the sequences $(\_array[0], ..., \_array[t-1])$ and $(\_array[t], ..., \_array[k-1])$ remain sorted.

By using the two loop invariants, we reinterpret the loops, and use the abstract values to check the explicit specification. Let $S_3 = (\tilde{\ }\_array = ARRAY_1)$ and $Input_1 = (ascending = true)$ and $Input_2 = (ascending = false)$ be used to execute the explicit specification. After the outer loop is completed, it is ensured that

Constraint 3.
$let(\tilde{\ }\_array = ARRAY_1$ and $len(\_array) = n$ and $ascending = true)$ in
$(k = len(\_array)$ and $0 <= k$ and $k <= len(\_array)$ and
$ascending = true$ and
$forall[j: [0, k), i: [0, k)]|i < j => \_array(i) <= \_array(j))$

Constraint 4.
$let(\tilde{\ }\_array = ARRAY_1$ and $len(\_array) = n$ and $ascending = false)$ in
$(k = len(\_array)$ and $0 <= k$ and $k <= len(\_array)$ and
$ascending = false$ and
$forall[j: [0, k), i: [0, k)]|i < j => \_array(i) >= \_array(j))$

Constraints 3 and 4 are consistent with the postcondition because we have $inds(\_array) = len(\_array)$. Hence the Property 1.3 gets approved with the aid of loop invariants. We then conclude that $Sort_2$ equipped with the explicit specification is satisfiable.

Note that the execution of the explicit specification relies on the loop invariants written by human engineers, but their effectiveness is not determined. A common approach is to, when writing loop invariants, write them in a form that is as close as possible to the postcondition [7]. A more sensible approach is to let the loop invariants be automatically generated on the basis of the explicit specification, which will be remained as one of our future work. In addition, when each statement be executed, there exists a fundamental belief that the invariants need to be held. It should be necessary to monitor the execution and analyze the state of the system at runtime, while a challenge still remains in that how the invariants can be handled in a cost-effective way.

3   Checking of Internal Consistency of CDFD

A SOFL specification is composed of a set of processes. A CDFD (*Condition Data Flow Diagram*) is used to integrate all the processes, and a formal module is used to define their semantics. In this paper we call a process a *starting* one if it does not consume any input or only consumes some input dataflows outside of the system. Similarly, we call a process an *ending* one if it does not produce any output or produces some dataflows transmitted to the processes outside of the system. Besides that every process in the specification needs to be satisfiable, the entire specification should be satisfiable (i.e., hold the internal consistency property).

Since a formal specification can be regarded as an abstract interpretation of a set of functional scenarios [8], the internal consistency of the specification can be checked by checking all of its functional scenarios.

3.1   A Scenario-Based Strategy

Let a SOFL specification *Spec* be composed of a set of functional scenarios $\{Scenario_1, Scenario_2, ..., Scenario_n\}$. Formally, we write it as

$$Spec \equiv \{Scenario_1, Scenario_2, ..., Scenario_n\}$$

where a scenario $Scenario_{1 \leq i \leq n}$ is defined as a deterministic sequence of (sub)processes that consumes a set of input dataflows and produces the output dataflows [9]. Let pre_Spec and $post\_Spec$ combine all the preconditions (of the starting processes) and all the postconditions (of the ending processes) of *Spec*, respectively. Let $pre\_Scenario_i$ and $post\_Scenario_i$ combine all the preconditions (of the starting processes) and all the postconditions (of the ending processes) of $Scenario_i$, respectively. We enrich the above formula with preconditions and postconditions, as

$$\{pre\_Spec\}Spec\{post\_Spec\} \equiv$$

$$\{\{pre\_Scenario_1\}Scenario_1\{post\_Scenario_1\},$$
$$\{pre\_Scenario_2\}Scenario_2\{post\_Scenario_2\}, ...,$$
$$\{pre\_Scenario_n\}Scenario_n\{post\_Scenario_n\}\}$$

A checking of the internal consistency of $Spec$ can be conducted through checking these scenarios, considering that all of the functional scenarios can be obtained. The internal consistency of $Spec$ can be evaluated through gradually checking three sub-properties.

Property 2.1. Any input satisfying pre_Spec can satisfy the precondition of at least one scenario. Formally, we have

$$pre\_Spec \wedge inv => (\bigvee_{1 \leq i \leq n} pre\_Scenario_i) \wedge inv.$$

Property 2.1 ensures that a legal input meeting pre_Spec can lead to at least one scenario $Scenario_i$ be selected to execute. For example, let $pre\_Spec = true$, $pre\_Scenario_1 = (x >= 0)$ and $pre\_Scenario_2 = (x <= 0)$. An x of any value can lead to either $Scenario_1$ or $Scenario_2$ be executed.

Property 2.2. Any scenario is interconnected by all the processes on it. More specifically, any output of an intermediate process of a scenario can be consumed by at least one of its successors as input. Otherwise the scenario is not feasible. Formally, let a process $Pred$ has a set of successors $\{Succ_1, Succ_2, ..., Succ_m\}$ in a scenario $Scenario$. We have

$$\exists \overrightarrow{x} \cdot post\_Pred(\overrightarrow{x}) \wedge (\bigvee_{1 \leq i \leq m} pre\_Succ_i(\overrightarrow{x})) \wedge inv$$

where $\overrightarrow{x}$ be a vector of dataflows transmitted between $Pred$ and its successors.

Property 2.3. Every scenario is internally consistent. That is, $Scenario_{1 \leq i \leq n}$ can consume some input satisfying $pre\_Scenario_i$ and produce some output satisfying $post\_Scenario_i$. Formally, we have

$$\exists \overrightarrow{x}, \overrightarrow{y} \cdot pre\_Scenario_i(\overrightarrow{x}) \wedge inv => post\_Scenario_i(\overrightarrow{y}) \wedge inv$$

where $\overrightarrow{x}$ (and $\overrightarrow{y}$) be the vector of input (and output) variables of $Scenario_i$. Note that the property also implies that some input satisfying $pre\_Scenario_i$ may cause another scenario execute.

For facilitating the checking of a specification against to the three sub-properties, we derive from the specification a set of scenarios covering all functionality the specification provides with, and then calculate their pre- and postconditions. Thus we at first define the order of the processes.

Let a process can be succeeded by its successors in two basic manners:

1. $Pred \rightarrow Succ_1|Succ_2|...|Succ_m$. It denotes that a completion of $Pred$ leading to only one of its successors to execute.
2. $Pred \rightarrow Succ_1 \cdot Succ_2 \cdot ... \cdot Succ_m$. It denotes that a completion of $Pred$ leading to all of its successors to execute.

$Pred$ can also be compositely succeeded by its successors. For example, $Pred \rightarrow (Succ_1|Succ_2) \cdot Succ_3$ means that after $Pred$ completes, either $Succ_1$ or $Succ_2$, along with $Succ_3$, is selected to execute.

Similarly we have

1. $Pred_1|Pred_2|...|Pred_m \rightarrow Succ$. It denotes that a completion of one of the predecessors leads to $Succ$ to execute.
2. $Pred_1 \cdot Pred_2 \cdot ... \cdot Pred_m \rightarrow Succ$. It denotes that a completion of all of the predecessors leads to $Succ$ to execute.

Scenario derivation can benefit from the slicing technique. Given a specification, we derive the scenarios by following the next steps. Although a derivation process, similar to an enumeration of all the possible scenarios, also faces a path explosion problem, a formal specification is usually abstract enough so that all the scenarios can be exhaustively enumerated.

1. Choose an arbitrary input i satisfying $pre\_Spec \wedge inv$ to begin with.
2. Simulate the execution of the specification, and record all the corresponding processes in a scenario.
   (a) If $Pred \rightarrow Succ_1|Succ_2|...|Succ_m$ and $Pred$ is completed, select any one of the successors to execute;
   (b) If $Pred \rightarrow Succ_1 \cdot Succ_2 \cdot ... \cdot Succ_m$ and $Pred$ is completed, select all of the successors to execute;
3. Take a backward execution of the specification, and record all the corresponding processes in a scenario.
   (a) If we have $Pred_1 \cdot Pred_2 \cdot ... \cdot Pred_m \rightarrow Succ$ and $Succ$ has been selected to execute, select all predecessors to participate in;
   (b) If we have $Pred_1|Pred_2|...|Pred_m \rightarrow Succ$ and no predecessors but $Succ$ has been selected to execute, select any of the predecessors to participate in.
4. Repeat Steps 2 and 3 until no processes can be included in the scenario.
5. Generate the pre- and postconditions of the scenario through combining all conditions on the scenario, as [9] explains.
6. Revisit the specification, and mutate a scenario to produce a new one.
   (a) If $Pred \rightarrow Succ_1|Succ_2|...|Succ_m$, select a new successor;
   (b) If $Pred_1|Pred_2|...|Pred_m \rightarrow Succ$, select a new predecessor.
7. Return to step 2.

The satisfaction of a SOFL specification to the properties 2.1 and 2.2 can be conveniently checked after all scenarios have been derived and their pre- and postconditions been generated. The property 2.1 is checked through finding some counterexamples, each of which can meet pre_Spec, but not the precondition of any scenario. For example, let

$$\{true\}Spec\{post\} \equiv \{(x > 0)Scenario_1(post_1), (x < 0)Scenario_2(post_2)\}.$$

Once a counterexample (e.g., $x = 0$) is found, the Property 2.1 is not satisfied. Some off-the-shelf SAT solvers (e.g., SAT4j [10]) can provide the engineers with support in finding the counterexamples of a propositional expression.

An interconnection of a scenario denotes that the entire scenario can work, if appropriate values are transferred among the processes. Any scenario can be determined to meet or violate the Property 2.2 by either using the human intelligence or using the typical SAT solvers to solve the constraints on the successive processes. For example, let a scenario segment be $Pred_1 \cdot Pred_2 \rightarrow Succ_1$, where $post\_Pred_1 = (x >= 0)$ and $post\_Pred_2 = (y >= 0)$, $pre\_Succ_1 = (x > 0$ and $y >= 0)$. The Property 2.2 is held when the outputs of $Pred_1$ and $Pred_2$ can be consumed by $Succ_1$. For example, $(x = 1)$ and $(y = 1)$ are valid values transferring from $Pred_1$ and $Pred_2$ to $Succ_1$.

The satisfaction of a scenario $Scenario_i$ to the Property 2.3 relies on $pre\_Scenario_i$ and $post\_Scenario_i$ as well the pre- and postconditions of all the processes on the scenario. Once again, the engineers can create some snapshots satisfying $pre\_Scenario_i$ and some others satisfying $post\_Scenario_i$. The intermediate snapshots and dataflow values are also created in order to demonstrate that the scenario is feasible. A scenario is feasible if the entire scenario can be instantiated, i.e., at each phase a snapshot and the dataflow values can be created. The specification meets the Property 2.3 if all the scenarios are feasible.

Next we will use a Sort-Search example to illustrate how the specification is checked with respect to the Property 2.3 and explain the strategies used.

3.2　A Sort-Search Example

For the sake of space, we link a process $Search$ with $Sort_2$ to form a SOFL specification, as Fig. 2 shows. In the specification, $Sort_2$ sorts a sequence of integers, and $Search$ then searches for an element in the sorted sequence. The process $Search$ is defined as

```
process Search(key: int, length: int) index: int
ext rd _array
pre   length = len(_array) and
      (forall[j: [0, length), i: [0, j)]| _array(i) <= _array(j) or
      forall[j: [0, length), i: [0, j)]| _array(i) >= _array(j))
post 0 <= index => _array(index) = key
      or index < 0 => forall[i: [0, len(_array))] | _array(i) != key
end_process
```

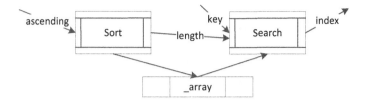

Fig. 2. A CDFD of the sort-search specification

Since the specification is of a simple structure containing two processes, only one scenario, which is same as the specification itself, is derived. Thus it can be concluded that the Property 2.1 is met by the specification. The Property 2.2 is also met by the specification in that some variable values (e.g., $S_2 = (\_array = [1])$ and $Output_1 = (length = 1)$), if produced by Sort, can be transferred to *Search*. Actually any sorted sequence can be consumed by *Search* as input in this example.

When check the specification against of the Property 2.3, the engineers can "execute" all the scenarios using the abstract or concrete values. An execution of a scenario is, in the sense of feasibility, to use the concrete values to instantiate the scenario. For example, let the pre-snapshot and the input of the process $Sort_2$ be $S_1 = (\_array = [2, 4, 8, 10, 7, 5, 3, 1])$ and $Input_1 = (ascending = true)$, and a post-snapshot $S_6 = (\_array = [1, 2, 3, 4, 5, 6, 7, 8])$ and an output $Output_3 = (length = 8)$ can then be produced. Let the pre-snapshot and the input for *Search* be S_6 and $Input_3 = (length = 8, key = 5)$. An output $Output_4 = (index = 4)$ can then be produced. Thus the scenario is feasible in that all conditions on the scenario can be satisfied, at least by the above values.

The abstract values can also be used to instantiate the scenario in order to demonstrate its feasibility. For example, let the pre-snapshot and the input of the process $Sort_2$ be $S_3 = (\_array = ARRAY_1)$ and $Input_1 = (ascending = true)$. As explained in Sect. 2.1, let $ARRAY_2 = [1, 2, ...n]$, a post-snapshot $S_4 = (\_array = ARRAY_2)$ and an output $Output_2 = (length = n)$ can be produced by $Sort_2$. Let the pre-snapshot and the input for the process *Search* be S_4 and $Input_4 = (length = n, key = n - 1)$. A post-snapshot S_4 and an output $Output_5 = (index = n - 1)$ can be produced by *Search*.

The explicit specifications can be available for all the processes on a scenario. We use the symbolic execution technique and loop invariants to execute the explicit specifications and find whether the scenario is feasible. For example, let *Search* be equipped with an explicit specification (a binary search algorithm) shown next.

```
process Search(key: int, length: int) index: int
...
explicit
ascending:boolean = forall[j: [0, length), i: [0, j)]| _array(i)
<=_array(j);
```

```
low:int := 0;
high:int := len(_array) - 1;
found:bool := false
while (low <= high and !found)
loop inv (3) high+1 <= len(_array) and
             0 <= low and
             forall[i:[0, low)]| _array(i) != key and
             forall[i:[high+1, len(_array))]| _array(i) != key;
begin
    mid:int = (low + high) / 2;
    midVal:int = _array(mid);
  if ascending then
        if (midVal < key) then low: = mid + 1
        else if (key < midVal) then high: = mid - 1
        else index: = mid; found: = true
  else
        if (midVal > key) then low: = mid + 1
        else if (key > midVal) then high: = mid - 1
        else index: = mid; found: = true
end;
if found = false then index: = -(low + 1);
```

The abstract values are used to run the scenario. As shown in Sect. 2.2, when $ARRAY_1$ is assigned to _array, an ascending array (say $ARRAY_4$) or a descending one (say $ARRAY_5$) can be produced. Let KEY be the key to search for. We deduce that

Constraint 5. found = true = >
   (low < = high) and (high+1 < = len(_array))
   and (0 <= low) and (forall[i:[0, low)] | _array(i) != KEY)
   and (forall[i:[high+1, len(_array))]| _array(i) != KEY)
Constraint 6. found = false = >
   low > high and index = -(low+1))
   and (0 < = low) and (forall[i:[0, low)]| _array(i) != KEY)
   and (forall[i:[high+1, len(_array))]| _array(i) != KEY)

Constraints 5 and 6 are consistent with *post_Search* in that (1) when *found* is true, we have $mid = index = (low + high)/2$, $midVal = \_array(mid)$, and $KEY = midVal$; (2) when *found* is false, no element in _array can be the key. Thus we conclude that the specification meets the Property 2.3, and thus is internally consistent.

4   Related Work

Specification verification is an important but intricate topic in software engineering. Theorem proving and model checking are two main approaches to formal verification [11]. The former consists of a systematically exhaustive exploration of the model. The latter consists of generating from the system and/or its specifications a collection of mathematical proof obligations, the truth of which implies conformance of the system to its specification. Having been pervasively used in industry, these techniques have not yet been used in verification of SOFL specifications. The main reasons include that the domain space can be huge, the proof obligations are not easy to define, and the inference rules for inferring some complex properties have not yet been established.

Some practical verification techniques exist in order to verify a requirement or design specification in a cost-effective manner. Alloy uses the modern SAT solvers such as SAT4j [10] to search for the domain space, and then checks the feasibility of an Alloy specification or finds some counterexamples [12]. USE verifies a UML/OCL design specification by using the system snapshots created by engineers [13]. Symbolic execution and concolic testing techniques and tools (such as NASA's Jave Pathfinder [14] and KLEE virtual machine [15]), are also developed, mainly to verify a program, through executing the program and explore the program paths. SPEC# is a tool designed by Microsoft in order to support the idea of design-by-contract in programming. It supports a modular verification of the program by using an SMT solver and an inference engine [7].

Specification review [1] and testing [3,4] are two techniques specially designed for verification of SOFL specifications. They can also be used to verify the specifications in other formal languages, with slight modifications. However, an application of these techniques in practice relies on either reviewers' experience to construct the review task tree, or the testers' intelligence to select the test cases. The two techniques also face challenges when the objective properties are too complex to decompose.

Inspired by the related work, we propose a hybrid approach in order to check the internal consistency of a SOFL specification. The hybrid approach integrates some typical used techniques, such as interactive theorem proving, symbolic execution, specification review and testing in order to make it easy to verify the objective specification. The different strategies are adopted in the hybrid approach to check whether the specification is internally consistent.

5   Conclusion

In this paper we propose a hybrid approach to verify the internal consistency of a SOFL specification. The internal consistency of the specification is checked through checking the satisfiability of each process on the scenario, and then checking the internal consistency of the entire specification. When check the satisfiability of a process, we often use the concrete or abstract values to run the process, and then gradually check whether the process meets three sub-properties. When check the internal consistency of the entire specification, we use the symbolic execution and the deduction techniques, and then determine the internal consistency of the specification through executing all its scenarios.

Although the hybrid approach provides a promising approach to verification of a SOFL specification, the internal consistency of a specification is not completely checked. For example, the Property 2.3 ensures that every scenario can be feasible, but it should not be concluded that the entire specification is always satisfiable. We would decompose the internal consistency property in a more rigorous manner. We would also develop the tool, which integrates an SAT solver and an interactive deduction tool, in order to automate the whole checking process.

Acknowledgments. We would like to thank the anonymous reviewers for their valuable and thorough comments. This work is supported by the National Natural Science Foundation of China (Grant No. 91118004 and 61100051) and Shanghai Key Laboratory of Computer Software Testing and Evaluating (Grant No. SSTL2011_02).

References

1. Liu, S., McDermid, J.A., Chen, Y.: A rigorous method for inspection of model-based formal specifications. IEEE Trans. Reliab. **59**(4), 667–684 (2010)
2. Liu, S.: Formal Engineering for Industrial Software Development. Springer, Heidelberg (2004)
3. Liu, S.: Utilizing specification testing in review task trees for rigorous review of formal specification. In: APSEC, pp. 510–519 (2003)
4. Liu, S., Tamai, T., Nakajima, S.: A framework for integrating formal specification, review, and testing to enhance software reliability. Int. J. Softw. Eng. Knowl. Eng. **21**(2), 259–288 (2011)
5. Sen, K., Agha, G.: CUTE and jCUTE: concolic unit testing and explicit path model-checking tools. In: Ball, T., Jones, R.B. (eds.) CAV 2006. LNCS, vol. 4144, pp. 419–423. Springer, Heidelberg (2006)
6. Ma, K.-K., Khoo, Y.P., Foster, J.S., Hicks, M.: Directed symbolic execution. In: Yahav, Eran (ed.) SAS 2011. LNCS, vol. 6887, pp. 95–111. Springer, Heidelberg (2011)
7. Barnett, M., DeLine, R., Fähndrich, M., Jacobs, B., Leino, K.R.M., Schulte, W., Venter, H.: The spec# programming system: challenges and directions. In: Meyer, B., Woodcock, J. (eds.) VSTTE 2005. LNCS, vol. 4171, pp. 144–152. Springer, Heidelberg (2008)
8. Liu, S., Chen, Y., Nagoya, F., McDermid, J.A.: Formal specification-based inspection for verification of programs. IEEE Trans. Softw. Eng. **38**(5), 1100–1122 (2012)
9. Chen, Y.-T., Liu, S., Nagoya, F.: An approach to integration testing based on data flow specifications. In: Liu, Z., Araki, K. (eds.) ICTAC 2004. LNCS, vol. 3407, pp. 235–249. Springer, Heidelberg (2005)
10. Berre, D.L., Parrain, A.: The Sat4j library, release 2.2. JSAT **7**(2–3), 59–64 (2010)
11. Clarke, E.M., Wing, J.M.: Formal methods: state of the art and future directions. ACM Comput. Surv. **28**(4), 626–643 (1996)
12. Vaziri, M., Jackson, D.: Checking properties of heap-manipulating procedures with a constraint solver. In: Garavel, H., Hatcliff, J. (eds.) TACAS 2003. LNCS, vol. 2619, pp. 505–520. Springer, Heidelberg (2003)

13. Gogolla, M., Bohling, J., Richters, M.: Validation of UML and OCL models by automatic snapshot generation. In: Stevens, P., Whittle, J., Booch, G. (eds.) UML 2003. LNCS, vol. 2863, pp. 265–279. Springer, Heidelberg (2003)
14. Pasareanu, C.S., Visser, W., Bushnell, D.H., Geldenhuys, J., Mehlitz, P.C., Rungta, N.: Symbolic pathfinder: integrating symbolic execution with model checking for java bytecode analysis. Autom. Softw. Eng. **20**(3), 391–425 (2013)
15. Cadar, C., Dunbar, D., Engler, D.R.: Klee: Unassisted and automatic generation of high-coverage tests for complex systems programs. In: OSDI, pp. 209–224 (2008)

Author Index

Chen, Yuting 175

Duan, Zhenhua 35, 48, 62, 76

Feng, Ruitao 154
Feng, Zhiyong 154

Hu, Jing 154

Li, Mo 118
Li, Xiaohong 154
Liu, Bo 76
Liu, Hongjin 35
Liu, Pan 17
Liu, Shaoying 3, 89, 104, 118, 135, 166
Liu, Yao 76
Lu, Xu 35

Miao, Huaikou 17
Miao, Weikai 89

Nakajima, Shin 3

Shi, Ya 48
Sulistiono, Wahyu Eko 166

Tian, Cong 35, 48, 76

Wang, Xi 135
Wang, Xiaobing 62

Yan, Lu 154
Yang, Hua 48

Zhao, Liang 62
Zhu, Shenghua 104